"To read *Living the* to set out on a journey v ter with the Lord, Jesus ... invitation to consider the final frontier: the infinite interior within. To take up this book is to be given a map which leads to the discovery of the mystery of oneself. Like his previous work, Fr. Bransfield's newest book possesses the remarkable capacity of great Christian authors like J. R. R. Tolkien to lift the heart and awaken within the reader wonder and awe at the human experience."

— *Mother Agnes Donovan, S.V., Superior General, Sisters of Life, Yonkers, NY*

"A portrait seen through a child's eyes takes on new meaning in Fr. J. Brian Bransfield's new book, *Living the Beatitudes: A Journey to Life in Christ.* As he presents a child's capacity not only to fantasize and pretend, but also to trust and believe, Fr. Bransfield explores the gift of childhood that led Jesus Christ to call for us to become like children if we wish to inherit the kingdom of God.

"Fr. Bransfield invites the reader to eavesdrop on the conversation between Jesus and the Samaritan woman at the well in the Gospel according to St. John as he weaves theology and spirituality with everyday life experiences, thus allowing the reader to follow the path on which Jesus answers the thirsts of life. The gifts of the Holy Spirit, virtues, and Beatitudes are explained in an easy and accessible manner for Catholics. Fr. Bransfield presents well the paradox of how the carefree walk of the child leads to a rightly ordered life with emphasis on God's will for our salvation. Ultimately the portrait revealed by these Beatitudes is the very face of Jesus Christ and the way in which a grace-filled imitation of him leads us to resemble the One who leads. I highly recommend this well-written book for the depth it will bring to readers searching for understanding and inspiration as they seek to answer the baptismal call to holiness."

— Most Reverend Joseph E. Kurtz,
Archbishop of Louisville, KY

" 'We all want to live happily; in the whole human race there is no one who does not assent to this proposition, even before it is fully articulated.' These words of Saint Augustine take us to the heart of Fr. Bransfield's engaging book. A woman of Samaria, drawn by her natural thirst for happiness, meets the Savior who also thirsts—for her faith. He, the fountain, surges up to transform her and send her forth. Fr. Bransfield reminds us that it is God who places the longing for happiness in our hearts in order to draw us to himself—for only he can fulfill our longing. Drinking of the wisdom of the Lord Jesus, engulfed by his love, we pass from fear, sin, and isolation, through the cross, to a new life of gratitude, virtue, and beatitude. This life of holiness is inspired and fueled by the Holy Spirit. Fr. Bransfield opens up for us the Lord's invitation to an intimate, eternal relationship, and the reader will find in these pages a gentle but sure guide for responding to that invitation."

— Most Reverend J. Peter Sartain,
Archbishop of Seattle, WA

LIVING THE BEATITUDES

LIVING THE BEATITUDES

A Journey to Life in Christ

Reverend Monsignor J. Brian Bransfield

Pauline
BOOKS & MEDIA
Boston

Library of Congress Cataloging-in-Publication Data

Bransfield, J. Brian.
  Living the beatitudes : a journey to life in Christ / J. Brian Bransfield.
    p. cm.
  Summary: "Find a new perspective on the spiritual life by taking a fresh look at the beatitudes"--Provided by publisher.
  ISBN 0-8198-4544-2 (pbk.)
  1. Beatitudes--Criticism, interpretation, etc. I. Title.
  BT382.B695 2011
  226.9'306--dc23
                                2011030904

Cover design by Rosana Usselmann

Cover photo: istockphoto.com

Published by Pauline Books & Media, 50 Saint Pauls Avenue, Boston, MA 02130-3491. www.pauline.org

Printed in the U.S.A.

Pauline Books & Media is the publishing house of the Daughters of St. Paul, an international congregation of women religious serving the Church with the communications media.

2 3 4 5 6 7 8 9   17 16 15 14 13

To my sisters and brother:
Margaret-Anne and her husband, Michael,
Mary Jane,
Paula,
and
Paul
with loving gratitude

Contents

PART I

PART II

Foreword

During the thirteenth century, when the Franciscans and Dominicans were busy arguing about which was the greatest of the religious orders and the Jesuits had not even been imagined, a German Dominican with the intellectual stature of Bede the Venerable and Anselm of Canterbury captured the importance of savoring the journey of life with the words: "Be willing to be a beginner every single morning."

At first hearing, Meister Eckhart's directive sounds very similar to the encouraging words of the many "feel good" experts found on contemporary television and radio programs. Although these present day "tele-philosophers" want us to believe that such insights are of their own making (or thinking), in reality they are repeating an old story that has never grown old.

For example, 600 years after Meister Eckhart, the American student of religious experience, William James, captured the identical sentiment in this way:

Seek out that particular mental attitude which makes you feel most deeply and vitally alive, along with which comes the inner voice which says, "This is the real me," and when you have found that attitude, follow it.

Then in our own time, the novelist Don Williams, Jr. added his voice to the mix when he wrote: "The road of life twists and turns and no two directions are ever the same. Yet our lessons come from the journey, not the destinations."

However or whenever it is said, the point remains the same. It is the journey that is most important, and the most important journey of all is the one we make to God, who is the source of all life. That, more than anything else, is the lesson to be found in Father J. Brian Bransfield's book, *Living the Beatitudes: A Journey to Life in Christ.*

Father Bransfield proposes the mysterious woman at the well as our guide to the Christian virtues we find presented in the Beatitudes, virtues for which we should strive: poverty of spirit, gentleness, solidarity with those who suffer loss, justice, mercy, purity of heart, peace, and the ability to suffer persecution for what is right. But, in fact, Father Bransfield is the guide, for he leads us to see how each beatitude invites us on a journey into a deeper communion with the very life of God.

Guides are helpful people. Anyone going on a journey to an undiscovered country can read a guidebook and learn the basics. But a guide who intimately knows the landscape can show the traveler places he or she never would have found and help him or her better understand what makes life meaningful for the inhabitants of the country.

The same is true of our spiritual lives. With the right guide, our soul, our spirit can travel to places we could never imagine. That is the journey *Living the Beatitudes* urges us to begin. It is a journey through ourselves—the way we think, the way we act—to the God who has made us in his own image and asks of us that we live and love in imitation and union with him.

Make no mistake about it, following Christ and living the Beatitudes demands courage and sometimes courage is in short supply. But as Blessed John Paul II so often reminded us, we need not be afraid. Jesus, who promised to be with us always, walks with us on the journey. When we drift from the path, he guides us back; when we hesitate with fear, he encourages us on; when we grow weary from the distance, he gives us heart; and when we fall, he picks us up so the journey to the one who is greater than ourselves, the one who realizes our hope, may continue.

In this book, Father Bransfield invites us to journey to fullness of life in Christ by utilizing the Beatitudes as lampposts along the way. If we accept his invitation to walk the road, we will never find it crowded, but we will find that it affords us an opportunity to allow Christ to shine through us, and through him our world will be redeemed.

Most Reverend George V. Murry, SJ
Bishop of Youngstown

Acknowledgments

Throughout the different seasons, patience alone is the foremost common element that unites the springtime and the harvest. More than pen and paper or keyboard and printer, patience is also the secret weapon of the writer. That is why there are so few of them. Patience grows the thought into a phrase and stretches the feeling into a word. Patience, alone, *attracts* words and pollinates them. In fact, patience is the story behind all words. The words in this book would not have been possible without the many patient words and kind actions that supported them.

Therefore, the first word of this book is one of gratitude.

I am deeply thankful to the many people who encouraged and supported me in my efforts in writing this book. My first and heartfelt thanks go to Most Reverend Charles J. Chaput, O.F.M., Cap., Archbishop of Philadelphia, for his interest in and encouragement of my work. I am deeply appreciative to

Cardinal Justin Rigali, the Archbishop Emeritus of Phila-delphia. I am likewise sincerely grateful to Most Reverend George V. Murry, SJ, Bishop of Youngstown and Secretary of the United States Conference of Catholic Bishops, for his gracious agreement to offer the foreword to this work. I deeply appreciate the gracious words of Most Reverend Joseph E. Kurtz, Archbishop of Louisville, and Most Reverend J. Peter Sartain, Archbishop of Seattle, regarding these pages. My thanks also goes to Mother Agnes Donovan, S.V., Superior General of the Sisters of Life, for her thoughtful and kind expression of support for this book.

Through patience, the word becomes a gift. I deeply value the gift of the daily opportunity to collaborate with the highly dedicated and professional staff of the USCCB, in particular my brother priests at the Conference, most especially, Reverend Monsignor Ronny Jenkins, the General Secretary, for his dedi-cation to priestly virtue, for his encouragement and example of expert scholarship, and for his friendship. I am indebted to my colleagues in the General Secretariat, and to Andrew Lichtenwalner. I am likewise grateful to my part-time col-leagues on the Pontifical Faculty of the Immaculate Concep-tion, which I serve in adjunct capacity, and to my students at the Dominican House of Studies in Washington, DC.

Patience is character. I cannot thank enough the Daughters of St. Paul, especially, Sr. Marianne Lorraine Trouvé, FSP, Sr. Maria Grace Dateno, FSP, and Sr. Sean Mayer, FSP, for the highly specialized professional efforts which character-ized their preparation of the text for publication.

Patience, that most extroverted of virtues, is also the liga-ment of friendship. On a personal level, I am happy to express special thanks to Martin and Cynthia Lutschaunig, and their sons, Christian, Daniel, and Andrew, for the gift they are in my life. Likewise, I am indebted to Brian and Joan Gail for their prayers, friendship, and continued encouragement. I appreciate the support of my brother priests, Reverend Monsignor David Malloy, Reverend John Pidgeon, Reverend James Olson, Reverend Stephen Dougherty, Reverend Eric Gruber, and Reverend Michael Gerlach. I am especially grateful to Father James Bajorek for introducing me to the writings of Saint Teresa of Avila.

Patience is most of all steadfast, and so I am most especially grateful to my family, for their steadfast love: my mother and father who have gone to God, and to my sisters and brother to whom this work is gladly dedicated.

Introduction

Belief comes easily to the child. So, too, does fantasy. But, of course, belief and fantasy are far different. To fantasize is to pretend that the real is something it is not. Children fantasize or pretend when they use their imagination at play. It does not take much conjuring for a young boy to transform an L-shaped twig into a pistol and pretend to be a gangster of old. A group of children playing in the neighborhood pool on a summer's afternoon easily imagine that the inflatable raft is a sleek pirate ship on the run. Pretending is the magic of childhood that can turn the backyard into a famous battlefield of history, or a doll into a baby as when a little girl plays house.

Belief, on the other hand, is the opposite of fantasy. Belief engages the real to form a relationship. A child who believes in his or her parents grows up with simple confidence that generally his or her basic needs will be met. Loving parents will provide food to eat, a warm bed to sleep in, and comforting voices in times of distress. The child knows that someone will be close by, the next day will dawn, and someone will smile and care. When a child believes in his or her teachers, coaches, classmates, and friends, a relationship opens naturally. Learning, training, camaraderie, and friendship arise from belief.

The child is an expert in believing. Even the everyday pressures, troubles, and fears of life become, for the child, an opportunity for belief. The sound of thunder is an opening to believe in the shelter of the home. Nightmares and even fictional monsters are openings to believe in the protection of guardian angels, the warmth of father and mother, and the security of family. The family and home are meant to become the enchanting locus of belief for the child.

Church, too, for the child, is a fascinating place of belief. The child's eyes widen to behold the images in stained glass windows depicting saints with swords conquering large dragons. Children scrutinize the shrines in the alcoves of a church. Such places serve to localize the belief that God guides and heals his people. The statues with arms spread wide seem larger than any danger the child will ever face. The stories of the Bible fill the child with the strong momentum of assurance that God knows what to do and delivers us in the end. The child can feel the relentless determination of the Wise Men, the courage of David before Goliath, the humble receptivity of the Virgin Mary, and, above all, the gentleness of Jesus. Children absorb every detail of the stories of the saints. Children believe the promise that God guides us and protects us in any peril. Children examine every inch of a holy card to see the attributes of the champions of belief. The child senses that the same God who led Abraham and stood by Moses will also act on his or her behalf.

Growing up can cramp our capacity to believe. The mystery was within reach when we were children: we *believed* it, and we believed God would protect us, be next to us, and guide us. We believed God was on our side. We also believed that it was good to be good. We felt the connection of the church building and the people in it, with the apostles and Jesus. We felt the link between the Church and the rest of the world. The God we prayed to in church would continue to guide us as we stepped outside of church.

But then something happened. As we grew up, the world became complex and often painful. We walked more quickly past the stained glass windows and allowed the alcoves to gather dust. We no longer lingered before the shrines and the statues. We experienced tests and trials. We learned what the word "cancer" means. Hollywood blockbusters began to take the place of the biblical stories. Highly-paid actors and actresses captured our fantasy world. The people we thought would live forever, such as our parents and close friends, died. The world we once trusted hurt us. Our early beliefs were challenged and the fantasies of the world seemed to offer a quick escape.

Instead of storms outside in the night, storms raged inside. We felt a hunger deeper than that for food. We sensed a darkness even when the lights shone. The angels seemed to fly away, back into the stories. Monsters began to take the form of a "business as usual" world of trying to fit in and competing to get ahead. The devil, who uses disguise as a standard operating procedure (cf. 2 Cor 11:14), seemed more comfortable seated behind a desk in a suit and tie rather than with horns, a tail, and a pitchfork. The holy water seemed unable to wash away the more complex evil stains. Holy cards became sad reminders of the most recent wake or funeral we attended. It was more difficult to connect the worlds inside and outside the Church. They seemed to stop fitting together and grew apart. Many people stopped being naïve, only to become depressed. Success was no longer about doing the right thing, but about doing my own thing. The connection between the Church and the rest of the world was severed.

This book is about restoring the connections. It is for faithful Catholics and for Catholics who want to be faithful. It is for the once faithful, and the less than faithful. This book is about making worlds fit together. It is about transforming our knowledge of faith into an accessible image, which will restore our capacity to believe and can then lodge deep in our memory. Adults long to access the spontaneous and ready faith of childhood that is still within us, waiting for us. We experience the daily thirst for a living relation and coherent connection between grace and daily life. We have seen enough of the world to know that sin exists. We want to understand not just how to be nice, but how to be *good*. Even though we may have been away from the practice of the faith for years, we sense the meaning of the sacraments in daily life. Yet, as adults, we often cannot find a way to reinvigorate our childhood beliefs and assimilate them into our adult faith. We thirst for the action of God to be relevant to the deepest questions of our life.

The primary tool in bringing the two worlds together is the ancient yet familiar image of the fountain that the Lord Jesus Christ himself used to describe God's action in the life of the believer: "Let anyone who thirsts come to me and drink. Whoever believes in me, as scripture says: 'Rivers of living water will flow from within him'" (Jn 7:37–38). This fountain is closer than we think. We are likely to hear its sound every Sunday. After the faithful have proclaimed "Holy, Holy, Holy" the priest prays the words of the Eucharistic Prayer. The former translation of the second Eucharistic Prayer begins, "Lord, you are holy indeed, the fountain of all holiness."[1] In the new

---

1. Second Eucharistic Prayer, *The Roman Missal*, revised according to the second typical edition of the *Missale Romanum* (1975), March 1, 1985, for use in the dioceses of the United States of America.

translation of the *Roman Missal*, the prayer begins, "You are indeed Holy, O Lord, the fount of all holiness."[2] These words go back to the second century of Christianity, to the ecclesiastical author Saint Hippolytus. These ancient words have stood the test of time. They remain with us today, common and familiar, yet unique and irreplaceable in the reality they describe. Grace, God's love for us, is a strong and persistent fountain that flows into our souls and shows forth in our actions.

Yet many have forgotten the path to this fountain. For many, the brambles of shame have snarled the path to happiness and a peaceful relationship with God. Years of fear and exclusive focus on fire and brimstone have blocked that path. Instead, the sad detour of spirituality-lite has replaced it, reducing the spiritual life to vague emotionalism and surface sentimentality. Promises betrayed and one hypocrisy too many have eroded the path to God. We have forgotten the maps that lead us to this life-giving fountain. The purpose of this book is to show us the way back to the fountain, to prune away the overgrowth, to clear the debris from the trail, to remove the boulders from the middle of the path, and to invite the reader to the fountain of all holiness.

A familiar Gospel figure can help us as we go about this task. One day Jesus met a person very much like us. She was a Samaritan woman in the midst of her daily routine. She remembered the greatness of her childhood faith and referred to it as the memory of "Our father Jacob" (Jn 4:12). Queen Esther from the Old Testament also recalled her childhood faith in her moment of desolation: "As a child I was wont to hear from the people of the land of my fore-fathers that you,

---

2. Second Eucharistic Prayer, *The Roman Missal*, revised according to the third typical edition of the *Missale Romanum* (2002), 2010, for use in the dioceses of the United States of America.

O LORD, chose Israel from among all peoples, and our fathers from among all their ancestors, as a lasting heritage, and that you fulfilled all your promises to them" (Est C:16).

The Holy Spirit revives our childhood faith in times of fear and pain, and encourages us in the words of the psalmist: "Cast your care upon the LORD, who will give you support" (Ps 55:23). The woman of Samaria lived with the pain of daily fear, hurt, and sin. Jesus knew the record of her painful past: "For you have had five husbands, and the one you have now is not your husband" (Jn 4:18). While the Lord Jesus is our ultimate guide, we will take as our helper this woman who met Jesus.[3] She is known only as "the Samaritan woman." We never learn her name. She is anonymous to us, but in many ways we know her very well. She is very much like us. She knows the world of forgotten promises and sin. She also knows the world of a remembered hope and grace. She reaches out her hand to us.

Method

This book is divided into two parts. The first part consists of four chapters that present the woman of Samaria as an image for modern Christians. She, in her thirst, meets the Lord Jesus *in his thirst.*

Chapter One describes the deeper meaning of the Samaritan woman's encounter with Jesus. She encounters Jesus while going about her routine tasks and her daily pain. Similarly, our routine tasks and ongoing wounds carry a deeper

---

3. Hans Urs von Balthasar notes the special character of every detail of the Gospel accounts in which Jesus meets the sinner. See *The Glory of the Lord: A Theological Aesthetics I, Seeing the Form* (San Francisco: Ignatius Press, 1989), 580.

dimension. Chapter One reveals that the invitation of Jesus surrounds us daily, especially in the place we are most wounded. His invitation is not an ultimatum, but a personal summons that addresses our deepest self. Jesus gradually introduces himself to the woman. For this introduction to be complete, she must allow Jesus to clear away her misconceptions and disordered attachments. So must we. The woman of Samaria can represent those who practice the faith regularly as well as those who have drifted. Jesus leads the Samaritan woman away from her fears and excuses to accept the gift that he offers. Jesus uses the image of the fountain to describe his gift. The gift Jesus offers is meant to become a fountain within the believer. The image of the fountain becomes the central image of the following chapters. This image is developed in such a way to help the believer understand the work the Holy Spirit carries out deep within the Christian.

Chapter Two propels us deeper into our own understanding of our identity. As we move past our fears, we discover that fear, despite its power, has a hidden gift. This chapter examines the popular understanding of identity as progress that so often drains the fountain from our lives and leads to emptiness and chaos. The authentic meaning of identity lies deep beneath our preconceived notions. To reach our deepest identity, we must pass through the common experience of fear. Only here do we discover the path to understand grace and virtue, not as antique theological terms, but as our daily energy and direction. Having moved through our fears we can begin to reach our hand into the gift of the fountain of God's grace.

Chapter Three invites us to consider images of the spiritual life and to reflect on the image of the fountain, especially the fountain of grace that flows from Jesus on the cross, as an effective and dramatic image for the spiritual life. This chapter begins by comparing our internal world to a treadmill of thoughts and worries that so often weigh down our approach to life and spirituality. God interrupts our worries and leads us to the rich source of grace. Rather than a treadmill, the great saints portray the spiritual life as a ladder by which the believer is led through the difficulties of life. The image of the ladder is similar to that of the fountain. Jesus himself uses this image with the Samaritan woman (see Jn 4:14). In the pages that follow, this image becomes the central image for the life of God within us. Fountains are a surge of natural generosity from deep within that transform pressure into beauty. Fountains well up to refresh, cleanse, and sustain us. The self-gift of Jesus on the cross is the fountain of life eternal.

Chapter Four revisits the mysteries of the Trinity, human sin, the cross, and the call to holiness through the help of the image of the fountain. This chapter contrasts the popular mental picture of God with the mystery of the Trinity. The unity of the Father, the Son, and the Holy Spirit is an eternal gift of self, one to the other. The eternal Triune gift of self is presented as the basis for the temporal gift of self at the heart of the identity of the human person. This chapter explains how sin sabotages this gift of self and reduces the flow of the fountain through the insistent impulse for self-taking. The human person struggles to live a life of self-giving, but is continually confronted with the tendency to sin, in particular through the seven deadly sins. The effects of sin fester in us, inclining us to sin. The Christian cannot conquer sin and its effects with his or her own efforts. This chapter presents the mystery of the cross as God's response to sin. God offers his own gift of self in his Son as the source of grace by which we can receive his mercy. This gift of God alone conquers human sin. The life of the Christian is therefore a response to the call to holiness offered in the grace of God through the sacraments. This does not happen in some remote, automatic, or magical fashion. The seven gifts of the Holy Spirit (cf. Is 11:2) build the seven virtues (cf. 1 Cor 13:13; Wis 8:7.) within the believer. The virtues then form the believer to live the Beatitudes (cf. Mt 5:3–12). The *Catechism of the Catholic Church* teaches that the "Beatitudes respond to the natural desire for happiness."[4] The relation of the seven gifts to the virtues and the Beatitudes is the way each Christian is transformed to live a holy life and respond to the natural desire for happiness. This chapter prepares for Part II by explaining the traditional influence of the seven gifts of the Holy Spirit to internalize the life of virtue so that we can live the Beatitudes.

The second part of the book consists of eight chapters on the Beatitudes. Each chapter focuses on a surge of the fountain of grace that the Holy Spirit longs to release in the heart of the believer. Each gift of the Holy Spirit strengthens a particular virtue in the Christian. The virtue, in turn, develops and forms the action proper to a particular beatitude. The gifts, virtues, and Beatitudes build on one another in a way similar to the upward surging momentum of a fountain. At the same time, a struggle ensues through battle with the seven deadly sins. The sins attempt to weigh down, dull, and curtail the life of grace so as to prevent the internalization of virtue. Each chapter deals with particular deadly sins opposed to a particular beatitude.

We now turn, then, to the Holy Spirit and ask him to take us to Jesus. We step onto the road together. We see a mysterious figure at a well. He looks up to us, and he turns to us, and he begins to speak to us. He is asking us a simple question.

---

4. *Catechism of the Catholic Church (CCC)*, no. 1718.

PART I

CHAPTER ONE

The Woman of Samaria, Then and Now

Timing Is Everything

One seemingly ordinary day Jesus was on his way from Judea to Galilee. The Gospel of Saint John tells us that to go from Judea to Galilee, "He *had to* pass through Samaria" (Jn 4:3). The Greek word used for *had* is *edei (ἔδει),* which means "it was necessary."[1] Why does the Gospel emphasize that it was *necessary* that Jesus pass through Samaria on his way from Judea to Galilee? He could have taken another route. It was not a *geographic* necessity that Jesus travel to Galilee by way of

---

1. For the significance of this term see Hans Urs von Balthasar, *The Glory of the Lord: A Theological Aesthetics VII, Theology: The New Covenant* (San Francisco: Ignatius Press, 1989), 316, and *Theo-Drama: Theological Dramatic Theory IV, The Action* (San Francisco: Ignatius Press), 234. See also, Larry Paul Jones, *The Symbol of Water in the Gospel of John* (Sheffield, England: Sheffield Academic Press, 1997), 95.

Samaria. So why did he choose that route? The first sentence of this Gospel passage suggests a task of urgent necessity is in the offing. The very first sentence already hints at the significance of the journey of Jesus: he had a *mission* on that journey. To find out the purpose of his mission we must follow Jesus in the Gospel passage and investigate further.

The passage continues as Jesus enters Samaria: "Jesus, tired from his journey, sat down there at the well. It was about noon" (Jn 4:6b). The route that Jesus has chosen has evidently taken its toll. The Gospel writer emphasizes that Jesus is tired from the journey and also notes it was noon. Jesus has traveled a long way and is now feeling the effects of the noon-time heat. In fact, Jesus is so tired that when he arrives at a well, he sits down. The facts appear ordinary enough: in the middle of a long journey, at the hottest time of the day, Jesus stops by a well for rest and refreshment. This happens every day. It appears the most ordinary of detours. Yet, that which appears ordinary, when taken into the mystery of Jesus, becomes extraordinary.

A well is no ordinary place. On the surface, a well is a source of water and refreshment. Yet, a well in the Old Testament is more than just a rest stop. Isaac and Rebekah (cf. Gn 24), Jacob and Leah, Jacob and Rachel (cf. Gn 29), Moses and Zipporah (cf. Ex 2), and Tobias and Sarah (cf. Tb 8) are all betrothed after meeting at a well. The well is the central place of communion in the biblical world. In the Old Testament, the well is a place of betrothal, the meeting place of spousal love.[2] On one level, the well is simply a place to pause for a drink of water. On a deeper level, the well is the

---

2. See Warwick Neville "Old Testament Spousal Narratives: A Contribution to the 'Nuptial Mystery'" *Dialoghi Sul Mistero Nuziale*, eds. G. Marengo and B. Ognibeni (Rome: Lateran University Press, 2003), 185–204. See also, Jean Daniélou, *Advent* (New York: Sheed and Ward, 1951), 45. See also, Larry Paul Jones, *The Symbol of Water in the Gospel of John* (Salem, WI: Sheffield, 1999), 91–92.

meeting place of chaste spousal love. Jesus always travels on the deeper level. Thus he arrives at the locus of spousal love.

The noon hour is no ordinary time. The notation of time appears at first to be an incidental detail to set the scene within the Gospel passage. But the detail has much to tell us. At noon-time, the heat of the sun peaks in intensity. The sun burns directly overhead, driving away any natural shadows in which to hide or seek shelter. People withdraw. It is the lonely time. Noon is also the time when, in just a few short chapters in the Gospel of Saint John, Jesus will enter his lonely suffering on the cross. Just as the sun reaches its peak, the Son will reach his. Jesus pauses on this necessary journey, at the place of chaste spousal love, at the same hour in which he will mount the cross in the ultimate act of love.

Next, a seemingly common event takes place: "A woman of Samaria came to draw water" (Jn 4:7). The need for water is among our most basic and common. Yet, something *uncommon* happens here. Most people come to the well in the cool hours of morning or evening to perform the arduous task of drawing water from a great depth and hauling it the long distance back home. This lone woman arrives at noon when the sweltering heat of the day peaks. Why does she approach a routine place for a routine task at this irregular and most *un*routine hour?

One reason may be her painful past, which Jesus will later point out to her: "For you have had five husbands, and the one you have now is not your husband" (Jn 4:18). She has been married and divorced five times. She is, by now, branded and burdened with a very public reputation. People talk about her and call her names. They point her out to others. Perhaps this is why she approaches the well at an unusual time. The crowd comes in the cool morning or evening. If she came at those times, the murmuring would be too much to endure. People would stare. They would warn their children, "Don't turn out like her; see what happened to her . . . listen to your parents, or else you'll end up like her." At noon, the crowd stays away because of the intense heat. Public opinion and gossip have segregated her to this worst, most arduous time for drawing water from the deep well. She would rather endure the scorching heat than the cruel, scornful glares of those who know her sinful past. She comes for the basic sustenance of life, but must do so in the pain of her daily exile. She can lament with the cry of the Old Testament: "At the peril of our lives we bring in our sustenance, in the face of the desert heat" (Lam 5:9). She arrives, at first, to draw natural water to quench a natural thirst. After hearing the word of Jesus she will cry out, "Sir, give me this water . . ." (Jn 4:15). Her physical thirst is a sign of her spiritual thirst. As she is led to recognize the divinity of Jesus, it is as if the words of the psalmist become her own: "O God, you are my God—for you I long! For you my body yearns; for you my soul thirsts, like a land parched, lifeless, and without water" (Ps 63:2). On this deep level, she fulfills the words of the psalmist: "In their distress they cried to the LORD, who rescued them in their peril, guided them by a direct path so they reached a city to live in" (Ps 107:6–7). The prophet Isaiah foretold as much: "The afflicted and the needy seek water in vain, their tongues are parched with thirst. I, the LORD, will answer them; I, the God of Israel, will not forsake them. I will open up rivers on the bare heights, and fountains in the broad valleys; I will turn the desert into a marshland, and the dry ground into springs of water" (Is 41:17–18). Isaiah repeats his prophecy: "Thus says the LORD . . . See I am doing something new! Now it springs forth, do you not perceive it? In the desert I make a way, in the wasteland, rivers . . . for I put water in the desert and rivers in the wasteland for my chosen people to drink" (Is 43:16a, 19, 20b).

The woman of Samaria was doing a routine daily task, following her regular pattern of behavior. She may have been bored or daydreaming, when suddenly, in her exile, she meets someone. This someone has an apparently ordinary request: "Give me a drink" (Jn 4:7). Thirst is a regular and predictable experience. Yet, that which has seemed ordinary thus far in the Gospel account has actually had a much deeper meaning. So too does this request of Jesus. He will utter the same request, close to the same noon hour on Good Friday when he calls out from the cross: "I thirst" (Jn 19:28). His true thirst is for salvation through the forgiveness of sins. Her thirst is wrapped up in fear of what others think, about her status, about her past and future. His thirst is about others; hers is about herself. The two thirsts meet. He is about to invite her, in the words of the prophet: "All you who are thirsty, come to the water" (Is 55:1).

It all *seems* ordinary enough, but just beneath the surface extraordinary events are aligning. She comes in her loneliness and pain as he sits down in the deep thirst of his mission; she comes to satisfy her thirst, and he asks her for a drink; he is on his journey and she is in her exile; it is noon, he thirsts, and calls out on his necessary journey. This apparently common series of seemingly chance happenings is actually forming one continuous dramatic event. It is a rehearsal for Good Friday, a walk-through of the mission of salvation.

As we follow the passage, the conversation between Jesus and this anonymous woman continues. After he asks for a drink, she points out in a rather rude and abrupt manner that he does not have a bucket and that the well is deep. She further points out that he is a Jew and she is a Samaritan. She identifies all the obstacles she has in relating to Jesus, all the reasons she cannot believe in him. Her excuses range from the practical to the prejudicial.

Consider again the opening sentence of the Gospel passage, which said it was *necessary* that Jesus pass through Samaria. It was not a geographic necessity; rather it was necessary that Jesus pass through *for this woman* and for her *salvation*. She has been exiled within the daily events of her own life. She has suffered much at the hands of many men. But only *one* man can save her. As the psalmist notes, her natural thirst is a sign of her supernatural longing: "My being thirsts for God, the living God" (Ps 42:3). Jesus extends his mission into her daily routine. He goes where she is. He necessarily passes by the well, the place of chaste spousal love, on his journey. He sits down at that well, with a deliberate stubbornness, as if to say, "Now I will teach her the source of true love . . . I will overflow the meaning of this well." Love alone holds the secret to the truth about life. It is the mission and the thirst of the Son of God to lead the sinner to the depths of his own mercy and love. The supernatural mission of Jesus is expressed in his natural thirst.

The Samaritan woman represents every sinner in the Church, of all times and places. She meets her Lord at this strategic intersection of the ordinary and the extraordinary, the painful and the routine. He invites her to spousal union with him in chaste love. It is as if he begins to hear her confession.[3]

Our life, too, has a well. It sits right in the midst of our daily routine of ordinary places and common tasks. Our lives might even have a place of exile, where we go to avoid other people and to forget the pain. Nonetheless, pain prompts us. The thirst goes deep, a thirst that exists not only in our throat but throughout our life.[4] If we look carefully and listen closely

---

3. See Balthasar, *The Glory of the Lord VI*, 120, and *Theo-Drama IV*, 386.

4. See Yves Congar, *The Revelation of God* (New York: Herder and Herder, 1968), 37.

in our exile, avoidance, and forgetfulness, we might see the figure of a man whose timing is perfect, who sits down and still thirsts. He looks up and turns to us with his request: "Give me a drink; I thirst."

Samaria Is Not So Far Away

The car door swings shut with a thud. A teenager shoves both hands deep into the front pocket of his hooded sweatshirt. He turns and strides slowly across the parking lot while the church spire stretches high above. Two more thuds follow in quick succession as his younger sister and father exit the car. They follow the teen's swaying path. The distance between them speaks volumes as they make their way across the asphalt. They climb the steps in the ritual Sunday morning trek to the church door. They have just finished the all-too-familiar pre-Mass argument about "going" or "not going" to church. The father's ultimatums filled the air in response to his son's complaints. After the grimly quiet car ride, they embark on this forced march to church.

Of course they keep secret their yelling and arguing. No one hears it except them. They believe they are the only family that struggles and yells at one another. The father strides the last few steps to the heavy door and wonders how things went wrong. *Why do we fight? Why do things have to be so tense? Isn't it enough that I have to work two jobs, and my wife works weekends to make ends meet? Why can't my family be more like other families who smile and seem so well put-together? The car doors will slam again in less than an hour . . . if we are lucky.*

What keeps this routine shuffle going nearly every week? What keeps them coming back? Is it the long, invisible arm of super-ego that points the way insistently to church? Do they go to church because it has been drilled into them? Does *guilt* pave the way to the church door? Or do they attend because they would feel left out if others in the neighborhood and at work were religious and they were not? Does *social convention* keep the routine going?

Or do they believe, almost superstitiously, that if they did not go to church, things in their life would get worse? Does *fear* push them along this path to church? And what about us? Do we, perhaps unconsciously, seek out religion as a solution to fix something in our lives? Do we sense we need healing and find something about faith that draws us? The modern sense of faith can easily slip into the belief that faith and religion are about fixing my life or the life of another. Such an understanding of faith can lead the seeker to try *to get something out of* religion. Most often, they seek emotional relief by which they try to maintain an equilibrium of life and navigate through the puzzles of day-to-day existence. Religious people want to be good, yet *good* means different things to different people.

Guilt, habit, fear, pain, self-improvement—curiously enough, the reasons some people attend church are the *same reasons* other people give for not going to church. The woman of Samaria is very familiar with guilt, habits, fear, and pain. She is familiar with our excuses because she has tried them all.

The reasons do deepen, of course. What are our reasons for attending Mass? Perhaps we want to set a good example for our children. Perhaps we have noticed we feel more calm and even more centered, if only for a short while, after Mass. Perhaps in church, we feel closer to obtaining something that seems missing in our lives. We come because we live the good example of our parents, or because we have made a long search and know intuitively that this is where we are meant to be. Perhaps the prayers of our parents have escorted us in, or the intercession of a saint. And, possibly, beneath all the seemingly superficial, mixed motives, we hear a distant echo of "something more" just behind the door.

The questions about practice of the faith all have to do with Catholic identity. What does our Catholic identity mean to us? Is it that we all do the same thing? Or that we make the same gestures, believe the same basics, or live in the same parish? Why do we attend Mass on Sunday? How do we maintain our Catholic identity through the week? Yet, we also are aware of the painful parts of our history. Catholic identity is a rallying point for some, while others seek to dismiss it as a diagnosis. As we examine our Catholic identity, we cannot simply rely on ourselves or the opinions of others. We must turn to the Holy Spirit. He acts in us in a way similar to that of a chiropractor who adjusts a person's spine. The Holy Spirit assesses the broad range of our Catholic posture and applies pressure and relief at various places in various degrees, realigning the familiar patterns we have adopted.

Today, so many of us are like the Samaritan woman. She came to draw water from the well. We also come to draw water from our faith lives. In the midst of our daily activities we maintain a general belief in God. We have participated in a more or less steady manner in religious ceremonies. Yet, so often, we regard religion as simply a private ceremonial event with no immediate relation to our lives during the rest of the week. Religion has become compartmentalized. We have drifted into understanding faith as a purely private matter.

As in the passage of the Samaritan woman, Jesus emerges during the hardest part, in the intense and oppressive heat of our lives. Yet sometimes we miss him. We may have passed him by dozens of times, or ignored him, or been drawn in another direction by failure, self-pity, drugs, alcohol, or indifference. Yet, Jesus waits. And one day he looks up and asks us for a drink.

More Wounded Than Skeptic

How many Catholics no longer saunter across the parking lot to church on Sunday mornings? How many do not keep pace with faith anymore? How many cast a measured, yet polite, look on the faithfulness they once held close?

In April 2008 the Center for Applied Research in the Apostolate (CARA) published *Sacraments Today: Belief and Practice Among U.S. Catholics*, a survey of adult Catholics in the United States commissioned by the United States Conference of Catholic Bishops.[5] Over seventy-six percent of self-identified adult Catholics say they are proud to be Catholic. Yet only twenty-three percent of self-identified adult Catholics attend Mass at least once a week. This means that fifty-three percent of adult Catholics are proud to be Catholic, but do not put that faith into practice by weekly attendance at Mass. Thus, they experience a notable gap between their Catholic identity and their Catholic practice.

What has caused this? Could it be that over-familiarity with the routine constrained the *practice*? Could it be that predictable and superficial answers were repeated once too often to hearts with wrenching questions? Could it be that the well-intentioned but unimaginative explanations offered for the problems of daily life just did not meet the expectations of those in church on Sunday morning? Have they, like the Samaritan woman, been hurt once too often by the world? Have they given up? Are they in exile? Do we who attend regularly look askance at those who do not? Do we consider them shallow or skeptics? Do we blame the ones who are not there on Sunday for being lazy—or do we *miss* them?

---

5. Center for Applied Research in the Apostolate, *Sacraments Today: Belief and Practice Among U. S. Catholics*, Georgetown University, Washington, DC, April 2008.

The misperception is that those who do not practice regularly are lazy, disorganized, convenience-oriented people who want their own way or are "writing their own ticket." Worse, they may be judged to be skeptics, doubters, fair-weather, or rule-shunning slackers. To label others is to solidify the distance created by fear. When we label other people we do not help them; we only protect ourselves. Fear does one of two things: it either condemns or shies away. Love, however, calls and creates. How do we reach the fifty-three percent of self-identified adult Catholics who are proud to be Catholic, yet do not attend Mass regularly? We have more opportunities than we may realize. We see the fifty-three percent rather often. Some of them attend Mass once or twice a month. Others come to marriage preparation and to celebrate at rehearsals and weddings. They come to grieve at funerals; we visit them in the hospital; they attend Baptism classes to prepare to have their children baptized. They attend similar preparation evenings or weekend retreats as their children prepare for first Penance and for Confirmation. They also attend back-to-school nights.

And they are wounded. They are wounded by misinformation, by lack of knowledge, and by the effects of an individualistic, materialistic, consumer-driven, utilitarian, and narcissistic culture in which the only sin is intolerance. Many today have a devalued sense of religion and dismiss obedience as unrealistic. Society dismisses rules and religious affiliation as external, authoritarian threats to personal autonomy and privacy. In this atmosphere, people lack informed positions on Catholic teaching. They also find a disconnect between identifying as a Catholic and practicing as a Catholic. We must face this cultural reality and respond with an original strategy.

The strategy must start on Sunday. Some come to Sunday Mass in business suits, and others in summer shorts. Some wear ties, and others tie-dye. Some come as families, and

others stand alone. If we arrive early, we have a period of
silence all around us. We select our pew, slide in, and wait. We
thumb through the missalette as others saunter past to their
places. Those who do not read the missalette or church bulle-
tin may simply gaze down at their shoes, or glance up to see
the sporadic parade of people finding their places in the pews.
Those few moments before Mass are probably the only time
all week we are silent while in the midst of a crowd.

We have had to wait at other times through the week: in
the check-out line at the grocery store, at the bus stop, for the
school bell, for the stop-light. But at each of those pauses we
always had a channel to change, a dial to turn, or a button to
press that would rescue us from the silence. The church pew
has no dials, buttons, or channels to make the silence go away:
no radio, no television, no cell phone, no music player, and no
computer. We feel lost and helpless without a remote control
in hand or a screen in front of our face.

What fills our thoughts as this waiting lingers? Have we
forgotten the old alchemy of how to convert *waiting* into
anticipation? Or do we take the nearest mental exit to daydream and set our minds to automatic pilot as our bodies
slouch low? We can easily remain right where we are as our
mind stealthily disengages and ducks away in escape. The
incense seems like anesthesia. The teen's thoughts rush ahead
to the future freedom of college-life when the Sunday morning fights will be far away and he can snooze away as if Saturday
morning lasted all weekend. As the father sits and waits for
Mass to begin, he replays the office skirmishes of this past
week. He thinks of what he really wanted to say, and rehearses
with precision his exit speech for that happy day when he,
against all odds, wins the lottery.

As we sit, we know what is coming. A priest will process
forward with some ministers. The congregation will stand,

some will sing. The priest will continue along the center aisle of the church to the altar. He will turn and begin with the routine words and gestures. Our minds may drift again, back to the office, beach, or ball field. We may think about how life has wronged us and rewarded others. Every now and then a lector, priest, or musician runs loud and disturbs our stream of consciousness. The usher may pass too close and bump us back into the present moment as he escorts a late-comer to the plentiful seats up front. When the daydreams run out, we may look around to see who else is here—and who isn't. After taking attendance, one can take in the latest fashions.

Instead of thinking how God created us and called us to life in his Church as we sit in the pew on Sunday morning, our minds can so easily drift to the abrupt meeting at work, the rift with the neighbors, the weeks until vacation, or the others here at church. Then we judge ourselves harshly for thinking of these distractions during Mass.

Or perhaps we are one of the late-comers. We plan to attend the 10:30 A.M. Mass. We get the kids ready, load the car, and realize we forgot the envelope for the collection. We run back in the house, get the envelope, drive to church, can't find a parking place, finally locate one a distance away, and cross the threshold during the *Gloria*. We are late. We grit our teeth and judge ourselves again. We worry about the example we set for our children, what others think as we squeeze into the pew. Then we try to settle down and listen.

The kids begin to move about, and push each other in the pew. We tell them to stop. They continue. We separate them, again judging ourselves, blaming ourselves for their behavior. *They should be more behaved in church. What am I doing wrong?* We try to concentrate again.

Just inches away, within and underneath the familiarity of our routine, someone else sits down. He has decided in his love that it is *necessary* for him to journey into our distractions, resistances, complaints, habits, and excuses. Our escape route is his familiar territory. He has been here many times before. He knows very well the paths we travel, and he wants to meet us there. He wants to convert our daydreaming into *imagination*, our distractions into *directions*, our resistance into *strength*, and our habits into *virtues*. He usually begins by asking us for a drink.

Invitation over Ultimatum

If Jesus is so close to us, why does it seem so difficult to find him? What stands in the way? So often we are too busy with distractions and fears to see Jesus. The Samaritan woman has been hurt so frequently that she instinctively pushes everyone away. When Jesus asked the Samaritan woman for a drink, she responded, "How can you, a Jew, ask me, a Samaritan woman for a drink?" (Jn 4:9). As is often the case today, rigid societal rules led to automatic and inflexible thinking. She responds with the prejudice and the false security of the old hatreds. Jesus, in turn, responds, "If you knew the gift of God and who is saying to you, 'Give me a drink,' you would have asked him and he would have given you living water" (Jn 4:10). The woman stops in her tracks. This is a new moment. She had gone to the old defenses, and he responded with *the new invitation* to the *gift*. She cannot remember the last gift she received. Other men would push her farther into the exile of ultimatums when she went to her defenses. They had cursed at her, insulted her, and used her as an object. Yet, this man is different. He speaks about a *gift* that he wants to *give* to her. He reveals the depth of his thirst, not for something to drink but a thirst for the *gift*, for the person to *receive the gift*. She is the most thirsty resident of that town. Jesus has begun to transform her thirst for passing things into the thirst for righteousness (cf. Mt 5:6). The Eucharist is the gift par excellence in which we receive refreshment and nourishment from the Lord Jesus. As Pope Benedict XVI emphasizes: "Precisely because Christ has become for us the food of truth, the Church turns to every man and woman, inviting them freely to accept God's gift."[6]

As Jesus begins to speak about the gift, she senses something deeper in what he is saying: *his thirst is not about himself.* His thirst is about *others.* She has not met this manner of man before. Already she has changed. Her conversion is beginning. As soon as he says the word "gift," her prejudices begin to loosen. The word of Jesus is the basis of her conversion and transformation. His word of life drills through all of the stubborn scars and buried pain. As the prophet Ezekiel says, "As he [the Lord] spoke to me, spirit entered into me" (Ez 2:2). The psalmist says that the Lord "sent forth the word to heal them" (Ps 107:20). Pope Benedict XVI teaches that the Word we hear proclaimed at Mass leads us to the spiritual fulfillment we desire, and it draws us to the presence of Christ in the Eucharist: "There is an intrinsic bond between the word of God and the Eucharist. From listening to the word of God, faith is born or strengthened (cf. Rom 10:17); in the Eucharist the Word made flesh gives himself to us as our spiritual food."[7] Transformed by his word, the Samaritan woman now addresses him not as "you, a Jew," as she had only moments before. She begins to recognize the presence of Jesus. She addresses him: "Sir, you do not even have a bucket and the cistern is deep; where then can you get this

---

6. Pope Benedict XVI, *Sacramentum Caritatis*, 2.

7. Ibid., 44.

living water? Are you greater than our father Jacob who gave us this cistern and drank from it himself with his children and flocks?" (Jn 4:11–12). She has gone from the harsh words of prejudice to the practical protection of excuses.

We make excuses too. Excuses are the opposite of commitments. Our excuses harden into complaints. Jesus tells us about the gift in many ways every day, but our defenses deter us: we have too much to do, the calendar is full, the times for Mass don't meet our schedule, the pastor only talks about money, we don't agree with or understand this teaching or that, we are tired of hypocrites, it's boring, we don't get anything out of it.

Jesus then states the case clearly: "Everyone who drinks this water will be thirsty again; but whoever drinks the water I shall give will never thirst; the water I shall give will become in him a spring of water welling up to eternal life" (Jn 4:13–14). Excuses do not quench our thirst. Everyone who drinks the water of prejudice or excuses will become thirsty again. But Jesus offers another type of water; the water of the gift that overflows and quenches our thirst.

The original Greek language of Sacred Scripture captures the conversation at a deeper level than the English translation does. When he speaks about the water, Jesus uses the Greek word pēgē (πηγή) (Jn 4:14), which means *fountain*, *spring*, or *source*. This water is lively, fresh, and clean. When she speaks of the water, the text uses the Greek word phrear (φρέαρ), (Jn 4:11), meaning a *water tank* in which water sits motionless and inactive.[8] Such water quickly becomes stagnant. The Old Testament account of Joseph and his brothers tells us that one day Joseph's brothers were tending their father's flocks at

---

8. See Jones, *The Symbol of Water in the Gospel of John*, 99.

Shechem (cf. Gn 37:12–13a). They were near this very well at which the Samaritan woman meets Jesus. In fact, Joseph's brothers, in their envy against Joseph, plot to "kill him and throw him into one of the cisterns" (Gn 37:20). They relied on evil schemes and stagnant cisterns to solve their problems.

The Samaritan woman sees water as a necessity and gathering it as a task. Yet, she will gradually and tumultuously come to learn the identity of Jesus. As we have seen, she first rudely refers to him as "you"; then prejudicially as "you, a Jew,"; then, after they have been speaking for a while, respectfully as "Sir"; and finally she will proclaim him as the "Messiah." We often mistake the well within us as a flat necessity: Baptism is a merely ceremonial action we do because this is what people do when they have a baby. We view Confirmation as an important ceremony, a step our children take with their classmates. But do we see these moments the way Jesus does, as *fountains* that spring up within us?

Many people in our world turn inward to find a water tank instead of a fountain. In this understanding, the water of our spiritual life does not move. In fact, the water tank itself is always in danger of leaking, and the water may become contaminated. Such water does not nourish or provide any fresh infusion of life.

The woman from Samaria lived from such a tank: She began every day with worldly fear. She lived on such a diet of fear, hurt, and negativity that she was defensive, depressed, and alone. The waters of depression never move. They only grow dark. Jesus steps into the darkness of the fear and offers the gift. As Jesus sits by that well, he is declaring that he is the fulfillment of everything that past generations sought from that well. Jesus himself *is* the fountain of new life. Jesus says that the water he gives will become in the one who drinks a fountain (genēsetai en autō pēgē; γενήσεται εν αντω πηγη). The psalmist proclaims that God can open up "springs and torrents" (Ps 74:15). The water that God provides is the Holy Spirit. Jesus's gift of the Holy Spirit becomes a source *within the believer himself.* The Holy Spirit is not meant to be isolated as a private possession of the person. Rather, from the very beginning of the Church, the presence of the Holy Spirit in the believer is visible to others (cf. Acts 6:5; 9:17; 11:24; 13:52). The *Catechism of the Catholic Church* describes the Holy Spirit as "the artisan of God's works."[9] He is the voice that speaks even in the midst of our pain. He summons us even in our symptoms. Transformed by the Spirit, the Christian enters more deeply into the painful places of the world to be a sign of God's grace: "As they pass through the Baca valley, they find spring water to drink" (Ps 84:7). The Holy Spirit enters the Christian in such a way that the source of the gift is located within the person, just as the apprentice internalizes the trade from the action of the master craftsman.[10]

To find the depths of our identity
we must pass through fear.

---

9. *CCC*, no. 741.

10. See Jean-Pierre Torrell, O.P., *Saint Thomas Aquinas: Spiritual Master,* vol. 2 (Washington, DC: Catholic University of America Press, 2003), 19–20.

Chapter Two

Identity, Fear, and the Problem of Progress

Identity: Layers and Labels

As we consider our inner world we also begin to reflect on our own identity. Think for a moment about your identity. *Who are you?* What comes to mind as you think about who you are? Some things come predictably to mind. We think of our nationality. *I am Italian. I am Irish. I am Polish. I am Hispanic. I am Asian. I am African-American.* We think of our occupation. *I am a banker, a teacher, a taxi driver. I am blue collar or white collar. I work in an office. I work from home. I travel a lot in my work.* We think of our blessings. *I am a husband and father. I am a wife and mother.* Like the woman of Samaria, we may also think of our pains and hurts. *My parents are divorced. My son is in jail. My daughter has an addiction. My children do not attend church. My parents are ill.*

But to find our identity, we must go deeper. As we peel back the initial layers of our identity we may also think of our attitudes or habits. *I am a responsible person. I like things to be predictable and neat. I am a last-minute person. I am an extrovert or an introvert. I work hard.* Reflecting on our identity also may include our hobbies. *I am an artist or an athlete. I like to read, watch movies, or listen to music.* We might also equate our identity with our physical appearance, which preoccupies us. *I am tall. I am short. I have dark hair, blond hair, red hair. I am neat, sloppy, meticulous, or lazy. My nose isn't right.* This often leads to comparing our looks with the looks of others. Inevitably, we find someone whom we believe is more attractive and charming than we are. Going on, we may equate our identity with our mood. *I am usually happy, sad, sensitive, demanding, quick-tempered, or patient.* Some people attach their identity to their salary. We often confuse our identity with a number: our debt, our savings, our credit score, our zip code, our weight, or the number of things we own. Popularity and cash flow are often quickly equated.

Our identity is more than the elements that distinguish our individuality.[1] As we move beyond appearances and peel back the layers even more, we drill down inwardly and reflect on our identity. We might claim to be the worst thing that ever happened to us. We equate ourselves with our wounds, our pains, our confusion, with the faults of our parents, the betrayals of former confidants, the many reversals of love. Those times in our life when we have wanted to shrink down, hide, or be invisible can leave a painful impact. Negative past events tend to linger in our memories. Our past pains can easily roar to life and haunt us all over again. We often confuse our self-esteem with our identity. Many mistake the way they

---

1. See Balthasar, *The Glory of the Lord I*, 26.

happen to feel about themselves *as* the inner self. This was the case for the woman of Samaria. She would rather endure hard labor in the noonday heat than the disdainful, scorching glares of her neighbors. This is why she lashes out at Jesus. Her experiences have trained her that relationship brings only pain.

It is easy to feel empty as we drift consciously or unconsciously over the many layers of our beliefs about the self. Many of us keep this feeling inside for a long time. Rarely do others see the pain, ambiguity, and loneliness. Instead, many people pretend to be happy. They do all the "right" things on the outside, yet on the inside continue to spiral downward. Some may feel they are being sucked into quicksand rather than being led into the refreshing fountain of which Jesus speaks. Many feel dried up with no buoyancy. In their dryness they settle for *feelings of satisfaction* rather than actual *fulfillment*. Some turn to self-help books, therapy-based television shows, and personality seminars. Some attempt to fill the inner emptiness with endless activities, substances, plans, or pleasures. These places of false refuge easily and quickly become patterns, habits, and even addictions. The downward spiral continues, and many begin to believe they are trapped by the things others have done to them.

At a certain point in life some people may begin to wish they were actually someone else or could start over with a different life. Those who experience pain can often fall into the trap of idealizing others. Often, in the early immature years, people wish they could switch places with a classmate or friend who seems to have it all: flawless good looks, high intelligence, the "perfect family," money, talent, popularity, expensive toys, the cleanest house, and athletic prowess. But before wishing for these things, people often blame themselves or others. It is so easy to blame others for all our problems and painful setbacks. We blame others for *who we are* rather than take responsibility for *who we will become*. Oddly enough, many who have a negative sense of themselves stubbornly refuse to work their way out of such pain. Instead, they blame, pretend, anesthetize, fantasize, and search for shortcuts that sometimes appear to pay off in the short run. It appears easier to wish for what we desire than to work for it.

Many escape routes lure us as we walk our personal Way of the Cross. We are tempted to break away and flee from our own powerlessness. Yet, in the Christian way of life, to escape our powerlessness is to forego our inheritance. Jesus invites us not simply to put up with our cross, but to take up our cross daily (cf. Lk 9:23). Saint Paul teaches that we are to be content with weakness, insults, and persecutions for the sake of Jesus (cf. 2 Cor 12:10). In the moment of weakness and self-surrender, we discover the moment of the gift.

Identity: Remembering What We Forgot

What were we human beings meant to be in our original, unfallen state? Who would we be if all the difficult and painful things had not happened? What would the world and human nature be if they had progressed in the way God had intended, without the influence of sin?

If we had remained in a state of harmony and perfection, our minds would know truth directly. We would not so easily give in to the temptation to cheat, lie, or gossip. Our will would seek authentic goods in a direct and unimpeded fashion. We would not be tempted again and again to get ahead at another's expense, to use others, or to manipulate them. Our appetites or passions would be ordered to the truly beautiful. People would not hurt one another, but would truly make a gift of themselves to each other in love.

Our experience is far different from this. Life quickly becomes complicated. The order and harmony for which we were created has become subject to evil, pain, pathology, imbalance, hardship, and malice. The difficulty is that evil *appears* to us to be good. We are taken in by *apparent* truths and *apparent* goods. A young couple who have fallen in love will move in together. They do not see the dangers and pain they are setting themselves up for. They do not want to wait in order to develop the necessary maturity that even love cannot sidestep or bypass. They give in to fear rather than give themselves away in love. It is only when we step back and look deeply at life that we see the finely grained movements by which we experience the authentically true and good. From the vantage point of mature experience we can detect our inner wounds. We find it difficult to know what is really true, and we find it difficult to do what is truly good. Our intellect and will are wounded and weakened. A break at the root of our identity has inflicted these wounds.

This break is known as sin. Sin is an offense by which we have opposed God in disobedience. When we sin, we consciously and deliberately reject God and his ways. We disobey and forget God. Sin separates us from God and delivers us to chaos, disorder, and emptiness. The chaos of sin would never look like chaos to the untrained eye, however. At first glance, the chaos of sin does not seem like bedlam or pandemonium. This chaos *appears* to be good and true. It pays its taxes. It mows its lawn. It is neatly cleaned and pressed, and always arrives on time, but it is deeply and perniciously evil. Sin has wormed its way deep inside us and has wounded our intellect, will, and passions. As the prophet Isaiah says, we are afflicted by "[w]ound and welt and gaping gash, not drained, or bandaged, or eased with salve" (Is 1:6b). We long for refreshment and healing, but very often our activity in the world only worsens the wound. Refreshment comes from only one source: God and his life of grace. Blessed Pope John Paul II taught that purity of heart and the life of grace are like a "hidden spring" that we must keep watch over lest our access to it be cut off. [2] The Holy Father notes that we must guard this "hidden fountain" like a "watchman." Sin and its effects threaten to obstruct our access to the fountain, so that we lose our way to its refreshing waters of grace and virtue.

An image may be helpful. When I was growing up, our family home was located on two lots. At the border of the second lot we had a dense thicket of hemlock (a variety of thick, needle leafed evergreen trees) over thirty feet long and eight feet high. Over the years, it doubled in height. The branches grew thickly together. But a variety of weeds sprung up in the soil beneath the beautiful evergreen thicket. This undergrowth of vines, ivy, and weeds grew more rapidly than the trees themselves. Every season the weeds would grow up through the hemlock, tightly intertwining with the trunks and choking the branches. The vines would even grow out through the top of the hemlock and droop over. Not only was it unsightly, but worse, the weeds were choking the life out of the hemlock. In the dense thicket, it was impossible to uproot the ivy, weeds, and vines; we could only trim them back.

Many people find that sin creeps into their lives in a similar way. They know they have patterns of sin and vice that are choking the life out of their marriages, families, and personal lives. Yet, they cannot find a way to clear out the roots. They may "trim back" the behaviors from time to time. They may make resolutions, renew good intentions, or seek some assistance. But they never seem able to pull out the roots. The

---

2. See Pope John Paul II, *Man and Woman He Created Them: A Theology of the Body* (Boston: Pauline Books & Media, 2006), 320, 326.

patterns, vices, sins, and pain always return and sometimes rapidly spread.

Eventually we had to cut down and haul away all the hemlock. We decided to plant grass seed in the expanse of brown soil where the trees had been, in order to flood the area with new life. But first we had to prepare the soil for the seed. When I tried to turn the soil over with a large shovel, I was thrown off balance. The dirt wouldn't budge, not even an inch. I tried again. Same result. I went to a different patch of dirt, but I couldn't even make the shovel go down half an inch. The roots of the weeds, vines, and ivy had grown so thickly in the dirt through all those years, that now they formed an almost impenetrable layer that prevented any access to the rich soil below. If I simply scattered the grass seed in this dirt, the roots of the ivy and vines would produce weeds that would overwhelm and choke off the new life. To prepare the ground for the grass seed, I had to use a small hand tool and slowly work through every inch of the soil to free it from the intertwined mass of roots. Only then did the dirt become true soil again, free enough to receive the new seed and to allow water to penetrate so that the seed might burst open and grow.

The tangle of roots symbolizes what sin, vice, and their effects produce in our lives. Just like weeds, the roots of sin weave a web of disorder all through the soil of our lives. For years, my family saw the weeds through the hemlock. We even trimmed them back, but we never realized how deeply they had penetrated. They not only choked off the life of the hemlock, but they also prevented new life from taking root.

The story about the hemlock is an image for the purgative way of the spiritual life. Just as I had to dig out the roots, in our lives we need to cut away all the barrenness and pain. We do this in our spiritual life through purification or what is called purgation, the first stage of the spiritual life. As God purges sin from our life, and we are docile to his great action, we begin to look for ways to plant new life.

God is the like a gardener, who through the Holy Spirit works patiently in every inch of our soul and life to free us from sin, vice, and their effects. In the Gospel of Saint John, Saint Mary Magdalen sees Jesus as a gardener after his resurrection (cf. Jn 20:15). The Bible speaks of three great gardens: the Garden of Eden, the Garden of Gethsemane, and the Garden of the Resurrection. We, like the soil of a garden, must be docile before the Gardener who longs to bestow the seed of new life deep in our hearts and to water it with his grace so that we grow in virtue. All of the pain of purgation, where we must be honest with ourselves and with God, prepares for new life and growth. The purgation can take years. Our best tools in this time are patience and humility. The moment we begin to crave progress in the spiritual life we are only adding to the roots of pride. As the purgative way clears the ground, new life can find an opening and sink deeply into our hearts. This begins the illuminative way, which follows the purgative way. The illuminative way is the time when, after the attachment to vice and sin is healed, God shows us the deep beauty of his mysteries. Then follows the unitive way, where we are united to God, and we grow deeply in his love.

Like the Samaritan woman, we may feel somehow marked by the seemingly unconquerable patterns of life, by pain on the one side and indulgence on the other. The weight and hardship of our poor decisions never seem far away. They certainly were not for the Samaritan woman.

She is particularly burdened by sin and its effects. Jesus notes that the Samaritan woman had five husbands. He brings this forward, not to embarrass her, but to confront her so that she can acknowledge the chaos and see it in its proper light—or darkness. He shows this to her in his mercy and attentiveness to her pain. As the psalmist says, "My wanderings you have noted . . ." (Ps 56:9).

Numbers are important in the Scriptures, and they often stand for more than a simple quantitative measure. The number five, such as the five husbands of the Samaritan woman, can also stand for other realities denoted by the number five. Saint Bonaventure taught that the number five in the passage of the Samaritan woman was connected to the number five in the account of the rich man and the poor beggar Lazarus in the Gospel of Saint Luke (cf. Lk 16:28). In that parable, Jesus tells the story of the rich man who now abides in Hades after he had feasted his whole life and neglected the poor man Lazarus at his gate. From his suffering in Hades the rich man looks up and sees Lazarus now comforted in heaven. The rich man fears that his five brothers, still living, will come to the same end as he did, so he asks Abraham to send Lazarus to the five brothers and tell them to repent while they have time. Saint Bonaventure says, "By the number five is understood that they had been given over to the five senses of the body, according to what is said to the Samaritan woman in John 4:18: 'You have had five husbands. . . .'"[3] The brothers represent the five senses, which the rich man had indulged. The reference to the five husbands of the Samaritan woman helps us recall the trap of indulging the five senses, an indulgence that causes her much pain and prevents her from relating to others. Yet, at some point in her choosing, that which was painful and hurtful *appeared* to be good and true.

---

3. St. Bonaventure, *Commentary on the Gospel of Luke* as in *Works of St. Bonaventure* ed., Robert J. Karris, O.F.M. (New York: Franciscan Institute Publications, 2003), 1545.

When we feel pain on the inside, we so easily use the senses and the body to attempt to feel good again. But Jesus knows this, and he goes out of his way to make it *a necessary and central part of his journey* to meet the Samaritan woman. Jesus also wants to meet us.

To respond adequately to the question of our identity, we must realize that descriptions of our habits, histories, or appearances do not explain who we are as *persons*. Our spiritual gravity must take us farther and deeper to the substance of our identity and meaning. Despite any indication otherwise, a consistent core lies beneath all the attributes that may describe us. This core can show forth the authenticity and originality of our identity. *Who are we?* What is our identity *in our deepest self?*

Admitting Fear

Understanding one's life and faith as a gift is not an idealistic, world-denying outlook or a naïve coping mechanism for the painful events of daily life. To live by the gift frees us from the self-centered attitudes that can weigh down our spiritual life. To live by the gift helps us climb out from under the load of negativity, impulsiveness, and routine fueled by our self-centeredness. To live by the gift turns our automatic reactions into authentic human responses.

Each person finds himself or herself alone at some point to reflect on the direction of one's faith journey. Perhaps we have taken a detour or wandered into an apparent dead end. We may have taken a circuitous route leading to consequences that we never imagined. The dead ends, blind alleys, and one-way streets in which we find ourselves so quickly cornered can actually lead us to step forth on a new pilgrimage. Our faith journeys can begin again, in an instant.[4]

But what happens when people give up instead? Decline in the practice of the faith evolves from various causes. Some persons have simply grown cold. Some drift because they have been conditioned by the worldly values, attitudes, and behavior of a secular culture.[5] Yet, the idea that the secularist should doubt faith is itself a *belief* of the secularist. Indifference becomes solidified over time and is actually seen as a good thing. Some disagree with a particular teaching of the Church, while others were treated rudely at one time or another. Adrenaline over such issues and experiences then fuels disagreement into dissension. Some turn away from the practice of the faith because of painful wounds from the past. Some have a crisis of faith in which they find little meaningful direction.

Outreach that is artificial or too intense can entrench misunderstandings rather than heal them. Even the attempt to identify common ground on an issue as a starting point can often provoke fearful suspicions and the taking of sides. Unless the common ground is holy ground, we are out of our element. The common good is the only truly common ground.

In order to find it, we must acknowledge a common experience. To reignite diminishing fervor, we must find a strategic location to begin building bridges over long-standing divides.

---

4. Hence the eminent Swiss theologian Hans Urs von Balthasar notes the attempt to capture the favorability of religion through a research poll or statistical measure of trends always falls short. The Holy Spirit confounds all measure. See Balthasar, *Theo-Drama IV*, 462, 480. Balthasar makes this point again when he notes that no statistic can capture the often hidden fruitfulness of the action of the saints, see *The Glory of the Lord VII*, 531. See also Balthasar, *Theo-Drama II, Theological Dramatic Theory: Dramatis Personae* (San Francisco: Ignatius Press, 1992), 29.

5. See Pope John Paul II, *Veritatis Splendor*, 88.

Oddly enough, the most common experience among human persons is fear. The modern world is preoccupied with fear.

This fear is not the dramatic, Halloween-style fear represented by the silhouette of a knife-wielding, masked intruder in a hallway. The excitement of suspense-fear that dissipates after the horror movie credits scroll away entertains us. But we face another type of fear, much more pervasive. This kind of fear wakes us up at 3:15 A.M., sits beside us at breakfast, and hides behind our tensions and odd behaviors. It fills us with anxiety and leads to ulcers, high blood pressure, migraines, and panic attacks. These afflictions result when we try to control fear by keeping it locked inside us. Control is power distilled into many forms: arrogance, entitlement, frustration, stubbornness, excessive rivalry, and resentment. All of these are based in fear. Why are we afraid to let others see our fears? Are we afraid to appear out of control? Ironically, chaos is actually synonymous with control, for the opposite of control is creativity. We so often resist the challenge of creativity because of our fears. Our fears walk up the steps of church with us on Sunday, sit between family members in the pew, and dream instead of live. Fear drains the fountain to a puddle.

To find the depths of our identities we must pass through fear. For many persons, fear can easily fill their experience of religion. Unfortunately, religion can often be misinterpreted and incorrectly seen as a means of control, constraint, and painful judging rather than as healing and direction. In such circumstances, misunderstandings about religion can be a source of debate. The debate is not understood as a learning experience, but quickly turns into a controversial and confusing argument. This can lead to anger that reminds people of early pain or trauma from the past: fights between parents who worked too much or drank too much, shouting matches about money, a screaming mother, an absent father, a teacher who ridiculed, or a coach who made an example *of* players rather than set an example *for* them. Arguments, control, and ultimatums simply reinforce worldly fear.

Worldly fear emerges from the pain of sin. Saint John is speaking about worldly fear when he says, "There is no fear in love, but perfect love drives out fear because fear has to do with punishment, and so one who fears is not yet perfect in love" (1 Jn 4:18). Love is given for all of us in the generous act by which God creates, and then saves, the world. You and I do not create love. We *share* in it. Love is uncreated, and, as such, it fills the universe. In order to give love, we must first have *received* it. We can receive love in two ways. First, we can receive it in the form of charity, authentic self-giving love that pours itself out for the true good of the other. This is the love to which Pope John Paul II refers when he says, "Man cannot live without love. He remains a being that is incomprehensible for himself, his life is senseless, if love is not revealed to him, if he does not encounter love, if he does not experience it and make it his own, if he does not participate intimately in it."[6] The second, and tragic form of encountering love, is in the form of fear, that is, wounded love. This kind of possessive love is self-taking and harms the true good of the other, turning the other to associate desire with worldly fear instead of with authentic love.

The experience of hurt, loss, rejection, and abandonment leads to deep, painful wounds, especially where we are most vulnerable—in the family. The individual who carries the weight of these wounds often tries to heal them through unhealthy means. Our wounds make us more desperate for the quick fix, when we easily let illusions deceive us. We are

---

6. John Paul II, *Redemptor Hominis*, 10.

meant for love, but when wounded, we distrust love and settle for power, that is, we settle for less. Rather than love, we focus on acquiring things and achieving status. As we grow more wounded by this process, we seek to acquire more and more to make us finally feel safe and worthwhile. Our drive to acquire must find a new trophy every day in order to be satisfied. We seek to do this efficiently and quickly. Everyone around us seems to be in a desperate rush. People move so quickly in the grocery store aisles, the highway lanes, and at work. It is as if they are searching for something beyond a loaf of bread, the next exit, or the next project awaiting them in their office. Speed and rushing do not simply indicate busyness; they signify anger. If the first car does not proceed immediately when the traffic light turns green, horns blare as if to say, "I am more important than the person in front of me, who does not deserve to be in my way."

Our fears circle around in our minds like a ferris wheel: one fear passes and another rides to the top. Our fears often run along particular lines: *I may not finish this project on time . . . What if my kids get sick? Can I afford the new roof? What if market conditions worsen? . . . Will I finish this report? . . . Do I fit in with my co-workers and friends? What does the boss really think of me? . . . How do I keep track of this hectic schedule? Why do I go to parties and feel alone? What if a pink slip appears in my inbox? Why do I over-analyze things? What if someone else comes along who is quicker, faster, and better looking than I am?*

Other fears often hit close to home. *What do the neighbors think of me? Why do my parents argue? Why are my circumstances so out of control? . . . Am I the only one who goes from laughing one moment to screaming the next? How do I keep my brother off drugs and on a payroll? Are my children's grades good enough? Can I make the tuition payment this quarter? Can I afford this mortgage? Will I get a promotion at work? Why does everyone else fall in love, while*

I can barely get a date? Why doesn't life add up? I didn't think my future would be like this. Why don't I get more out of life?

Our fears thrive on measurement and lead to unrealistic expectations. *I need to cram all this knowledge into my head so I can get an A on the test. If I get an A on the test, I'll do well in the course. If I do well, I'll graduate with honors and be accepted into a prestigious college, be more likely to get a high-paying job, and marry a beautiful person. If I do that, I'll have a wonderful life, meet no resistance, and thrive in all I do. If I don't . . .*

We face personal fears. *What will they think if my voice cracks during speech class? Can they hear my mom and dad arguing? What if I go to dance and do the same move twice . . . ? What if I drop the ball?*

We face all kinds of fears. We have fears about performance, heights, water, abandonment, health, public speaking, and so on. Our fears take the form of worries, anxieties, and preoccupations. Sometimes other people see the symptoms of our pain. Occasionally, we may admit our weakness to ourselves. We suffer from the need to control. We feel the gnawing hunger to receive approval from our boss, our spouse, our parents. We often seek to manage the symptoms of our distress rather than heal the cause of our pain.

Most of our fears do not strike terror into our hearts; they are more like background music that only our heart hears, while our head deals with the residue anxiety and passes the effects on to our body as ulcers, hypertension, headaches, and fatigue. Our fears inwardly trouble us as low-dose, chronic anxieties. Saint Paul experienced this too: ". . . we were afflicted in every way—external conflicts, internal fear" (2 Cor 7:5). Elsewhere he speaks of his daily pressures and anxieties (cf. 2 Cor 11:28–29). By its very nature, fear leads us to live impulsive lives of hurried confusion. Beset by fear and the superficial activity it engenders, we are ill equipped to deal properly with love. This is the wound of fear: it deters love, and therefore the gift of self which is the very nature of life and spirituality.

What are we afraid of? What lurks beneath our daily fears of making an incidental mistake, of being late, of public speaking, of raising our hand and getting the answer wrong, the generalized fear that "something" bad will happen? What is the fear that slumbers beneath our random fears? It is the fear that despite all my activity, work, and commitments, *I really don't matter, don't belong, don't fit in, and may actually be a loser.* The subtle sense that I may not matter is the basic fear, the root and meta-fear, variations of which we experience a hundred times a day, and from which all other fears spring. We are afraid that we will end up dissatisfied, incomplete, and unhappy. Fear arises from the often less than conscious, yet haunting preoccupation that no one would notice if I ceased to be. This is the fear that lurks behind all others and forms a common ground that ironically can unite us. Fear is the cause of low self-esteem. A person with poor self-image believes in the fear rather than the gift. So often, in response to low self-esteem, people seek ways to reach an artificial "high," a temporary escape route through misuse of a substance or activity. In all the fears, the fountain of our inner life slows to a trickle and the world becomes a dry chore of one obligation after another.

When fear besets and confines us, our wishes more easily consume us. We begin to daydream and begin the "if only" thinking. *If only my parents had been wealthy. If only I had just gotten in early on the dot com craze . . . had a box office hit . . . started a fashion line. If only I had the talent to be a pop-star . . . was discovered. . . . If only I were better looking. If only I were more extraverted. . . . If only I were smarter.* We begin to live between our fears and our wishes. This puts pressure on us, like a vacuum sucking out air. Because of this pressure, when we do act, we misfire.

We volley back and forth between anxiety and frustration. This ambivalence often spawns a double life. We try to relieve fear by acting out the exotic wish, but the controlled life of fear breeds only regret and guilt.

The fear-or-wish cycle leads to the whirlpool of infatuation. Instead of confidently acknowledging our real possibilities, we see the confidence we desire elsewhere, "out there," in someone else's words, actions, attitudes, and posture. Seeing this, we idealize it and idolize it. We want to feel on the inside the way someone else looks on the outside. We seek to imitate their imagined greatness.[7]

Fear hibernates in our daily endeavors. Just like the heart of the bear that slows to an almost imperceptible beat when it hibernates over the winter in a cave, so too a baseline fear pulses slowly beneath our daily intentions, circumstances, and actions. A key movement of the spiritual life is the capacity to recognize this fear that lies twined so closely to our very personality that sometimes we confuse the two. Our fear must be transformed. Unless we take this step, all other movements in the spiritual life remain cosmetic.

Fear's Hidden Gift

Fear is not all bad news, however. Fear holds a precious clue. The experience of going to church cannot be disconnected from the context of our daily fears. Where does fear come from? Ultimately, it comes from sin, but just how does sin cause fear? You and I experience the *desire* for fulfillment. The *Catechism of the Catholic Church* teaches that, "The desire

---

7. Thomas Merton, *No Man Is an Island* (New York: Harcourt, Brace and Company, 1955), 125.

for God is written in the human heart, because man is created by God and for God; and God never ceases to draw man to himself."[8] The *Catechism* also notes that fear and desire are among our principal passions.[9] In fact, fear is closely related to desire. Desire can prompt us, through the aid of prudence and courage, to overcome unreasonable fears. And reasonable fear, through prudence, can assist us to forego illicit desires. Desire for the authentic good supplies an inner energy to propel us forward. This longing is the yearning for happiness,[10] which entails more than our passing interests, limited goals, or self-centered demands. This desire is reflected in but cannot be reduced to our basic cravings for shelter, pleasure, nourishment, and company. As we look around the world we cannot find the ultimately satisfied person. Despite their millions of dollars and fashion plate good looks, celebrities need yet another blockbuster movie and wrinkle-free skin. Despite a record-breaking winning streak, the star athlete needs one more victory. Despite the straight A report card, the academic wants one more top notch performance. Despite the platinum hit, the recording artist needs one more tour. The ultimately satisfying experience or situation eludes us. We always want one more ride. It seems that the more we get of anything, the more we want, but the less it satisfies.

This yearning offers a clue to our identity: we are meant for more. Surrounded by the finite, we yearn for the infinite; encircled by the measurable, we seek the immeasurable; racing against time, we reach out for eternity. Not only do disasters, calamities, and our apparent curses remind us of this, but so do

---

8. *CCC*, no. 27.

9. *CCC*, no. 1772.

10. See Pontifical Biblical Commission, *The Bible and Morality: Biblical Roots of Christian Conduct* (Roma: Libreria Editrice Vaticana, 2008), Preface.

our discoveries, comforts, and blessings. This reaching for more is not a sign of greed but of greatness. We did not invent our yearning for fulfillment. We did not decide one day to seek for more. The inner dynamic of our yearning comes from beyond us and calls us farther still. This experience had to *come from* somewhere. We cannot fulfill this desire by ourselves, because it did not come from us; we are only finite. It did not come from money, fame, pleasure, or power, because these do not fill it.[11] Since no effect is greater than its cause, that which gave us this infinite yearning must itself be infinite. The greatest fulfillment can only be given by the greatest good. This yearning deep within us, before which we are so often fearful, is the thirst for God.

The Problem of Progress

We often mistake the craving for passing satisfaction as the call of authentic desire. We are meant for more, but we often look for it in the wrong places. Those of us who grew up in the latter half of the twentieth century face a particular difficulty with our identity and faith life. We have been taught from childhood to approach study, exercise, and work with a conquering and industrious spirit, and then look for results. When we study, we want to see speedy returns and advanced grades; when we exercise, we want to see firm muscles immediately; when we work, we want quick results and noticeable returns. We become trained in the paths of unreasonable fears, and suspend our healthy desires. We fear what will happen if we do not "fit in," so we hold back on pursuing authentic truth and goodness. We continuously estimate, measure, and

---

11. See Pope Benedict XVI, *Verbum Domini,* 10.

evaluate progress, and will tolerate nothing less. The spirit of the Industrial Revolution is alive deep within us. Our lives become an assembly line along which we seek to consolidate our efforts with all we do.

There were three sustained revolutions in the past 200 years that have greatly influenced our identities: the Industrial Revolution, the sexual revolution, and the technological revolution.[12] The Industrial Revolution marked the frantic chase after happiness through acquiring things as they came off an assembly line. Consumption and acquisition became the measure of meaning. The infrastructure required for industry stole the father from the family home. After profits and business superseded marriage and family, it was time to get down to pleasure. The same frantic search drove the sexual revolution, not a search for things, but for pleasure. Such efforts do not bring happiness, but only compound the wound in our heart. The anger left over must find an outlet in an even higher rate of frenetic searching. Sex for pleasure became an industry for profit.

This higher speed in the search for happiness drove the technological revolution. Technology has turned sports from a contest of talent and skill into an industry of salaries that defy gravity and news stories from information into entertainment. Our social networks come more and more through a machine. My machine "talks" to your machine. Our work, too, is changed from skillful accomplishment to a race to five o'clock with a quick, or not-so-quick, stop at the bar to try to anesthetize the pain from the day. We check our e-mail and our voice mail at work and at home. Sooner or later we just want someone to hear us for real.

---

12. For more on this topic, see J. Brian Bransfield, *The Human Person* (Boston: Pauline Books & Media, 2010).

The cascading trilogy of the Industrial, sexual, and technological revolutions have saturated the consciousness and categories of modern man: If it can't be quickly acquired with pleasure, it is simply not important. Consumption, pleasure, and profit with speed and efficiency have become the measure of meaning and worth. The contemporary person is encumbered by a demand for efficiency to such an extent that the natural is foreign to us. This is the recipe of the new fundamentalism that is geared to replace the sacred with the disposable. This closed cycle ironically spreads and expands as it feeds on society. The result is a black hole that absorbs and discards all meaning of the gift: family, marriage, human life itself. The person who has experienced early family pain and has developed painful patterns of dealing with that pain then absorbs the culture's answers to pain: find relief through acquisition, achievement, pleasure, power, efficiency, and control. The person thus develops familiar pathways that are essentially self-centered and, while pretending to relieve the pain, only intensify it.

Advertisers would have us believe that we can find "instant beauty" in an over-the-counter product. We cannot. Beauty is not a product. It doesn't come in a bottle or a cream. Shampoo products are advertised as "self-adjusting." But shampoo has no "self"; only persons have a self. The cultural awareness of the meaning of the human person and the meaning of the most classical and sacred institutions in society is deeply fragmented. The horrors of abortion, euthanasia, contraception, divorce, deliberate fatherlessness, human trafficking, and domestic violence proceed directly from such fragmentation. The first enemy of the three revolutions is its consistent victim: the child. The child is the target, because only the child reflects the newness, originality, and spontaneity that can slay the toxic attitude of consumption, pleasure, and efficiency. The devil hates the child. Even after two thousand years, abortion is the devil's temper tantrum at the Incarnation—that the Son of God did not assume angelic nature, but chose to become man as a child in the womb of the Virgin Mary.

We continuously seek a greater return from any investment we have made. We believe that the more we do, the more our value should increase, and the more we should *feel* our value increasing. We can't tolerate ambiguity. We calculate the return on our investment for our education, recreation, and occupation. Undeterred progress becomes our center of gravity and the touchstone of our reality.

This view of identity, besides not being true for our education, occupation, recreation, and family, also creates difficulties for our faith life. We understand faith and religion as an investment. We may have attended religion classes, gone to church, read the Bible, and now teach our children to be good, even sending them to religious education. We pray, attend Mass, and try to live good, honest lives. With such a portfolio, we believe we should receive profits that we can easily measure. If the profits are delayed, or come in a form other than what we expected, we assess our faith practice so that we can feel better spiritually. With faith, as with anything else, we want to gauge the results and maximize our returns. We evaluate our relationship with God by counting blessings and rewards. We often look for God in the results rather than in the signs he provides. It is easy to think that the results *are* the signs. The search for results is not only the enemy of prayer, it is actually the *opposite of prayer*.

The investment-return schema of the spiritual life is at best unpredictable and, at worst, a sticky web. Such a schema clearly does not work with faith, which is a gift, not an investment. The nature of faith as a gift is not so easy to understand. As we turn to our faith lives, we default into automatic thinking. *If I believe in and worship God, then my life ought to show the results. Since I am such a good person and keep the rules of faith, God should see this and answer my prayers so as to arrange my life comfortably. My relatives should be off drugs and on a pay-roll. When I pray I ought to feel secure and sense God's nearness regularly. I should always have more than enough money to pay the bills. None of my loved ones should get cancer, but if any do, God has to heal him. The retirement I dreamed of is the retirement I should have. When I volunteer at the soup kitchen my car should be safely parked around the corner. With the life of faith, as with other categories of life, I should be able to count on the returns.*

Our tendency to measure progress and relate it to our personal self-worth can easily sabotage growth in our relationship with God. My desire to gauge the relationship by the returns is ultimately *more about me* than about God. It is about my control, my need to be certain rather than the gift of faith. The tendency to keep looking for the next result takes us farther away from the fountain. Again and again in the Bible, we see that God calls a person to uncertainty, to a lack of palpable results, and therefore to total reliance on him alone. God summons us to a relationship, not to an analysis. He calls us to be faithful without conditions.

As a result, you and I must train ourselves to a new disposition as we seek to encounter God in the Church. We cannot measure life, especially the life of faith, by our usual standards of fairness. Life is not fair. Life is free. Freedom is not immunity from coercion, but rather a desire for the authentic good. If we look closely, with a new and original vision of faith, we can begin to apply the history of salvation to our own lives. We can see that where we thought God was absent, he was, in fact, present. Where we thought we had nothing, we had the gift.

Chapter Three

The Work of Grace in Us: Three Images

The Treadmill

Physical exercise is very popular today, boosted by health plans, infomercials, and gym ads that promote its benefits. In-home treadmills purport to make exercise more accessible. They require no monthly membership fee, no driving to the gym, and offer the opportunity for convenient exercise. Commitment to the routine, however, is not as easy as it sounds. Boredom steps in as we walk in the same place, seeing the same four walls. The monotony can weigh down and thwart even the best intentions. Treadmills often end up as dusty, yet expensive, hangers for heaps of clothes rather than as health machines.

While the treadmill can be a challenging commitment in our outer world, it is a very helpful image for the traffic of our inner world. Not only do we think a lot, but we also tend to go over the same things in our thoughts. In fact, our inner world can quickly become so busy that it paralyzes our outer spontaneity. We step on the inner treadmill as soon as we awake, as our thoughts race ahead into the day. *What time is the staff meeting? Do I have my presentation prepared? Did I sign the homework? Did the kids study? I forgot to pick up milk last night, is there enough for breakfast? Did I get the clothes from the dryer last night? I have to pick up the medicine, return the library books, check in on Mom and Dad. . . .* We think about our life with its problems, benefits, results; we *think* about how we *feel,* and this makes us even more vulnerable to the ups and downs of daily life. We begin with a low-level preoccupation, pacing through the hours before they arrive. Ironically, as the external treadmill is designed to lower our blood pressure, our internal treadmill raises it.

A sea of worry submerges our natural buoyancy. As the psalmist says, "Fear and trembling overwhelm me" (Ps 55:6). The worries appear to be bona fide concerns of daily life: *Will I make the rent? Can I afford the rising price of education, car insurance, health care and even groceries? Are my children safe when they go out? How do I protect my children from the violence they see on TV? Do I eat the right foods? Is that a new wrinkle . . . a grey hair . . . an extra pound? Are my aging parents still able to care for themselves? Why is my husband always coming home later and later? Are my child's test scores high enough? The busier I am the lonelier I become.* A problem arises not in having daily concerns, but when the worries go into overdrive. Then we face high levels of stress and low levels of enjoyment in our lives. Worries direct us away from the real world into ambition for an illusory ideal. We make decisions based on profit and appearance rather than principles and character.

People react to worry in various ways. Some people try to control themselves and others. Some people escape into drugs or behavioral addictions. Some pursue volume after volume of self-help literature or seek out the latest self-help guru on TV. Some dreamily escape into Hollywood gossip and fashion magazines, imagining themselves as celebrities living in a nonstop whirl of excitement. But we cannot reach into a picture, television show, or someone else's house and become another person. We are created to be ourselves. God has placed within our reach the key to solve our worries.

If we could use a microscope to detect the DNA of worry, we would discover a mixture of obsessive thoughts, compulsive actions, and anxious dispositions that lead to feelings of depression or anger. This mixture clogs the natural circuitry of spontaneity and jams our capacity for original thinking. Worry always makes a difficult situation more complex. Worry is like penance in reverse. *If I endure this preoccupation now, somehow the later situation will turn out okay.* But worry does not work. Ever. Attempts to reach certainty on all issues only multiplies internal friction. The anxiety that comes with our tendency to over-think so often pervades our lives so that we can't escape it. Ironically, we are hardly even aware of *how much we think*. We approach life as if it were a chess game in which we always have to figure out our next move. Worse, we approach God's will as if it were a bomb to be defused rather than a gift to be received. We believe that if we think hard and long enough we will find the key to understand the meaning of life, with its relationships, work, and problems.

In this whirl of thoughts and feelings, religion ceases to be about the fundamental mystery of God. Instead, religion is easily reduced to a set of personal and private beliefs that help us manage our lives and become more effective. The odd thing about this is that it often makes us feel worse and regret our actions and decisions. We blame ourselves when things do not turn out as we wished. Or we may blame others, including

God. The catalog of worries becomes self-defeating and God-defeating. Then we start thinking again about what to do next. We regroup, move on, and try another way to be happy. The conveyer belt in our mind never tires, yet we end up exhausted. Worn out, it seems easier just to give up. But as the woman of Samaria did, we discover the difference between giving up and *surrendering*.

God and his grace remains the answer to anything that confounds the human spirit. We can't control grace. The treadmill approach to life, especially to the spiritual life, insists that if I do the right things or say the right words, God will automatically fix whatever is wrong. The treadmill did not work for the woman of Samaria. Her predictable patterns could not protect her. The treadmill she marched upon took her to all the same places, repeated all the same patterns, and always arrived at the same dead end. She could have tried to track down all the reasons for her bad choices: her parents loved her too much or too little; they were too strict or too loose; she hung out with a bad crowd; or perhaps she just had bad luck. Jesus alone introduces the new detour toward life by his Word that flows like a fresh fountain: "If only you knew the gift of God . . . you would ask him and he would provide living water . . . a fountain within leaping up to eternal life" (Jn 4:10).

Grace is not a genie in a bottle who grants all our wishes as long as we go through the motions and say the correct words. Grace is not an automatic, do-it-yourself reality. Grace is a *gift*. It is God sharing his life with us in the history of salvation. Yet the gift of grace doesn't mean that our life will be painless and carefree. If we think that, we would fail to grasp the nature of love and authentic strength in the first place.

Grace operates in us in a way similar to good exercise. For example, I love to swim. But when I stopped swimming for several years, it was very difficult to begin again. First, I had to find an affordable indoor pool that fit my schedule. Even though my doctor had told me I should exercise more, I did not feel like going out and searching for the right pool. I tried a couple of pools, but they were either too far away or too crowded. I wasn't willing to make the commitment that swimming required. Then, when I found a suitable pool, I would swim three laps and my muscles would scream. I would stop early, not staying long enough to receive any benefit. After that I would put swimming off. It wasn't until I became docile to the firm commitment and sacrifice that swimming required, that I was able to swim for twenty or thirty minutes continuously. Swimming cost me. It meant I only had twenty minutes for lunch. Or on some days it meant I had to wake up an hour earlier and go outside on a cold morning.

After staying with swimming for eight months, I began to look forward to it, enjoy it, and feel its many benefits. This is not to say that grace depends on our efforts. God bestows his grace with incomparable freedom. The health benefits that come from swimming do not come from my finding the right pool, buying a swim suit and goggles, making time in my schedule, and driving to the pool every day. These things dispose me for the exercise of swimming, which helps my bodily systems to operate in harmony and boost my health. So, too, do many activities dispose us to grace, but we do not control or direct the actual experience of grace. As we approach the sacraments, pray, do spiritual reading, and practice the virtues, God acts first, all the time. Through his grace, he makes us sensitive to eternity and frees us for authentic knowledge of himself and his inner mysteries. Sin dulls our capacity to intuit the world and reality as proceeding from the action of God and finding completion in his plan. Grace restores this capacity in a new and wonderful way. The traditional understanding of virtue is that virtue is a good quality of mind by which we can act rightly. We cannot make bad use of a virtue, because if we did, it would not be a virtue, but a vice. But this good quality of mind is worked in us not by our own good intentions or firm will, nor by our simple cooperation with God, but by God working in us, without us.[1]

We receive the action of God upon us in grace, not in a passive way, but in a receptive way characterized by the classical notion of docility. The Holy Spirit is always acting. He prompts the believer by means of the grace of God. We are pliable in God's hands. He molds us to be like himself. This molding takes place over time, because our patterns of self-concern, sin, and worry yield only gradually to concern for others, grace, and faithful originality. If we are to stay on the path of grace, we need a schema or image by which to understand the ethos of grace and our response. Images can assist us in grasping the reality they represent.

Our docility to the action of God does not translate into a porcelain, fragile existence. The word "docility" comes from the Latin *docere*, to teach. Docility is teachableness, and as such is a robust claim of trust.[2] Pope Benedict XVI highlights the importance of this docility: "Created in the image and likeness of God who is love, we can thus understand ourselves only in accepting the Word and in docility to the work of the

---

1. See *Summa Theologiae,* Ia-IIae, q. 55, a. 4. See Cardinal Justin Rigali, *Let the Oppressed Go Free: Breaking the Bonds of Addiction* (Dallas: Basilica Press, 2009), 42.

2. See Servais Pinckaers, *The Sources of Christian Ethics* (Washington, DC: Catholic University of America Press, 1995), 160, and his work in *The Pinckaers Reader: Renewing Thomistic Moral Theology*, John Berkman and Craig Steven Titus, eds. (Washington, DC: Catholic University of America Press, 2005), 63, 68. See also Balthasar, *The Glory of the Lord: A Theological Aesthetics VI, Theology: The Old Covenant* (San Francisco: Ignatius Press, 1991), 127. See also Livio Melina, *The Epiphany of Love: Toward a Theological Understanding of Christian Action* (Grand Rapids, MI: Eerdmans Press, 2010), 18. See also John of St. Thomas, *The Gifts of the Holy Ghost* (New York: Sheed and Ward, 1951), 71.

Holy Spirit."[3] Docility calls us to approach mystery with active and eager resiliency. Docility facilitates our response in faith to revelation, and it enhances and integrates the human person's reception of God's grace. The ability to be docile before the grace of God allows us to be attentive to the deeper currents of reality and the experience of people. Religion, without docility, can appear to come on too strong, to be simply about changing other people's minds rather than transforming their hearts. Attentive and vigorous docility offsets skepticism and disarms secularism.

The Ladder

The image of the treadmill does not fit the spiritual life based on the gift of God's love, but in fact is just the opposite. Christians have always recognized the importance of the *journey*. As we mature we actually move from one stage to another through life. The early Christians associated growth in the spiritual life with upward movement. This upward movement is not the same as contemporary "upward mobility." It is not about a superiority that looks down on people. The classical cosmology of heaven being "up there" in the sky supported this image. The image of the mountain captures this understanding. In the Old Testament, the patriarch and prophet frequently ascended the mountain to speak with the Lord: Noah landed on Ararat, Abraham climbed Moriah, and Moses ascended Sinai (cf. Gn 8:4; 22:2; Ex 19:11). The psalmist asks: "Who may go up the mountain of the LORD? Who can stand in his holy place?" (Ps 24:3). The journey to the presence of

---

3. Pope Benedict XVI, *Verbum Domini*, 6. See also 80, 87.

God is often fraught with difficulties like thunderstorms, so the one who is to enter God's presence must be prepared to face obstacles.

In the New Testament, Jesus finds refuge on the mountain in prayer (cf. Jn 6:15), and he teaches on the mountain (cf. Mt 5:1ff.). The crucifixion takes place on the mountain of Calvary. The account of the Ascension emphasizes upward movement (cf. Mk 16:19; Lk 24:51; Acts 1:2). Growth in the spiritual life was often associated with upward movement.

Similar to the upward movement required to meet God on the mountain, Jacob dreamed of a staircase that ascended to the heavens (cf. Gn 28:12). The ladder became a classic image for growth in the spiritual life. Saint Augustine taught that the gifts of the Holy Spirit are a series of steps that gradually ascend.[4] Saint Irenaeus referred to the Holy Spirit as the ladder by which we ascend to heaven.[5] John Climacus (A.D. 579–649) penned *The Ladder of Divine Ascent* as a guide to living a holy life.[6] Guigo, the twelfth-century Carthusian, wrote the *Ladder of Monks* to describe the ways of prayer.[7] Saint Bernard of Clairvaux, the renowned abbot and Doctor of the Church, wrote *The Steps of Humility and Pride* to assist his brothers in their spiritual journey.[8] The path to holiness

---

4. Cf. Is 11:2. See St. Augustine, *Our Lord's Sermon on the Mount*, ed. Philip Schaff, DD, LLD, *Nicene and Post-Nicene Fathers*, vol. 6 (Peabody, MA: Hendrickson Publishers, Inc., 1994.), bk. I, ch. IV, 11.

5. See St. Irenaeus, "Adversus Haereses," in *Ante-Nicene Fathers*, vol. 1, ed. Alexander Roberts and James Donaldson (Peabody, MA: Hendrickson Publishers, 2004), bk. 3, ch. 24, 1. See also Pinckaers, *The Sources of Christian Ethics*, 151.

6. John Climacus, *The Ladder of Divine Ascent* (New Jersey: Paulist Press, 1982).

7. Guigo II, *The Ladder of Divine Ascent and Twelve Meditations* (Kalamazoo, MI: Cistercian Studies, 1981).

8. Bernard of Clairvaux, *The Steps of Humility and Pride* (Kalamazoo, MI: Cistercian Publications, 1989).

has often been depicted as a journey by which one ascends through stages to reach spiritual maturity.[9] The ladder serves to illustrate that God provides the way, and his grace supports our steps by the structure of his plan. He provides the means for, and guides the way of, our upward movement. When we fall in sin, we descend and regress on the journey. God's grace can then restore us and lift us upward.

Jesus introduces the Samaritan woman to an image similar to the ladder, but one with an even more concrete image of how God acts in our lives: the fountain. "You would have asked him and he would have given you living water . . . whoever drinks the water I shall give will never thirst; the water I shall give will become in him a spring of water welling up to eternal life" (Jn 4:10, 14).

The upward movement of the fountain preserves us from mistaking ourselves as the main actors in the drama of salvation. This universal and practical image, based on the words of Jesus, is easily understood and recalled by the average person. Pope Benedict XVI, calling our attention to the words of Saint Bonaventure, reminds us that the knowledge of sacred Scripture flows from Jesus as if from a fountain.[10] In *The Roads to Zion Mourn*, thirteenth-century Carthusian, Hugh of Balma, describes the action of the Holy Spirit in the spiritual life as an indwelling upward surge that cleanses the human spirit, dissolves the residue of sin, and creates an opening for deeper illumination.[11] Etienne Gilson likens supernatural truth to a river that comes from God and passes over waterfalls as

---

9. See Melina, *The Epiphany of Love*, 94.

10. Pope Benedict XVI, *Verbum Domini*, 29.

11. Hugh of Balma, *The Roads to Zion Mourn* in *Carthusian Spirituality: The Writings of Hugh of Balma and Guigo de Ponte*, The Classics of Western Spirituality Series (New York: Paulist Press, 1997).

it surges toward us.[12] The image of the fountain protects us from mistaking grace as simply an automatic reality that arises because of our own efforts.[13] The image of the fountain refreshes us in the face of so many rigorous and lax metaphors, and guides us to the words of Jesus.

The Fountain

Fountains capture our attention. Cleverly designed indoor and outdoor fountains adorn our shopping malls, gardens, office buildings, and monuments. When I was little, the shopping mall we occasionally visited had a large circular fountain. The pool of water, while only about a foot and a half deep, was about thirty feet in diameter. It was located beneath a huge curved glass dome that allowed a cascade of sunlight to stream through and offered an expansive view of the sky above. Water gushed from the center of the pool and shot high into the air. A large ornate clock hung over the fountain and chimed every fifteen minutes. People would sit on the marble benches around the fountain to watch the water. It seemed almost animated as it shot up as high as it could, then hovered for a moment before falling downward again.

Fountains fascinate us. They create a sense of anticipation and expectancy. The surge of water rising to a height and falling in sheets back to its source appeals to the human psyche and mesmerizes young and old alike. The shimmering water

---

12. Etienne Gilson, *The Christian Philosophy of St. Thomas Aquinas* (Indiana: University of Notre Dame Press, 1956), 12. Balthasar emphasizes water flowing from a spring as one of the four nature symbols for generation, see Balthasar, *The Glory of the Lord a Theological Aesthetics II, Studies in Theological Style: Clerical Styles* (San Francisco: Ignatius Press, 1984), 285.

13. See Torrell, *Saint Thomas Aquinas,* vol. 2, 125, 199, no. 65, 209.

invites people to cast in coins that dot the inlaid designs on the bottom of the pool.

Famous fountains are found in the world of literature and fable, and some, such as the mythical fountain of youth, are also elusive. The ancient world relied on fountains as the foundation of communities. Strategic proximity to water was vital for any civilization. The town center had to be far enough to avoid floods, but close enough to slake the thirst of generations. Hydration was crucial and drought catastrophic. Town squares developed around fountains that emerged from distant and deep sources via the natural forces of gravity. Sources of water routinely form the center around which life gathers.

As an upward surge that moves forth from strong and abundant foundations, the fountain is also an image for the spiritual life. In fountains, water leaps into action. So, too, in us, as Blessed Columba Marmion emphasizes, through Baptism and Confirmation the Holy Spirit becomes a living fountain in the soul of the Christian.[14] Balthasar draws on the same image.[15] The Holy Spirit surges within us, not to control us, but to prompt, influence, and direct us in the way of God's grace. He is not like a water cannon that compels and forces us; he is like that fascinating fountain that invites us and calls us deeper. He bestows sanctifying grace on the soul so that the Trinity may dwell within us and we may become a new creation.

Especially significant for the spiritual life, fountains are a natural symbol of generosity. They well up, pour forth beyond themselves in the act of giving, and are graciously offered back

---

14. See Columba Marmion, *Union with God: Letters of Spiritual Direction by Blessed Columba Marmion,* ed. Dom Raymond Thibaut (Bethesda, MD: Zaccheus Press, 2006), 6.

15. Balthasar, *The Glory of the Lord VII,* 253. See also Jean Daniélou, SJ, *The Presence of God* (Baltimore: Helicon Press, 1959), 27.

to their source only to overflow again, springing forth in a new fruitfulness. God generously pours his life into us. The fountain is an image of a gift of self. The energy of the spring flows upward as it generously proceeds from deep within, and is then scattered and shared with whatever enters its realm. God's grace seeks to transform our pressures, faults, and pain into a gift of self. His grace unleashes the gifts of the Holy Spirit in our lives, to propel us more deeply to the life of virtue based on living the Beatitudes. The *Catechism of the Catholic Church*, at the very beginning of "Part Three: Life in Christ," emphasizes that the gifts of the Holy Spirit make us capable of leading "a life 'worthy of the Gospel of Christ.'"[16] The *Catechism* elaborates on this by stating that in the formation of our conscience, "We are assisted by the gifts of the Holy Spirit, aided by the witness or advice of others and guided by the authoritative teaching of the Church."[17]

The image of the fountain reminds us that God's action in our lives always comes first. His grace moves in us, loosens our complacency, and urges us toward new life and authentic love. Through his refreshing influence, the Scriptures we have heard take on a new meaning. Even though we may sit in a familiar pew, we take on a new perspective. The Mass comes alive for us, instead of being something we simply watch, and we approach the sacraments as opportunities rather than obligations. Fountains change and refresh the world. God's grace changes and refreshes our hearts.

As noted, in the teaching of Pope John Paul II the image of a fountain, or a hidden spring, stands for some of the deepest mysteries of the spiritual life.[18] This image assists us to

---

16. *CCC*, no. 1692.

17. *CCC*, no. 1785.

18. See Pope John Paul II, *Man and Woman He Created Them*, 320, 326. See also Yves Congar, *The Revelation of God* (New York: Herder and Herder, 1968), 29.

envision the momentum of faith, anchoring it in something familiar. The Sacred Scriptures also attest to the importance of the fountain from the very beginning.

Fountains in Sacred Scripture

The Book of Genesis contains two accounts of creation. The first is the staccato-like, seven-day account of creation (cf. Gn 1:1–31). God utters a series of commands and the cosmos arises. On the sixth day, God withdraws into himself and decides to create man, male and female, in the midst of that cosmos.

The second account of creation, which is the older account, takes on a different style (cf. Gn 2:4b–25). It is story-like, and takes place in a garden that God had planted.

> At the time when the LORD God made the earth and the heavens—while as yet there was no field shrub on earth and no grass of the field had sprouted, for the LORD God had sent no rain upon the earth and there was no man to till the soil, but a stream was welling up out of the earth and was watering all the surface of the ground—the LORD God formed man out of the clay of the ground and blew into his nostrils the breath of life, and so man became a living being. (Gn 2:4b–7)

The story moves so quickly that we might miss some elements. Read the above passage again, noticing the portion enclosed by the dash marks, where the author "interrupts" the sentence. Without that portion, the verses simply announce the creation of man from clay and breath. The portion within the dashes appears to contain an incidental fact: there was no field shrub or grass, because there was no rain, and no man to till the soil. But the account has more.

Notice that the author is saying there was no vegetative or human *life*. Without rain, there was no water, and so no *life*.

Even the clay that God takes up depends on the *water*—from the "stream [that] was welling up." Water is the gift of God that propels and prepares for the creation of life.

The stream welling up, or fountain, is a very important, and seemingly required, element in the creation of the human person in particular and of life in general. The human person is created only after the fountain of life wells up in Genesis. It is as if the water welling up in the second account is similar to the "mighty wind" (Gn 1:2) that swept over the waters in the first account. Both symbolize the action of the Holy Spirit.

Water and the fountain are not only significant at the beginning of creation, they are also central to God's saving actions in history. Numerous key events of salvation history happen at streams and wells in the Old Testament. The fountains of the deep purify the earth through the flood of Noah (cf. Gn 7:4, 12, 23b). As noted earlier, the well is a significant place of betrothal. It is also a place of encounter with God. Jacob wrestles with the angel by the side of a stream (cf. Gn 32:23–25). In the face of the thirst of the Israelites, God instructs Moses, "I will be standing there in front of you on the rock in Horeb. Strike the rock, and the water will flow from it for the people to drink" (Ex 17:6). God then makes a fountain surge from a rock to nourish his people. The prophet Isaiah recalls this event: "They did not thirst when he led them through dry lands; water from the rock he set flowing for them; he cleft the rock, and waters welled forth" (Is 48:21). Likewise, the psalmist proclaims: "He split the rock and water gushed forth; it flowed through the desert like a river" (Ps 105:41). Saint Paul, too, explains, "[Our ancestors] all drank the same spiritual drink, for they drank from a spiritual rock that followed them, and the rock was the Christ" (1 Cor 10:4; see also Dt 32).

At the crossing of the Red Sea, God turns the sea into a fountain on either side through which the Israelites safely pass (cf. Ex 14:22; Ps 77:15–21). The psalmist announces, "As they pass through the Baca valley, they find spring water to drink" (Ps 84:7). In the Book of Numbers, Balaam announces the favor of God upon his chosen people: "They are like gardens beside a stream. . . . His wells shall yield free-flowing waters, he shall have the sea within reach" (Nm 24:6a, 7a). Even foreigners are cleansed by the fountain at the word of the prophet: "So Naaman went down and plunged into the Jordan seven times at the word of the man of God. His flesh became again like the flesh of a little child, and he was clean" (2 Kgs 5:14; cf. Lk 4:27).

The prophet Isaiah speaks of a fountain that never runs dry (cf. Is 58:11). He also cries out: "Streams will burst forth in the desert, and rivers in the steppe. The burning sands will become pools, and the thirsty ground, springs of water" (Is 35:6b–7a). The prophet Daniel proclaims: "You springs, bless the LORD" (Dn 3:77). The psalmist echoes: "He changed the desert into pools of water, arid land into springs of water" (Ps 107:35). The Lord discloses himself as "the source of living waters" to the prophet Jeremiah (Jer 2:13). Isaiah promises that the elect will draw water with joy from the "fountain of salvation" (Is 12:3). The psalmist proclaims to the Lord: "From your delightful stream you give us drink" (Ps 36:9b). In the New Testament, Jesus announces salvation to the Samaritan woman at the well, as we have seen, and he proclaims that living waters well up within the believer (cf. Jn 4:14). The fountain refers to the Holy Spirit within the believer.[19] Jesus transforms water into wine at

---

19. Jn 7:37–39; see Balthasar, *The Glory of the Lord VI*, 421, 424–425.

the wedding feast of Cana (cf. Jn 2:1–11). He walks on the sea to show his power over creation (cf. Jn 6:16–21). The man carrying the jar of water guides the way to the Last Supper (cf. Mt 26:17–19; Mk 14:12–16; Lk 22:7–13). Jesus washes the feet of his apostles as a share in his inheritance (cf. Jn 13:1–20). The Book of Revelation announces that those who are thirsty shall drink of the Lord's "gift" which flows "from the spring of life-giving water" (Rv 21:6b; cf. Rv 22:1). The Holy Spirit is the fountain spoken of in the Book of Revelation.[20]

Today, the thirst for spirituality is on the rise, yet spirituality means different things to different people. Some step onto the treadmill every day. The hectic pace, worry, and avoidance never slakes their thirst. Spirituality-lite and self-help tomes do not fill us. But in the midst of all the distractions, another path leads to the fountain. We can easily remember this image and call it to mind throughout the day. It reminds us that our spiritual journey begins with and is renewed by the action of God within us. His action of love gives buoyancy to our response to him. If we believe our spiritual life is up to us, it becomes another task on the list rather than a response to God who is already at work within us.

The Fountain of the Cross

The image that Jesus uses in his conversation with the Samaritan woman is also directed to us: Jesus on the cross is the fountain of all holiness in his self-gift of love to the point of death. We must focus again on Jesus Christ and his gift of self on the cross for us. As his body is pierced on the cross, blood and water pour forth (cf. Jn 19:34). A few earlier verses

---

20. See H. M. Féret, OP, *The Apocalypse of St. John* (Westminster, MD: The Newman Press, 1958), 72.

foreshadow this, when the disciple whom Jesus loved leaned on the side of the Lord at the Last Supper (cf. Jn 13:23). The beloved disciple already senses and follows the intuition of love. He is already aware of the great treasures and blessings that will flow from this place. In only a few short hours, he will still be standing by this great source as the side of Christ is pierced and opened on the cross.[21] As the prophet Zechariah foretold: "I will pour out on the house of David and on the inhabitants of Jerusalem a spirit of grace and petition; and they shall look on him whom they have thrust through, and they shall mourn for him as one mourns for an only son, and they shall grieve over him as one grieves over a first-born" (Zec 12:10), and, "On that day there shall be open to the house of David and to the inhabitants of Jerusalem, a fountain to purify from sin and uncleanness" (Zec 13:1). Likewise the prophet Ezekiel proclaimed: "I saw water flowing out from beneath the threshold of the temple toward the east . . . the water flowed down from the southern side of the Temple" (Ez 47:1).[22] As the life of the Lord pours forth on the cross, he places it at the disposal of the Church, so that this life may flow continuously as an inexhaustible fountain.[23] The water from the side of Christ evokes the water to which the psalmist refers: "Streams of the river gladden the city of God, the holy dwelling of the Most High" (Ps 46:5). Our attempts to pray, to

---

21. Cf. Jn 19:26. See Yves Congar, OP, *The Mystery of the Temple or The Manner of God's Presence to His People From Genesis to the Apocalypse* (Westminster, MD: The Newman Press, 1962), 76. See also Yves Congar, OP, *Christians Active in the World* (New York: Herder and Herder, 1968), 45. See also Pope Benedict XVI, *Verbum Domini*, 5.

22. Balthasar lists numerous Scripture verses that refer to grace repeatedly likened to water that springs forth from God, see Balthasar, *The Glory of the Lord VI*, 146–147.

23. See Adrienne von Speyr, *The Letter to the Ephesians* (San Francisco: Ignatius Press, 1996), 180.

follow our vocation, to return to or participate in the sacraments, to obtain grace in our struggle with sin, to simply go to church again, and to find the healing we need all flow first from the self-gift of Jesus on the cross. Our journey to holiness begins with that fountain of grace.

In his encyclical letter on the Holy Spirit, Pope John Paul II teaches that the Lord gives the Holy Spirit through the wounds of his crucifixion.[24] Hans Urs von Balthasar notes that Saint Thomas Aquinas describes the streams of grace flowing through the wound in the side of Jesus as a living fountain.[25] The wounds of Jesus allow us to peer into his divinity.[26] Just as the Son eternally gives himself away in love in the divine relations of the Trinity, he gives his riches away as a self-gift to humanity lost in sin, so as to lead each person back to the life of the Father through the power of the Spirit. The human person is redeemed only after the fountain of grace wells up in Jesus on the cross and is poured forth through the wounds of his crucifixion.

In its original Latin meaning a wound is a *vulneras*, a vulnerability before the other person. Vulnerability accents the wound not in the negative sense, but in the positive sense of *opening* toward the other. This positive vulnerability allows for a true and authentic relation and the gift of new life. Cardinal Joseph Ratzinger noted, as had Pope John Paul II, that the wound in the side of Adam from which God creates Eve is not a negative reality, but a positive wound: Adam and Eve's

---

24. See Pope John Paul II, *Dominum et Vivificantem*, 24. See also Pope Benedict XVI, *Jesus of Nazareth* (New York: Doubleday, 2007), 305.

25. See Balthasar, *Theo-Drama: Theological Dramatic Theory V, The Last Act* (San Francisco: Ignatius Press, 1998), 31, 60–61, 462, 470. See also Torrell, *Saint Thomas Aquinas,* vol. 2, 156.

26. See Speyr, *The Letter to the Ephesians*, 25–26.

"being turned toward each other . . . is shown in the wound, which is present in all of us and which leads us to turn to each other."[27] Similarly, in our own lives, this vulnerability gives us an openness before the other who is different, yet similar to ourselves. The mystery of salvation offered in Christ conveys that even our negative wounds, the wounds of sin, can be and are transformed into openings for grace and new life. Unlike a bodily wound, the "wound" or vulnerability before God that leads to union with him is healed only by being deepened.[28]

The Image of the Fountain in the Spiritual Life

The open and heightened receptivity of the believer is inspired first by the faith that the fountain that is the life of God wells up endlessly.[29] The image of the fountain is crucial to the spiritual life. We are so thirsty after pursuing the ways of the world. We return parched after attempting to satisfy our thirst elsewhere. The water Jesus gives us, as he tells the Samaritan woman, will become a fountain within us (cf. Jn 4:14). A fountain is guided, yet natural, spontaneity; the fountain's source is known only through the action of the fountain. We can receive the water of the fountain, but we cannot grasp the fountain itself. The fountain never bubbles up in the same exact way twice. While the source is often steady and even predictable, the surge is always original and spontaneous, reaching for new places. A fountain is always being propelled outside itself. The strength of the fountain is distributed behind the substance of the water. A fountain's

---

27. Joseph Cardinal Ratzinger, *God and the World: A Conversation with Peter Seewald* (San Francisco: Ignatius Press, 2002), 80.

28. See Balthasar, *Theo-Drama V,* 430, 477–478, 481.

29. Ibid., 393, 397–398.

wild spontaneity is guided by its source. This is how the Holy
Spirit operates in us. He surges forth from underneath in his
unique motion of love, from places that we may not even
know. Saint Teresa of Avila, the seventeenth-century Spanish
mystic, said, "For I don't find anything more appropriate to
explain some spiritual experiences than water. . . . [I] am so
fond of this element that I have observed it more attentively
than other things." [30] We know that the Spirit is there, just as
we know that the water of the fountain flows beneath the well
and in the earth. Yet, once unleashed, we can't predict where
the Spirit will act as he flows forth: "The Spirit blows where
he will" (see Jn 3:8). We can't confine the Spirit, who is faithful originality.

As we look for signs of the fountain within us, we can
sometimes drill in the wrong places or in shallow water.
Sometimes we confuse the spiritual life with "being nice" or
making sure we do the correct religious practices at the correct
times. We later drop such practices due to boredom or perceived lack of results. We think that religion is simply "not
hurting anyone." The only dogma of such watered-down spirituality is that there are no dogmas. Religion entails far more,
however. In faith we seek out the Triune God who sent his
Son for our salvation, and whose Holy Spirit brings that salvation through the Church. We must drill down through our
fears to the gift of God's love.

---

30. St. Teresa of Avila, *The Interior Castle,* in *The Collected Works of St. Teresa of
Avila,* vol. 2, trans. Otilio Rodriguez, OCD, and Kieran Kavanaugh, OCD (Washing-
ton, DC: Institute for Carmelite Studies, 1980), IV:2:2, 323. See St. Teresa of Avila,
The Book of Her Life, in *St. Teresa of Avila: Collected Works* vol. 1, trans. Otilio Rodriguez,
OCD, and Kieran Kavanaugh, OCD (Washington DC: The Institute for Carmelite
Studies, 1976), 11:7, 113. Torrell notes that there is a fountain that continuously
springs forth from the Word of God, see Torrell, *Saint Thomas Aquinas,* vol. 2, 83.

CHAPTER FOUR

Revisiting the Mysteries

Trinity

The image of the fountain can help to renew the conceptual image of God we have in our minds.[1] How do we picture God when we think about him? The image of God as an old man with a white beard is very common. God the Father is pictured above the heavens seated on a royal throne, with the Son and the Holy Spirit close by. Angels and saints surround them in adoration. Picture Bibles convey such anthropological and cosmological images to correspond to the concrete thinking style of young children. The image is meant to convey wisdom, majesty, and power, in order to help us understand God as all knowing, all loving, and all powerful. The image remains with many of us as we move into adolescence and

---

1. See Balthasar, *Theo-Drama V*, 393, 397, 433, 462, 477, 503; and *The Glory of the Lord I*, 616.

adulthood, even though we have a difficult time squaring this image with the complex events of adult daily life. But this image does signify true realities that we need to bring into adulthood with us.

This perspective is illuminated in a striking way by the relationship between the Persons of the Trinity. Each of the three divine Persons is the divine Substance, each is truly and completely God, and the Persons are perfectly united in the one divine Substance. The Trinity is absolute unity; the three divine Persons are pure relationality. The reciprocal transparency among the divine Persons is total and the bond between each of them complete, since they constitute a unique and absolute unity. God desires to incorporate us into this reality of communion as well: ". . . that they may be one, as we are one" (Jn 17:22). The Church is a sign and instrument of this unity.[2] Relationships between human beings throughout history cannot but be enriched by reference to this divine reality. In particular, in the light of the revealed mystery of the Trinity, we understand that true openness to others does not mean loss of individual identity but profound communion.

The early teaching of the Church sought to help people understand the revelation of the nature of God as contained in Sacred Scripture,[3] based on the revelation of Jesus: God is a Trinity of Persons, Father, Son, and Holy Spirit. As mentioned above, the three distinct Persons are perfectly united in one divine Substance. The eternal relationships between the divine Persons constitute the one substance or nature of the one God. The one God is the inner relationship of the Father, Son, and

---

2. See Benedict XVI, *Caritas in Veritate,* no. 54.

3. See Mt 3:17; 17: 5; Jn 16:17, 28; 1 Pt 1:17. See Balthasar, *Theo-Drama IV,* 327.

Holy Spirit.[4] The three divine Persons give themselves eternally, immeasurably, and infinitely to one Another. The three divine Persons thus exist in eternal relatedness. This describes the generous and genuine superabundant nature of the living triune God. The Trinity of persons are unsurpassable in their sovereign goodness and might. Thus, God decides to create man and the world out of the abundance of his generosity.[5] He causes time and all within it to exist on the basis of his self-giving love. Therefore, the self-gift of love is the essential action of existence.[6] The previous sentences seem very philosophical and complex. They seem to be a far cry from the image of the man with the white beard above the heavens with the Son and Holy Spirit next to him. But the man with the white beard was meant to convey perfect knowledge, perfect strength, and perfect love. We must recall that God is love, and love exists in unity and relation. This is a simple explanation of holiness: A mysterious relation of union brought about by the authentic gift of self.

As the *Catechism of the Catholic Church* emphasizes, "The mystery of the Most Holy Trinity is the central mystery of Christian faith and life."[7] We begin each prayer, each Mass with the Sign of the Cross as we call upon the Trinity. The Church dedicates one Sunday each year to focus specifically on the mystery of the Trinity. One of the readings for Trinity Sunday, the Sunday after Pentecost, is from the Book of

---

4. See Pope Benedict XVI, *Caritas in Veritate*, 54. Balthasar relies on the image of the fountain in his description of the Trinitarian life, see Balthasar, *The Glory of the Lord II*, 288.

5. See St. Thomas Aquinas, *Summa Theologiae*, Ia, q. 32, a. 1.

6. See Balthasar, *Theo-Drama IV*, 323ff.

7. *CCC*, no. 234.

Deuteronomy. Moses said to the people: "Ask now of the days of old, before your time, ever since God created man upon the earth; ask from one end of the sky to the other: Did anything so great ever happen before? Was it ever heard of? Did a people ever hear the voice of God speaking from the midst of fire, as you did, and live?" (Dt 4:32–33). Moses speaks to the people about an awareness of God that should pervade their whole life. It is as if he is saying to them: "Think of the earliest beginnings of things. Think of the time *before* time. What is most original in all the universe and in all existence? What *underlies* everything else? *God does*. But this is not some remote, arbitrary, distant god who just causes things to happen and has all the power, who will win in the end anyway, so you had better be on his side or else." Moses points out that we have heard the *voice* of God, and the greatest thing before we heard his voice was *creation* itself. All our successes, adaptations, and so-called advances pale in comparison to the mystery that God has created us, revealed himself to us, and spoken to us. More, he is steadfast and everlasting in his faithfulness to us, even though we routinely turn away from him.

If we examine all of history we will not find greater events than our creation, redemption, and God's revelation, his speaking to us. Nothing compares: the great Pyramids, the mysteries of mathematics, national conquests, Olympic feats, space travel, architectural wonders, fabulous treasures, and natural phenomena all fade when compared to our creation by God, our redemption in his Son, and his speaking with us. We often value the notion of God speaking to us if we discover something about life that helps or protects us. But the sheer fact that God *is*, and he has caused us *to be*, and that he longs to *interact* with us is already, before whatever else he says, a tremendous event in our daily lives. It does not make us arrogant, but refers us in humility back to the utter mystery of God.

God has reached out from his eternity into time, from his infinite existence to our finite existence, from his immeasurable and unlimited being to our measured and limited being. He has reached out as absolute love in an unsurpassed event of complete generosity. He has permitted us to be, and then willed to converse with us. The word "event" conveys more than the stale fact of a happening.[8] The original notion of "event" is "a dynamic coming forth from." When we speak of the "event of the cross" or the "event of salvation," we refer not simply to a past arbitrary case in point, but to an exciting, forceful, and effusive moment. It follows through and continues into the future with all the original, overflowing, essential burst of meaning that expresses most fully the contour of the love of God.[9] Love is always a giving forth.

This is apparent when Jesus speaks to the Samaritan woman of the gift of a fountain welling up within. This fountain is the eternal love by which she was created and for which she yearns. Every action and miracle of Jesus in the New Testament manifests unity and relation. When Jesus heals, he speaks to the person in front of him, restoring the afflicted person to physical unity. When Jesus confronts the Pharisees, he invites them to change their hostility to unity. When Jesus multiplies the loaves, with that abundance he shows God's relation of love with the world. In the Sermon on the Mount, Jesus relates to the painful situation of the world, which results in a wondrous unity of the call to a life of holiness.

The Trinity is a mystery of unity and relation. Human beings are created in the image of God. Therefore, unity and

---

8. See Melina, *The Epiphany of Love*, 35. See also Balthasar, *The Glory of the Lord I*, 64, 473–474, 530.

9. See Balthasar, *Theo-Drama V*, 91, 96. See also Bruno Forte, *The Trinity as History: Saga of the Christian God* (New York: Alba House, 1989), 16.

relation are at the central core of human meaning. Every hunger of the human heart has to do with unity and relation. Day to day, hour to hour, minute to minute, we are relating one to another in various levels of unity. Ways of relating that turn the self or the other person into an object to be used are wrong. Every pain we experience is a wound to unity and relation. We often simply "try to keep things together" in the family, at work, and at school. Trying "to keep things together" is reaching out for unity. How we relate as we try to keep things together is *relationship*.

All day long people seek to grow in unity with one another by relating more closely. When people seek emotional therapy, they are usually dealing with issues about unity and relationships. A wound in unity in families or at the office drives up blood pressure and underlies tension, addiction, and heartache. The lack of unity and the distorted relations of dysfunction may remain painful memories for years.

Charity unites. Pope Benedict XVI notes, "Charity is love received and given. It is 'grace' (*cháris*). Its source is the wellspring of the Father's love for the Son, in the Holy Spirit."[10] When we make the Sign of the Cross our hand moves from our forehead to waist to shoulders while we announce: "In the name of the Father, and of the Son, and of the Holy Spirit. Amen." This action and phrase begins the Mass, other liturgical celebrations, and our prayers. It is used for blessings. These words and actions are not just ritualized ceremony, but they actually *bring something about*.[11] They *confess* our faith in the Triune God and unite us to him. Where God is present, evil cannot be present; therefore these

---

10. Pope Benedict XVI, *Caritas in Veritate*, 5.
11. For example, see Jean Daniélou, *Advent*, 132.

words and actions enfold us in the presence of God and thus drive away the influence of evil.

The Son of God reveals to us the depths of the fountain of love. The second Person of the Blessed Trinity, the Son of God, took flesh in the Incarnation. The archangel Gabriel announced to the Blessed Virgin Mary that she was to be the mother of the Son of God (see Lk 1:26–38). When Mary said yes to God's plan, the Son of God took flesh in her womb by the power of the Holy Spirit. At this moment, as the Son of God assumes our humanity, he also begins to take on himself all the wounds of humanity. At the moment of the Incarnation, Mary conceives Jesus in her womb. Jesus seeks to be present in our hearts through the gift of his grace given us especially through the sacraments. The fountain Jesus speaks of with the Samaritan woman is not a technique or method. It is not located in a distant place. It is right next to her: "I am he, the one who is speaking with you" (Jn 4:26). He wants the fountain to be within her through his word and the action of the Holy Spirit. God, unforced, intervenes in history from the depths of his love.

Human Sin

The human person was created in the image and likeness of God. Before the fall, man enjoyed friendship with God and had the capacity to know God and relate to him without the burden of sin. Satan tempted man, who turned away from the original trust he had in God. This act of disobedience, known as original sin, disturbed and wounded man's harmony with God. Once it was shattered, man experiences the tragic consequences of sin. Jesus restores our union with God in his saving death and resurrection, by which he delivers us from sin and death. Yet, we still experience temptation and the effects of sin, which present false goods to us.[12] The grace of Jesus Chris, which saves us from sin and death, also strengthens us to live lives of virtue and thus avoid sin. With the help of God's grace and the teaching of the Church, we must discern how to identify true goods and pursue authentic happiness. We still desire this happiness, but, due to the effects of sin, can more easily turn from true goods to false goods.

Often, what people name as love is only *apparently* love. Sin thrives on counterfeits of love, when we redirect our desire for the true good to an apparent good. We then diminish our desire for the authentic good to simply a craving for a momentary satisfaction. Satisfaction is not the same as *happiness*. Ironically, gratifying the senses actually dulls their sensitivity, blocks their proper function, and weighs them down. This undue gratification conditions and adapts the senses to the inordinate pursuit of pleasure, and it blinds the person to the true, good, and beautiful. Seeking pleasure then becomes the primary underlying purpose in day-to-day life. The intellect and will are thus deterred from the true and the good in favor of seeking pleasure and avoiding pain. Rather than seeking to give, we seek to possess, dominate, and control.

Sin sabotages the gift. Sin attempts to grasp and possess rather than to receive. Those who desire to possess replace the gift with force, by which they seek to control others. They restructure the events of life to be about themselves rather than the purpose and meaning of the task at hand. But mercifully, the gift always eludes all attempts to control and dominate it. Boredom is sin's exhaust. It is frustration at the inability to

---

12. See Aquinas, *Summa Theologiae*, Ia, q. 114.

contain the unattainable. The attempt to possess brings only desolation, loss, sorrow, and isolation.

Sin is the choice to use something less than God to satisfy the longing for God. By attempting to fill our longing for God with possessions, we actually *wound* our ability to desire.[13] The wound of sin leaves its effects in us. Instead of living with the natural desire for fulfillment through the ordinary events of daily life, we now seek out the extremes of desire: fears and wishes.

It is unpopular to mention sin today. Our popular understanding of sin sees it as a mark that contaminates us because of an action, thought, or even a feeling. At some moment, because of something we have done, we have crossed a line and are somehow farther from God and have lost his love. Some may even begin to worry that something bad will now happen in this life, and certainly in the next, if the sin is not removed. Elements of this description require a deeper understanding.

This popular idea of sin as an amorphous stain deep inside may have caused a knee-jerk reaction in the other direction: the notion that there is no such thing as sin. The contamination image was so overwhelming that, rather than seek forgiveness of the sin, some people sought to simply remove the entire *category* of sin.

Sin must be properly understood. Sin is an offense against God that arises not simply from crossing a line, but from a disobedient choice to reject his love (cf. Rom 5:12; Gn 3:1–7). This disobedient choice to oppose God is the decision to love an apparent good instead of the true good. Sin is the choice for something that only appears to be true, good, and beautiful, but is really false, evil, and ugly.

---

13. See Balthasar, *Theo-Drama IV,* 73, 152, 190, 372.

Sin substitutes self-taking for self-giving. All of the major sins are types of self-taking. Gluttony is love of taking too much food or drink for the sake of self-indulgence. Lust is the taking of sexual gratification. Greed is the taking of wealth. Envy is the desire to take the good of another. Anger is the taking of offense. Sloth is the taking of undue rest. Pride is the continuous taking of self to the center. Sin is the futile act of satisfying a craving rather than the fruitful engagement of real desire.

When we sin, we experience tragic consequences.[14] We lose our affection for what is authentically true. Sin slows down and narrows our abilities to see what is absolutely good. The choice to do evil inhibits our future attempts to recognize the beauty of the virtuous gift of self, making it easier to sin the next time. Once we choose sin, we cannot, on our own, rid ourselves of it or its effects on us and in our world. Only love can free us from sin—not just any love, but love in the form of the grace of Jesus Christ.[15] After we sin, and without the grace of Christ, instead of discerning the true, good, and beautiful in our choices and actions, we find a dense resistance, like scar tissue. It impedes our sensitivity for what God intended. In sin, we cut corners around the gift of self so that our actions shy away from self-giving to self-centered taking. We cheat on our taxes rather than contribute to the common good. Those whom we charge with administering the common good sometimes swerve off in other directions. We would rather work on the computer than talk to a friend. We fall into prejudice instead of appreciating the meaning and importance of differences. We choose the quick reaction of violence instead of the

---

14. See *CCC,* no. 399.

15. See Adrienne von Speyr, *The Letter to the Colossians* (San Francisco: Ignatius Press, 1998), 116.

assertion of love. Gossip seems to flow through the air vents in the workplace.

Instead of communicating, we gossip. Information is power, and gossip turns information into competition. The poisoned grapevine causes some of our deepest wounds. In fact, gossip is the exact opposite of the Sacrament of Penance. In confession, we tell the priest our own sins; in gossip we tell an acquaintance someone else's faults, whether real or perceived. In confession, we can only tell one person, who is bound by a sacred seal to never tell anyone; in gossip we tell people knowing that they will tell others. In confession, we carry out the penance; in gossip, we impose the penance of defamation on someone else.

The action of sin, that is, the neglect of love, choosing self-taking over self-giving, has natural consequences. It's not that God simply gets angry at human beings who do not follow his commands. God has established a universe in balance with natural laws. He did not simply post a list of rules, his favorite do's and don'ts, expecting us to behave like robots. God established a world of harmony in which free and intelligent creatures could live in peace. When the free and intelligent creature, man, turned against goodness, truth, and love, and sought himself as his own end and refused the gift, natural consequences followed. Since nature is in balance, consequences occur when we disrupt that balance.

Sin has effects, first of all on our relationship with God. Original sin is the disobedient action performed by our first parents at the beginning of history that caused them to lose the state of original innocence. We inherit the stain and the effects of original sin. Baptism fills us with grace, removes the stain, and *weakens* the effects of original sin, but the effects do remain. Due to these effects, called concupiscence, the human person experiences an inclination to sin, a tendency to choose self over God. This makes it easier for us to be self-seeking rather than self-giving. The effects of original sin become clear as selfishness dominates families and society. The effects are seen in our tendency toward skepticism and self-interest rather than self-gift; our inclination to suspicion and division rather than unity; and the substitution of fear for love in relationships. The effects of sin leave us blind to the full truth and goodness that exist all around us.

When we turn against the true, the good, the ordered, and the virtuous life, the natural alternative is ignorance, malice, concupiscence, and weakness. These things tempt us to believe that what is false is actually true. We experience the power and influence of an entrenched resistance within ourselves that makes us fall victim to illusion. For example, a married couple who routinely argue give in to the notion that this time when they yell and scream, the other spouse will understand. Concupiscence prompts a neighbor to stir up controversy by gossiping rather than seeking a creative outlet for the need for attention and recognition.

While we still desire God, we find it difficult to discern the proper way to God. We mistakenly believe the way is through our own advancement and betterment. Because of concupiscence, we get entangled and easily mistake the obstacle for the answer. We experience a tendency to lie, to mistake an apparent good for a true good, and to indulge our appetites or passions. We may find violence easy, anger opportune, greed rewarding, lust satisfying, and power compelling. This situation spreads deeper and deeper. But God does not assign concupiscence as an arbitrary punishment. It is the natural effect of turning against the truth to sin. Though created to give ourselves as a gift of love in communion with others, we now prefer our private "right" to be the rugged, autonomous individual.

Sin is a self-taking that is disguised to look like self-giving. The self-taking of sin can be venial or mortal. Venial sin wounds and injures our relationship with God, weakening but not destroying it. Venial sin is self-taking in such a way that we, in routine matters, assert our own will as most important. From this first step, a disposition toward self-centeredness impedes our everyday relatedness to God, neighbor, self, and the created world. Mortal sin is self-taking, carried out in a gravely serious matter, with sufficient reflection and full consent of the will such that it immediately kills the life of God within us. Mortal sin destroys the life of grace in the soul. The effects of personal sin plunge us farther into the spiritual swamp of concupiscence.

Why does someone choose to sin? A person sins when he or she disobeys God. Disobedience to God arises from giving in to worldly fear.[16] Worldly fear is refined into seven types of action, called the seven deadly sins: gluttony, lust, greed, anger, envy, sloth, and pride. The Desert Fathers, in particular Evagrius Ponticus and John Cassian, taught about the seven deadly sins in their spiritual writings.[17]

Worldly fear operates in different ways. For example, the honor student who has worked hard for good grades might never think of cheating on a test. But then, on the morning of a crucial exam that will largely determine whether or not the 4.0 stands or falls, the notion of having a backup plan appears

---

16. See Balthasar, *Theo-Drama IV,* 148.

17. The seven deadly sins are based on the eight deadly thoughts in the synthesis of Evagrius Ponticus (345–399), see Evagrius Ponticus, *The Practicos: The Chapters on Prayer*, trans. John Eudes Bamberger, Cistercian Studies Series, no. 4 (Kalamazoo, MI: Cistercian Publications, 1970), 6. John Cassian (365–435) formulates the same as the eight principal vices, see John Cassian, *The Conferences,* trans. Boniface Ramsey, OP (Mahwah, NJ: Paulist Press, 1997), fifth conference. See also John Cassian, *The Institutes*, trans. Boniface Ramsey, OP (Westminster, MD: The Newman Press, 2000), Book Five. For a concise description of the manner in which the seven deadly sins operate, see Simon Tugwell, OP, *Ways of Imperfection: An Exploration of Christian Spirituality* (Springfield, IL: Templegate Publishers, 1985), 25–32.

the most prudent thing in the world. *After all, I studied well, so why should I lose my place because of a teacher known for grade-busting? What harm is there in scribbling down the major theorems that I already know anyway? It will just even out the unfair odds, and maintain what I worked so hard for.*

The truth goes deeper. The ultimate goal of education is not the perfection of the grade received, but the perfection of the one who *receives* the grade. If one cheats, by that fact one cannot *receive*, but only *take* that which is not theirs. In fact, academic cheating, when seen from the shadows, appears to be profitable, reasonable, and efficient, but can ultimately call into question the student's entire history of academic effort and success, destroying the very thing he or she hoped to achieve. In every situation, disobedience leads to a network of disillusionment and disappointment. That which we hoped to achieve by shortcutting truth and goodness is actually, in the end, a tedious detour that blocks the self from love. Once disillusionment and disappointment set in, doubt and denial never lag far behind. Denial and doubt of the truths of faith always begin as defense mechanisms for a person who has compromised, taking some shortcut around obedience to try to get to the true and the good. The overlapping network of sin reaches its full strength in the ideologies of the culture of death: individualism, egoism, narcissism, skepticism, materialism, consumerism, utilitarianism, hedonism, and utopianism.

Sin wraps itself in the guise of something good, deceiving us as to its full nature. It cleverly attempts to break down our defenses, assuage our wearied neediness in superficial ways, and smuggle evil into our hearts. Through a series of apparently innocuous concessions, it initiates a pattern of vice. Temptation never appears ugly but always seems alluring. The wound of self-centered sin darkens our vision, blinding us to everything except our own immediate needs. While focusing on the alluring options, we rarely contemplate the painful consequences that will swiftly follow and the good from which we turn away.

Temptation induces us to see our desires only as superficial realities, never as connected to the deep meaning of life. We need real wisdom to detect the true and authentic good. The life of virtue restores our Christian vision, shaping it to notice the naturalness of the good. The virtue-driven life always seeks union with the true, the good, and the beautiful such that truth, goodness, and beauty become principles *within* the person that guide one's actions and become a sign to others of the way to virtue.

The futility of sin knows not the gift, but only the grasping. God is not deterred by our experiences of futility and neediness. In fact, as with the Samaritan woman, as we walk along in the midst of our pain, we are likely to find him just ahead of us, in the midst of the ordinary events of daily life. We might mistake our own stubbornness for his delay, but there is no telling when he will ignite our next step.

The Cross

The central invitation of Jesus is to "follow me." If we follow him, the Way leads to a cross. Jesus did not command us to simply *put up with* the cross. He commanded us to *take up* our cross. Jesus suffered his passion and death *for us*. His cross and resurrection are eternally prolonged moments. In these infinite moments his divinity fully permeates all that is human. These actions forever open up our understanding that humanity is meant always to be understood through love.[18] The cross

18. Balthasar, *The Glory of the Lord I*, 672.

thus provides a glimpse of the gift of self as a total surrender in absolute and utmost love for the genuine good of the other. In this, the cross is the indescribable moment of superabundant grace.

The cross of Jesus is the fullest expression in time of that which the Trinity is in eternity. The Holy Spirit rejoices in this sacrificial gift of the Son to the Father, and makes this gift fruitful in the Church for our salvation. Because the Son stands with the sinner, after the cross, whenever God the Father encounters the sinner, he always first meets the Son whom he loves, and the love of the Father becomes mercy for the sinner.[19] This mercy emerges from the heart of the sacrifice of the cross.

The saving action of Jesus on the cross is a total outpouring of self in love. This act is the ultimate and unimaginable source by which the entire range of sin, throughout all of history is utterly redeemed. He answers every sin with his act of love.[20] His infinite, faithful, and compassionate love responds to every form of abuse, neglect, loneliness, violence, disaster, war, injury, curse, and exploitation. He experiences every death camp, gulag, and torture chamber. By his steadfast, eternal love, he responds to every twisted upheaval and riotous rebellion. By his unfaltering obedience he responds to every act of disobedience. By his faithful sacrifice he responds to every self-centered act in history. No technicality or circumstance escapes the offer of his love. The depths of his Godhead meet the abysmal depths of sin. He empties himself out in love before every transgression and floods all alienation with his compassion. And he does not do this *from the outside*, but he does all of it *from the inside*. He does not intervene in an

---

19. See Speyr, *The Letter to the Colossians,* 124–125.

20. Pope Benedict XVI, *Verbum Domini,* 12.

external manner, but in an *internal* manner. He truly experiences each slight, fault, pain, cruelty, attack, trauma, collapse, and exile. He absorbs every humiliation, disorder, tragedy, insult, wrong, betrayal, abandonment, infidelity, and abuse. He does not simply wave his hand to amend all wrongdoing. Rather, he bears each transgression in his crucifixion. God is indivisible in his unity and relation of love. This is the substance of God, his very nature, perfect unity in a relation of love that takes the form of a gift of self. He freely empties himself to save us from sin. This is the love that never ends. Jesus alone, since he is true God and true man, can take into himself all the divisions of the human race and heal them. Jesus takes on our divisions without losing the perfect unity that is his as God. Jesus, the Son of God, since he is true God and true man, communicates the indivisible generosity of God to our humanity, along with God's mercy.

The response of God to human sin is always compassion. In the face of human sin, God does not just inflict punishments and utter commandments. He does not say, "I told you so," and then try to save us just to save face. God is love and he responds with love. But love does not mean that God looks the other way when we sin. Nor is his forgiveness simply an arbitrary wave of the hand that dismisses the guilt of sin with no account. Human sin offends God. The degree of the offense of sin is measured by the dignity of the one offended. Because God's dignity is infinite, sin is an infinite offense against God. There is no way that the human person, who is finite, can make up for an infinite offense. To be faithful to himself and the freedom and love by which he creates us, God, in his justice and love must receive an infinite satisfaction for the offense of sin. In order to do this, the Son of God takes our place. He takes flesh and becomes true man without ceasing to be God. The Son, fully God, retains the infinite dignity of God, and as true man, can stand in our place, in solidarity with man. On the cross, the Son offers to the Father infinite and complete satisfaction for sin.[21] The Son takes every pain and pays every penalty.

Some of the apostles and early disciples of Jesus mistakenly thought he was a military Messiah who would deliver them from Roman oppression. They were surprised when they found out that Jesus was a Suffering Servant Messiah. Some even left him when they found this to be the case. We can fall into the same trap. We want Jesus to defeat the Romans in our lives. We want him to cure our loved ones, right the wrongs, and fix the difficulties. We mistake his mission. When he communicates his life to us, he does not do so for a victory the way we or the world define success or triumph. Something much more powerful takes place in his powerlessness.[22] He feels, to the depths, every crushing blow. He answers each cruel use of power by becoming powerless. When the Almighty becomes powerless, a new and overwhelming beauty is unleashed throughout existence in the form of an unimaginable, superabundant love. This crucified love is beautiful. The Crucified One, who offers himself completely for others, is more than beautiful. More, he *is* beauty itself.

Through the self-gift of Jesus on the cross, we receive the gift of the grace of God, made visible and active in the face of sin. This grace can be applied to all of our wounds, no matter how severe or long lasting. Jesus's gift of self brings about a new communion through unity and relation. He gives the new gift of unity and relation to a world in which evil and sin have sought to disfigure and destroy love. This new love of Jesus, then, necessarily takes the form of suffering, because it is

---

21. See the meditation on the Cross by Daniélou, *Advent,* 125–138.

22. Balthasar, *The Glory of the Lord VII,* 65, 321. See also *Theo-Drama IV,* 335.

inevitably attacked by the powers of sin and evil. The shape of love is always cruciform. In his one saving act, a new and inexhaustible brilliance permanently breaks forth upon the world: the mystery of eternal love. He changes darkness by bringing the light and disfigurement by the radiance of his beauty. When he had taken all of this upon himself, he meets the final enemy, which is death. He dies *for us*. And in death he performs the ultimate action that crowns the entire passion: he trusts in the Father's faithful and merciful love. This trust is answered by the Father in the moment of resurrection on the third day. The splendor of Christ, risen from the dead, is his beauty. The beauty of Christ *changes* us. His beauty enlightens us—he is the light that radiates throughout all of history, time, and space. And his unsurpassable light calls out to us persistently from its hidden source. His light illuminates, overtakes, and reshapes everything through his limitless love. Grace alone allows us to withstand this light.[23]

Far from dispensing us from the communion of the Church, this love draws us all the more close. Once the shaft of this light spreads across us we are changed, sealed, and marked forever. No more can one say, without hiding, "I don't need to go to Mass on Sunday, I just talk directly to God on my own. I am spiritual, but not religious."

The teachings of the Church are not static world views, abstract policy positions, or theoretical scholarly opinions that we evaluate to determine if we agree with them or not. Divine revelation is the free disclosure of God. Sacred Scripture and the living Apostolic Tradition are the two ways that God has chosen to reveal himself to us. The revelation of God, given in and authentically interpreted through the Church, is actually a living content that influences us in our

---

23. Balthasar, *The Glory of the Lord VI*, 9.

day-to-day lives. We must respond to this call. The act of faith is the living response. The revelation of God is a light that penetrates us and actually assists and strengthens our act of faith. The content of revelation begins to unfold, extend, and spread into the most unlikely places of our lives. Suffering calls on the deeper love that alone is the answer to human evil and sin. We can take two directions: We can either choose sin in self-centered pride, or grace in other-centered love. Suffering is the sign that we are making the choice to be either self-centered or other-centered.

His saving act on the cross radiates from Christ through his Church throughout history. No matter how busy we are or how bitter we have become, no matter how faithful we may believe ourselves to be or not be, no matter where we began our faith practice or how far we have drifted from it, this action of Jesus, in and through the Church, radiates to us today, in this hour, at this moment. The enormous act of Jesus is the eternal moment that unfolds and stands at the center of everything else. This is why we wait in the rain to pick our children up from retreats and Catholic education. This is why we go to Mass and receive the sacraments. This is why we pray, why we feed the hungry, embrace the poor, welcome the stranger, participate in stewardship. This is why we are patient and persistent with skeptics, why we do not sell out and take the easy road, why we protect the inviolable dignity of all human life, and celebrate the sanctity of marriage as a permanent, faithful, fruitful union of one man and one woman. We do all this because the cross is the inexhaustibly fruitful spousal act of love from Jesus to the Church, through which we receive the grace to live the life of virtue. The cross casts a light, not a shadow. This light is poured into the sacra-ments. The sacraments are the channels by which the Holy

Spirit communicates the saving action of Jesus to us, so that he truly dwells within us.

On the cross, Jesus pours forth mercy as a new dispensation of love. Coming forth from love, his mercy simultaneously provokes love. The Roman centurion standing near the cross of Jesus had not seen any of his miracles. This anonymous soldier had not heard the Sermon on the Mount, nor seen the lame walk or the hungry fed. For this guard, it was just another ordinary day. Yet simply by seeing how Jesus died, the centurion was brought to faith: "Truly this man was the Son of God!" (Mk 15:39; cf. Lk 23:47). Mercy is the "radically new re-creation of all meaning."[24]

This mercy heals all our wounds. Jesus saves, fulfills, and redeems the human race by incorporating us into his death and resurrection, which is his obedient yes on the cross to the Father, who saves us from every no we ever uttered to authentic love. Sin and evil did their worst to the Son of God on Calvary. Since he is true man, he tasted the depths of all the sins of all time and communicates the perfect self-gift of divine love that conquers sin and death. By his love Jesus created a path through suffering to new life. This same love communicates the power that is made perfect in weakness: the power of endurance and charity. Whatever suffering the Christian encounters is already conquered. In the moment of suffering, each Christian can choose to cling to Christ or to the world. Jesus Christ is the one Mediator. He assimilates all into himself and in his headship he heals and renews each person by giving a new measure of his immeasurable love.

The Church applies the merits of the self-gift of Jesus on the cross to every human situation. She applies this as grace,

---

24. Balthasar, *The Glory of the Lord I*, 549.

the effective love of God given to the human person in and through the sacraments and her ministerial action. The sacraments strengthen us to live a life of unity and relation: to live the holiness of life proclaimed in the Beatitudes.

The Call to Holiness

God's generosity is rooted in his undivided love. This is God's unique nature: a communion of eternal love exchanged between Father, Son, and Holy Spirit. God shares this generous love with us in the form of grace. When God's grace influences us we act with charity, another word for love. This charity transforms us in pivotal and practical ways. A doctor who has performed abortions and one day realizes the evil he is doing and stops, does so because he has finally become alert to the charity of God. A person who has not practiced his or her faith for a long time stops by a church or picks up a Bible. An impatient and grumpy person smiles and holds the door for another. A person caught in the cycle of sin begins to think about going to confession. A married couple who argue stop and wonder where things went wrong and see for a moment the person they fell in love with. God's generous love, given to the Christian through the Holy Spirit, alerts us to the sublime nature of God and his mystery. Other things may influence these transformations, such as scientific information or a frank conversation with a colleague, but their root cause is the grace of God that operates in the believer as charity. We must return often to the sources, reminding ourselves that the gift of self is the way of life. The sacraments are the primary and crucial ways God communicates the Holy Spirit to us, and through his power we are led to participate in the the life of grace through the gift of self and charity.

Under the influence of God's grace, even seemingly small actions stand out in bold relief for the Christian. We can find many opportunities to practice charity: showing courtesy in traffic despite a bad mood; showing patience to a family member in an argument; foregoing the recitation of the same old litany of grievances, and instead seeking new ways of relating to loved ones; and refraining from gossip because we know it is wrong. These choices are not simply attempts to introduce civility in place of rudeness. In these moments we reach into the gift of God himself who strengthens us to love. We are transformed by the Holy Spirit to act in a new way. When we participate in God's life at these moments we always experience them first as a form of suffering, as if we are foregoing something we would like to express. At first, actions of charity may feel like a cross because our wounds distract us from the beauty of the gift and lead us to cling to self-centeredness rather than self-gift.

We are also strengthened by reminders of God's love. Religious images such as a crucifix displayed in the home remind us of the gift of self. Taking five minutes in the morning to pray a decade of the Rosary begins the day with an act of self-giving. When we meet difficulties in our day, with the psalmist we can say, "Hear my cry for help, my king, my God! To you I pray, O Lord; at dawn you will hear my cry; at dawn I will plead before you and wait" (Ps 5:3–4). Starting the day with less rush, noise, and chaos can be more important than an extra fifteen minutes of sleep and will help us carry out our professional and familial duties with serenity. Reading Bible stories to our children begins to form in them the foundation of the gift of self. We must slip away for even brief moments of silence with God, not out of duty and obligation, but to offer them as a gift. No matter how small, the gift allows us to empty ourselves of what we would otherwise be doing, and thus creates an opening through which God can pour into us his own gift. God pours himself out for us so that we can pour ourselves out to others in love. In the gift we hear, see, speak to, and touch God.

The Son of God chose out of free obedience to make a gift of self on the cross to the Father. His self-gift never passes away: It continuously flows as a living fountain from the cross through the Church and into the sacraments. Just *how* does God bring his gift of self into our hearts through the sacraments? He does so through the seven gifts of the Holy Spirit. The prophet Isaiah names these seven gifts: Wisdom, Understanding, Counsel, Courage, Knowledge, Piety, and Fear of the Lord (cf. Is 11:2). The gifts of the Holy Spirit open the heart of the Christian and continuously and progressively form the believer so that the he or she conforms more closely to Christ.[25] The gifts of the Holy Spirit illumine the heart of the Christian and manifest an interior impulse deep in the soul. This illumination shapes the intellect and will of the believer to attune him to the mysteries of the faith.[26] The gifts do this by establishing and building the seven virtues in the Christian: the theological virtues of faith, hope, and love, and the cardinal virtues of prudence, justice, fortitude, and temperance (cf. 1 Cor 13:13; Wis 8:7). The Holy Spirit's action in and through his seven gifts is central to the moral life.[27] Pope John Paul II's famed Theology of the Body culminates in his exposition of Saint Paul's treatment of life in the Spirit. The radiance of the Holy Spirit opens the heart of the believer, stirs up faith

---

25. See Hans Urs von Balthasar, *Explorations in Theology IV: Spirit and Institution* (San Francisco: Ignatius Press, 1995), 328.

26. See John of St. Thomas, *The Gifts of the Holy Ghost* (New York: Sheed and Ward, 1951), 28, 45–46, 56–58, 63.

27. See Melina, *The Epiphany of Love,* xviii, 22, 61. See also Balthasar, *The Glory of the Lord I,* 292.

deep within, and communicates God's grace to our hearts. He lays the foundations that guide the Christian to live daily life in harmony with the divine mysteries. We can discover true and authentic happiness only through conversion of heart. This is the way of virtue. The *Catechism* explains, "[The seven gifts] complete and perfect the virtues of those who receive them. They make the faithful docile in readily obeying divine inspirations."[28] Virtue is the inward capacity that forms and deepens in the believer an affection and an inclination to steadfastly make authentically good choices and carry these through in corresponding action. Faith, hope, and love are the actions by which we join ourselves to God.

God sends his Holy Spirit to continuously sanctify, transform, and strengthen the intellect, will, and passions of the person who is burdened by temptation, sin, and the effects of sin. The theological virtues are the way God shares his life with us so that we can live the Christian life. Our reason guides us in our day-to-day life. It is part of our human nature that through observation, experience, measurement, and basic learning, we have the capacity to know and understand the daily functional realities of life. Yet, these realities *point* to something beyond themselves. Our finite nature can scratch against a permeable ceiling. The created things we encounter give us a hint of a *more than*, a *beyond*, that our finite mind alone cannot grasp. Saint Paul says, "Ever since the creation of the world, his invisible attributes of eternal power and divinity have been able to be understood and perceived in what he has made" (Rom 1:20). Solomon calls those people "foolish" who do not succeed in knowing God "from the good things seen … and from studying [his] works" (Wis 13:1). As we become

---

28. *CCC*, no. 1831. See also John of St. Thomas, *The Gifts of the Holy Ghost*, 67–68.

aware of the cycle of the universe, the systems of the human body, and truth, beauty, and goodness, we do see that all these must emerge from the transcendent Truth, Beauty, and Goodness. The finite yearns for the infinite, and the measurable reaches out for the immeasurable. Yet, the transcendent and incomprehensible God goes well beyond our nature. Our efforts to reach him always fall short. In his love, God reaches out to us, illumines us with his truth, and invites us to relationship with him. The virtues are the way God gives us, through grace, to be united to him. Faith, hope, and love, as Balthasar noted, always remain a "leap" for us, because they are the way that we finite creatures can relate to the infinite God.[29] When we have faith in God we are uniting ourselves to his *truth*. The faith we express is more than believing *that* there is a God. It is believing *in* God, *in* a divine Person who reveals himself to us in and through the Church. When we express hope in God we are uniting ourselves to God's goodness. Often, God's providence brings us goodness in ways we would never have imagined. We always want the express route to what we decide is good for us. God guides us along the local route to what is good in itself. Often, as we try to undo the knots of our lives we make them worse. We wish that God would airlift us out of trouble. His plan is far more faithful and providential. When we express our love for God, we are uniting ourselves to his beauty. Then we adhere to God because of himself, not because of anything he can do for us.

The cardinal virtues strengthen the believer to faithfully practice faith, hope, and charity as he or she pursues the Christian life despite difficulties and obstacles, including our own frailty. The life of virtue gradually transforms our

---

29. See Hans Urs von Balthasar, *The Christian and Anxiety* (San Francisco: Ignatius Press, 2000), 145.

appetites, inclining us to pursue the good and true. The virtues strengthen us to live the Beatitudes,[30] which Jesus gave us in the Sermon on the Mount. They are in a sense his self-portrait.[31] The *Catechism* explains that "The Beatitudes are the heart of Jesus' preaching," and that "the way of Christ is summed up in the Beatitudes."[32] In his *Christifideles Laici*, John Paul II says we take the first step to imitating Christ when we embrace the Beatitudes, the first stirring of the life in the Spirit.[33] Living the Beatitudes typifies the life of Jesus.[34] They are the way to live the gift of self in the world. The Christian is transformed through grace and virtue to respond to the call to holiness. The gifts, the virtues, and the Beatitudes form the central basis of moral theology.[35] They are not three separate lists, but they are one contiguous body by which the new evangelization brings about an abundant harvest.[36] Taken together, the gifts, virtues, and Beatitudes form a ladder, and, more so, a *fountain*, by which the Christian ascends to holiness of life with the strength of the Holy Spirit. Christ is our virtue, and we become conformed to Christ through the gifts of the

---

30. Mt 5:1–10. See Pinckaers, *The Sources of Christian Ethics,* 145–155; 162–163, 178, 163, 225, 369. See also Pinckaers, *The Pinckaers Reader,* ed. John Berkman and Craig Steven Titus, 15, 22, 28, 80, 82.

31. See John Paul II, *Veritatis Splendor*, 16. See also Pope Benedict XVI, *Jesus of Nazareth* (New York: Doubleday, 2007), 74.

32. *CCC,* nos. 1716, 1697.

33. John Paul II, *Christifideles Laici*, 16.

34. See Pontifical Biblical Commission, *The Bible and Morality: Biblical Roots of Christian Conduct* (Rome: Libreria Editrice Vaticana, 2008), 101, a. See also H. M. Féret, *The Apocalypse of St. John,* 36–38, 138.

35. See Aquinas, *Summa Theologiae*, Ia-IIae, q. 68. See also Balthasar, *The Glory of the Lord I,* 372; *The Glory of the Lord II,* 320. See also Torrell, *Saint Thomas Aquinas: Spiritual Master,* vol. 2, 207–208, 212, 217. See also Pinckaers, *The Pinckaers Reader,* 16, 29, 93.

36. See Pope Benedict XVI, *Verbum Domini,* 96. For a meditation on how God makes things new as no one else can, see Balthasar, *Theo-Drama IV,* 200.

Holy Spirit. The sacraments form grace and virtue in us and thus conform us to Christ. Through sanctifying grace we become by grace what Christ is by nature.

SEVEN GIFTS	VIRTUES	BEATITUDES
The Kingdom		Blessed are the persecuted
Wisdom	Love	Blessed are the peacemakers
Understanding	Faith	Blessed are the pure of heart
Counsel	Prudence	Blessed are the merciful
Courage	Fortitude	Blessed are those who hunger and thirst
Knowledge	Faith	Blessed are those who mourn
Piety	Justice / Temperance	Blessed are the meek [37]
Fear of the Lord	Hope / Temperance	Blessed are the poor in spirit

The sacraments form the believer to live the Beatitudes, which are the very structure of the Christian life. Living the Beatitudes is not simply a matter of gritting one's teeth with cold determination to do good. The Holy Spirit knows us in

---

37. The Latin Vulgate tradition used by many of the Fathers of the Church places "Blessed are the meek . . ." as the second beatitude. See Pope Benedict XVI, *Jesus of Nazareth* (New York: Doubleday, 2007), 80, 86.

depth, in every detail of our life histories and personalities. He strategically places invitations in our paths. Even as we practice the spiritual life, we may easily miss these invitations because we are still immersed in the world. Even if we are already trying to do good and avoid evil, the Holy Spirit seeks to direct our lives in order to configure us more fully to Jesus Christ.

Pope John Paul II taught that we do not earn the love of Jesus on our own merits. Rather, we become capable of receiving and acting according to the love of Jesus through a special gift we receive—the gift of the Holy Spirit. God's love is poured into our hearts only through the Holy Spirit (cf. Rom 5:5). Through his love, the Holy Spirit opens up a new possibility: his love heals and transforms us, enabling us to keep the commandments and live the life of virtue. His love always comes first. Through his love, we realize the extent to which sin has entered our lives, made us feel powerless, misled us, and wounded our hearts, families, and relationships. We then freely ask for and receive a deeper share of life in the Spirit.[38]

Life in the Spirit means living the Beatitudes. For many of us, the Christian life involves practices centered on participating in Sunday Mass, such as receiving the sacraments. We may also see the importance of prayer, obeying the commandments, and trying to live the life of charity. But we are also aware of our shortcomings despite our good intentions. As we hold to the practices and beliefs of our faith, the Holy Spirit always searches for ways to help us do this in a deeper, more interior way. He wants us to adhere to the Christian way of life, to keep the rules not simply because they are rules, but because through these actions, practices, and beliefs we are joined by the power of the Spirit to Jesus Christ.

---

38. See Pope John Paul II, *Veritatis Splendor* 22–23, and *Man and Woman He Created Them: A Theology of the Body*, 329ff.

Through this internalization, the Christian life becomes a broad way of life marked by a return to the simplicity of childhood wisdom. We still adhere to the same beliefs and practice our faith, but we now see and sense the connectedness between our interior world, our exterior actions, and the life of God's grace. We do this not with any euphoric fanaticism, but with a deeper understanding of the spiritual life, our interior world, and our relationships, all understood in the light of Jesus Christ. We understand in new ways the same beliefs we have always held; they become deeply personal. The Spirit cultivates an inborn awareness by which we personally share in the grace of God offered to us through the practice of our faith, especially the sacraments, and living a life of charity.

The call to holiness is not an anxious search, but a patient and trusting openness to growth: "This is the will of God, your holiness" (1 Thes 4:3). Holiness is not about a neat, pristine, polite demeanor that is controlled, unfeeling, or remote. Holiness is about loving God by the action of God himself: through sacrifice, the hardship of things not fitting together perfectly, disappointment, and waiting in the deep understanding that God alone can give. Holiness comes from the action of God, and the first lesson is that the world cannot satisfy our thirst. Pope Benedict XVI explains, "The Lord Jesus, 'the way, and the truth, and the life' (Jn 14:6), speaks to our thirsting, pilgrim hearts, our hearts yearning for the source of life, our hearts longing for truth. Jesus Christ is the Truth in person, drawing the world to himself."[39] After we have attempted to find holiness in a thousand other places by practices, intentions, imitations, and schemes, our thirst leads us to God. At this realization, the pieces begin finally to fit. This is the docility that flows from love, not servile or neurotic

---

39. Pope Benedict XVI, *Sacramentum Caritatis*, 2.

obedience, but filial obedience. Holiness is a new song that only God can teach (cf. Ps 144:9).

In responding to the call to holiness, the believer must first be trained to turn away from self-taking and toward self-giving in the school of virtue. God trains us: "Blessed be the Lord, my rock, who trains my hands for battle, my fingers for war" (Ps 144:1). Jesus Christ alone is the answer to our pain. His gift of self leads to the communion of love. We must grow to detect in each of our actions the motivation of Jesus Christ acting within us. We open ourselves to the Holy Spirit and cease living for measurable and meager results. Even in the midst of mixed motives, our search for God is already gaining traction. We begin to recognize his action not in extraordinary ways, but in the moments we have always had before us and stopped recognizing years ago. Generous procreation and education of children conquers the fear of not leaving our mark in the business world. Noble service and dedicated work defeats our anxieties about getting ahead. The shortcuts of anger, greed, and illicit pleasure are revealed as folly. We detect meaning in sacrifice and are willing to pay the price for our commitments. We begin to value the meaning of the experience of Jesus and the salvation he offers. Our sense of the nearness of God is more his action than our own. We begin to realize that our previous efforts, while well meaning, may have emphasized our spiritual feelings as the measure of progress. Now, we look to God.

The sacraments drench us in the outpouring of the power of the passion, death, and resurrection of Jesus. His outpouring of self on the cross replenishes the fountain in such a way that the fountain of life is entirely new.[40] We receive the action of his inexhaustible *kenosis* offered on the cross, of his self-

---

40. See Balthasar, *The Glory of the Lord VII*, 253.

emptying which is a self gift.[41] His self-emptying is also a self-opening. This is the fountain of eternal life and a call of salvation to those in exile. Grace infuses the fountain from its original source: the wounds of Jesus's self-gift. The gifts, virtues, and Beatitudes are like the waters of a fountain that surge forth. This fountain proceeds from Fear of the Lord to Wisdom. Wisdom is the uppermost surge of the fountain, the top of the ladder, the highest reaches of charity. Fear of the Lord is the beginning of Wisdom, the initial surge of the fountain from which all else flows. We reach the surge where we love God not because of obligation, duty, guilt, fear, or reward, but because of *God*. For the Christian, a new, self-replenishing reality is at work in the world: the living waters that flow from God himself and maintain the childlike disposition of the Christian.[42]

The Surges of the Fountain

Each surge of the fountain represents an influx of the gifts of the Holy Spirit that purify and cleanse the heart of the believer. The Holy Spirit *generates* something new within the Christian. The Spirit creates and provokes pliability in our otherwise hardened hearts so that we can begin to untangle life's complications. The gifts provide the Christian with the strength to fulfill the summons to conform his or her actions to Christ as proclaimed through the new law inscribed in our hearts. The Christian must therefore exercise discretion about what enters the heart, because that which enters the heart spreads. If grace enters the heart, the gifts of the Holy Spirit

---

41. See Phil 2:7. Balthasar, *The Glory of the Lord VII*, 208, 379.

42. Rev 22:16ff. See Balthasar, *The Glory of the Lord II*, 88.

nurture the life of virtue that flourishes in living the Beatitudes. If sin enters, the network of the deadly sins brings chaos and disorder, which harden the heart. The fountain of grace provides the momentum of conversion by which the believer turns from the folly of sin to the life of virtue.

The spiritual life has frequently been broken down into a series of steps. While helpful, this image can easily depict the spiritual life as a kind of treadmill that we control and measure, rather than an action of God that transforms us. The image of the fountain, instead, refocuses the action to come from *outside ourselves,* from God. The surging momentum of the fountain provides a substantial image for the manner in which the divine mysteries unfold in the life of the Christian through grace and virtue. The Gospel of Saint John presents this image: A large number of sick persons waited for the stirring of the waters in the pool of Bethesda (cf. Jn 5:3). They hoped that the first to enter would be cured. Jesus came and healed a man who could not get to the water in time. Thus, Jesus is shown to be the fountain that surges forth for those who cry out. Healing comes from the person of Jesus.

The following chapters treat each Beatitude individually as they coalesce in the life of the Christian. The treatment of each Beatitude will explain the Gift of the Holy Spirit that internalizes the particular virtue associated with each Beatitude. In turn, this leads to the development of the Beatitude in the believer. The seven deadly sins work against the seven gifts of the Holy Spirit.[43] The Christian life thus takes on the character of combat: The believer attempts to resist temptation in the ongoing struggle of conversion as he or she seeks to remain faithful to the life of grace and virtue (cf. Gal 5:13-26). The gifts, virtues, and Beatitudes work as an antidote to the

---

43. See Balthasar, *Theo-Drama IV,* 209.

network of the seven deadly sins. The seven deadly sins or eight deadly thoughts are not found in an explicit list in the Bible. While an example of each of the deadly sins is found in the Scripture, the explicit list as such came together through the wisdom of the Desert Fathers. These early monks distanced themselves from worldly schemes and processes so that they could examine the deeper motivations and movements of the heart. They began to see that sin formed a network in the life of the human person. One sin leads to another until the self becomes a desert. The vice of pride leads one to view the self as entitled. This entitlement tempts one through greed or gluttony to take more than one deserves, or through envy or lust to treat others as objects, or through sloth to treat work as optional. Greed, lust, and sloth were never far from anger, impulsiveness, and violence. The desert of sin always requires the healing fountain of the gifts of the Holy Spirit, virtue, and the Beatitudes.

PART II

Chapter Five

The First Surge of the Fountain: Blessed Are the Poor in Spirit

From the outside, faith looks as if it is all about being sure that God exists. Externally, it would seem that faith is about knowing and keeping the rules of our religion, performing various practices, or perhaps mastering compelling arguments as to why people should practice one religion rather than another. While these things have their proper place, the truly distinguishing mark of the Christian rests elsewhere. Hope is the hallmark of the Christian. Hope is not merely a happy disposition about the future; it is a virtue. Hope grows in the believer not by simple advice, reasoning, or turning away from negativity and pessimism. Hope is built up by the Holy Spirit. Hope is what the Holy Spirit produces in us when we are confronted by the temptation of worldly fear. Remember, to find the depths of our identity, we must pass through fear. We must *mature* through fear.

The Holy Spirit begins the work of hope in us through his gift of fear of the Lord. This is the first step, the first surge of the fountain of all holiness. The Holy Spirit wants to build two virtues in us by means of fear of the Lord: the first one is the virtue of hope and the second is the virtue of temperance.[1] These virtues heal the Christian from the influence of gluttony and lust. Through the healing and nourishment of hope and temperance, we are strengthened so that we may live according to the first beatitude: "Blessed are the poor in Spirit, for theirs is the kingdom of heaven" (Mt 5:3).

Fear of the Lord

Fears arise even as we yearn for fulfillment. Fears can hold us back or steer us in the wrong direction. For the Christian, however, fear can be transformed into a pivot, pointing the believer in a new direction. Seen in the proper light, fear, once transformed, can guide us to a blessed life.

Fear is akin to hitting rock-bottom. Once we know we are afraid, we have nothing more to run from and can stop pretending. We can then be real from the bottom up, at a grassroots, everyday level. Fear is not meant to be a roadblock or a cliff. Fear is a path. Saint Bonaventure and Saint Thomas Aquinas taught that there are four types of fear: worldly fear, servile fear, initial fear, and filial fear.[2] Both saints taught that as the Christian grows in the spiritual life, he or she moves from one fear to the next, aiming for the goal of transformed fear, known as filial fear born of love.

---

1. See Aquinas, *Summa Theologiae*, IIa–IIae, q. 141, a. 1, ad 3. See also John of St. Thomas, *The Gifts of the Holy Ghost*, 175.

2. Aquinas, *Summa Theologiae*, IIa-IIae, q. 19, a. 2–9. See also John of St. Thomas, *The Gifts of the Holy Ghost*, 197.

Worldly Fear

The spiritual life lived from the bottom up confronts the believer with the common experience of worldly fear. At first, believers find themselves surrounded by the ways of the world: fascination with power, pursuit of pleasure, fixation on getting one's own way, abuse of others, broken promises, deceit in business, short-term thrills, and useless worries. Christians can easily become absorbed by the ways of the world, the ways of worldly fear. These fears quickly become obsessions that subtly fill everyday thoughts, perceptions, and feelings. It is easy for Christians to awaken in the middle of the night doing mental gymnastics, trying to figure out how to manage things well beyond their control. Control always interrupts us. We try to control because we sometimes participate in worldly schemes of use and power.

Worldly fear ensnares us to live by the possessive way of the world rather than by the way of the gift. Through this fear we refuse to use our freedom as a gift, and use it instead to express our power to possess things, people, situations, and even the future.[3] Fear frustrates the human thirst to go outside oneself as a gift of self. Fear converts our thirst for the gift into the will for power. Power then leads us to manipulate and make demands.

Fearing failure, we follow the false ideal of perfectionism, to acquire pleasure quickly, and to fear the effects of falling behind, of being seen as second-rate. Fear saturates us with worry as we try to control our worlds of education, occupation, finance, family life, entertainment, and recreation. Back room deals, cloak and dagger politics, deception, manipulation, lies, and greed become the all too subtle, yet very present, norm. In

---

3. See Balthasar, *Theo-Drama IV*, 148ff.

fear, we quickly abandon ethics for political maneuvers. Fear thwarts the fountain and turns it into a water tank in which our desire for God grows shallow and still instead of ready and open.

Servile Fear

Worldly fear is the fear most of us experience day to day in the marketplace. It is the fear of not making it, the fear of being labeled, betrayed, or taken advantage of in the plots and ploys of the world. When we turn away from the law of the jungle to the law of God, the first step is to move from worldly fear to servile fear. This fear is, on the popular level, commonly associated with Christianity. Servile fear is approaching God out of the fear that if I do something wrong he will send me to hell. Unfortunately, this fear has been emphasized beyond its proper understanding. It was thought that the best way to get someone to heaven was by scaring the hell out of them with reminders of eternal damnation. While separation from God is a possibility, this is always understood in the light of God as a loving Father, not a cruel and harsh punisher. Servile fear is a step along the way, not a destination. As we turn away from the world in a moment of conversion, we nonetheless still bring the attitude of the world. If one has lived by worldly fear on a secular level, one can bring those concepts to his or her initial steps in the life of faith. At first, we believe that God will deal with us as the world dealt with us: that he will cast us off if we step out of line. Through the gift of fear of the Lord, the Holy Spirit works to purify us of this fear. The fear of hell and eternal separation from God is not negative. It is positive and healthy. One can love God immensely from the basis of fearing eternal separation from him. Yet, God desires more than this. He leads us farther through his gift of Fear of the

Lord. Just as he led us from worldly fear to servile fear, the Holy Spirit desires to lead us from servile fear to initial fear.

Initial Fear

Initial fear carries some residue of servile fear. The person in initial fear still fears the loss of heaven and dreads the pains of hell, but also realizes that this fear is *based on* the love of God. One seeks to avoid hell not only because of dread of separation, but also due to a growing love for God in one's heart and soul. In initial fear the person moves back and forth between two poles: doing good things because of a fear of punishment, and doing good things because these flow from positive love for God himself. One is motivated not just by what one may lose, but by who one is growing to love: God in himself. Over time, the Holy Spirit works patiently to lead us from initial fear to filial fear.

Filial Fear

Filial fear is the fear of a son who has a good relationship with his father. The son looks on the father and believes in the deep and tender bond of love that unites them both. The father's presence does not cause anxiety, but brings security, humble confidence, and assurance. So, too, in filial fear with God we have a sense of his kindness and love. Through the gift of Fear of the Lord, the Holy Spirit works in the soul to alert us to the care God has for us. This care is expressed in the Scriptural accounts that reveal the strength of God's love and his determination to offer his salvation to the world. Filial fear inspires us to lower our defenses and raise our trust, even when we feel weak and lost. According to the prophet Isaiah, the Fear of the Lord is one of the great treasures of Zion (cf. Is

33:6b). The Fear of the Lord, based in the filial relationship to which God invites his people, underlies the covenant framework of biblical morality: the Christian lives a moral life not out of fear of violating a norm, but out of filial love for the author of that norm.[4]

Fear and the Moral Life

The Samaritan woman shows us that when we follow the path of Jesus, he will transform our lives. He heals memories, forgives past sins, and helps us change our habits to transform our lives. Just as the word of Jesus begins to transform the Samaritan woman, it will transform us too. Jesus leads her from worldly fear, through servile fear, past initial fear, into filial fear. As the psalmist says, "I turn my feet from evil paths to obey your word" (Ps 119:101). With fear so prevalent, it is no wonder that anxiety and unease often predominate when Christians approach faith and the moral life. We can be preoccupied with the same old fears for years. They can be like a boulder that blocks the path to the fountain. Even our attempts to change our lives can seem frought with fear. On a popular level, and often in media, Catholic morality is equated very quickly with juridical obligations or imposed sanctions.

But the authentic ambit of Catholic morality begins in a much wider context.[5] Morality begins in the framework of an adequate and robust sense of what and who the human person is: this study is known as anthropology. The third pillar of the *Catechism of the Catholic Church* treats our lives in Christ, which is more commonly known as moral theology. This section does not begin with rules, commands, or lists of do's and

---

4. See Pontifical Biblical Commission, *The Bible and Morality,* 29, 102.2.

5. See Torrell, *Saint Thomas Aquinas: Spiritual Master,* vol. 2, 12.

don'ts, but with the human person created in the image and likeness of God.[6] This means that we are called to an authentic communion of persons united in love. God wants each person, with body and soul, to use reason and free will to seek the true and authentic good that fulfills human nature. The call to love God and neighbor is not imposed on us externally as a random and arduous task, but emerges from deep within us. Though we are wounded by sin, God supplies his grace and virtue to us so that we may live anew as his sons and daughters. This grace is not automatic, but a gift we must receive in docility.

Our sense of what it means to be human impacts the way we live and behave. The human person does not exist simply in a courtroom. Rather, the person exists in the context of a relationship that God freely initiates. This relationship is not ambiguous, nor created by God on a whim. God has desired to speak to us. God has told us about our relationship with him. The two overarching realities are that God has *created* us and *called* us. God has created the human person in his image and likeness and has called the human person to a relationship with him. God himself has designed this relationship, which is never arbitrary. Our relationship with God is not "private" in the individualistic sense. Our relationship with God is personal, and, as such, takes place always in and through his Church. The fact that it is a personal relationship does not mean that it is self-created or isolated. The living God, out of the depths of his own generous initiative, freely chooses to disclose himself to us. God reveals himself in history and makes known his wise and loving plan. He establishes a personal relationship with humanity by means of a covenant

---

6. *CCC,* nos., 1700–1709, esp. 1702–1703.

relationship. Through the Law, the prophets, and the writings in the Old Testament, God teaches his people to look forward to the promised Messiah. Divine revelation reaches its highpoint and culmination in Jesus Christ, the Son of God incarnate. The Gospels proclaim the message of Jesus, the coming of the Kingdom of God. The climax of divine revelation takes place in the passion, death, and glorious resurrection of Jesus. God has chosen to make known the knowledge of his mysteries so that these may be proclaimed to all people in and through the Church. Jesus called twelve apostles to be his witnesses. The apostles appointed successors to whom the Apostles passed on the fullness of the Sacrament of Holy Orders, who receive from the Apostles the office of shepherding the Church. This unbroken line endures to this day. Sacred Tradition is the living transmission of all the truths revealed by the Lord Jesus Christ and the authoritative truths which derive from his revelation as authentically interpreted and faithfully passed on by the apostles and their successors in the doctrine, life, and worship of the Church. Sacred Tradition is thus the perpetual renewal of all that God has revealed as true and unchanging.

Sacred Scripture teaches without error the truth which God, for the sake of our salvation, wished to convey. Sacred Scripture is read within the living Tradition of the Church. The teaching authority of the Church, the Magisterium, is entrusted with the task of authentically interpreting Sacred Scripture. The Holy Spirit, who guarantees the truthfulness of divine revelation, dwells in the Church and draws the whole body of the faithful to the response of faith regarding the authentic teaching of the Church.

The moral teaching of the Church is based on the Ten Commandments and the Sermon on the Mount. The teaching of the Church does not contradict right reason and accords with the unchanging principles and universally valid norms of the natural law. We do not rely on polls, Hollywood, the news media, the latest statistics, or politics. The graces of the sacraments form the life of virtue within us so that we have the strength to live the moral teaching of the Church. The Holy Spirit, by his seven gifts, which are given in Baptism and strengthened through our reception of the sacraments, bestows grace by which we freely allow the Holy Spirit to shape our intellect and will so that we internalize the authentic moral teaching of the Church into a daily way of life. The way we behave and live our lives flows from our relationship with God. God has thus revealed a morality, a way of life, which is, at the same time, a profound experience and an authentic teaching.

Yet many Catholics find it very difficult to grasp the notions of morality. North Americans have often fallen into the trap of compartmentalizing their life of faith. Under this tendency, the truths of faith are seen as an internal, private spiritual matter, while our actions and behavior are a separate, secular matter. Further, North Americans in general do not easily grasp how a seemingly private action such as cohabitation, contraception, divorce, abortion, or greed can affect or influence others beyond the self. Therefore, the popular view resists any attempt to coerce or limit my otherwise "private" actions, seeing them merely as lifestyle choices. This is the popular yet misguided understanding of freedom. More properly, it is individualism, relativism, and subjectivism. The autonomy that arises from individualism is only a facsimile of freedom. One of the great tragedies is that North Americans are thus insulated from the true nature of their actions. They claim to be free, but rarely realize freedom as the original and spontaneous response of the entire person to authentic love. Of its very nature, love is never private, and it always seeks the genuine fulfillment of communion as a response to the profound and complete truth.

The moral teaching of the Church authentically guides us to the truth. Moral theology is the science that explains the Church's teaching. At the Second Vatican Council, the Church called for the renewal of moral theology. This meant that the Church sought to reinvigorate the way she explained her authentic teaching on the moral life. The renewal of moral theology does not mean simply offering more convincing reasons for the already existing do's and don'ts. For 400 years prior to the Second Vatican Council, moral theology had focused almost exclusively on the tedious examination of judgments that persons made in various situations. The Council recognized the proper role of moral theology concerning judgment of conscience and action. But it also sought to integrate into moral theology the teaching of Sacred Scripture and the Church Fathers on configuration to the Person of Christ. Under the influence of the Holy Spirit, this configuration actually forms believers to live a life of virtue.

Before we can examine our own actions for their moral quality, we must understand how God works in our regard. He has taken the initiative in each of our lives. Today, even faithful believers often do not sufficiently value the way God has taken the initiative in creating and offering redemption to every member of the human race. Instead, popular conceptions of faith regard God as a type of insurance agent in the sky. God is supposed to take care of everything: keep our family healthy, ensure we get good grades, give us clear weather, and make everyone get along. We then pay our premium of prayer and worship. But if something bad happens, we are tempted to withhold our premium. We stop praying and going to church, and we let our beliefs and practices lapse. After all, God did not uphold his part of the deal, why should I then uphold mine? We then revert from the legalism of the insurance agent God to the freewheeling therapist God, who asks nothing but that we buy the newest best-seller from the latest guru.

The "God as insurance agent" notion leads to a very constrained understanding not only of God, but also of the human person. With this outlook, we see our relationship with God as one in which both God and man keep a ledger of requirements the other must make good on, rather than as a commitment of fidelity. If the requirements are not fulfilled we give up and abandon the relationship in anger.

God as an insurance agent is not the proper conception of God. God has revealed the truth of himself as a God of goodness who is love. Therefore, my first consideration and primary moral coordinate becomes: *How do I respond* by my life *to the God who has created me and initiated a relationship with me?* Since God is a God of truth and goodness, then my response to God must be characterized by truth and goodness as he has revealed these to be. God makes this revelation through Sacred Scripture and Tradition interpreted in the authentic teaching of the Church.

My journey of faith starts with God's invitation, which calls me to a new way of living. He addresses this invitation to me primarily and extensively in a very personal way. This personalization includes and is compatible with a crisp juridical application in extreme instances. But that is not the primary way God invites us to a deeper relationship.

From the first moment of existence, the human person is in a relationship with God, who always invites the person into a deeper relationship. The people who walk across the parking lot to church on Sunday morning may not be able to articulate their experience of God. Their experience may remain only vaguely conscious. Through its teaching and pastoral care, the Church helps them to better understand the action of God as it takes place in their lives.

The Holy Spirit illumines our hearts to understand that we find fulfillment and happiness through the self-gift of love. Fear deceives us about what is real. To acquire pleasure quickly does not bring us happiness, and does not heal pain. Only the communion of authentic self-giving love can heal pain. And love is the only proven way to change behavior permanently over time. Fear jams our radar for love and directs us to be self-centered and avoid the gift of self. The first action of love within us is to transform our fear into freedom.

Freedom from fear comes only from God: "I sought the LORD, who answered me, [and] delivered me from all my fears" (Ps 34:5). Only the gift of love creates communion, and we are created for communion. The Holy Spirit teaches us a new meaning of fear: "I will teach you the fear of the LORD" (Ps 34:12), so that we can then say, "Happy are those who fear the LORD" (Ps 112:1; cf. Ps 128:1). This Fear of the Lord is reverence, pausing before the magnitude of the gift of self. The sacraments are a school in which the Holy Spirit transforms us to take on the new heart of Christ: "Give me insight to observe your teaching, to keep it with all my heart" (Ps 119:33b). The psalmist understands healthy fear as leading immediately to the virtue of hope: "But the LORD's eyes are upon the reverent, upon those who hope for his gracious help," (Ps 33:18).

This gift is not fear in the sense of worldly or servile fear, regretful or nervous anxiety about God.[7] Fear of the Lord is a veneration and awe before the mystery that God *is*, and that

---

7. See John of St. Thomas, *The Gifts of the Holy Ghost*, 198.

he has permitted that we may exist through his love. Fear of the Lord teaches us to read deeply into God's ways of acting and dealing with us. Fear of the Lord is deepened by reading the Bible and learning how the figures of salvation history clung steadfastly to God no matter the circumstances.

Hope

Hope is the virtue that builds poverty of spirit in the Christian. Hope is not mere optimism or a positive outlook that we conjure up when things get bleak. Optimism is concerned with conveniences such as good vacation weather, and smooth driving. Christian hope is an unexpected resilience that the future will be good despite difficult situations. The *Catechism* teaches that "Hope is the theological virtue by which we desire the kingdom of heaven and eternal life as our happiness, placing our trust in Christ's promises and relying not on our own strength, but on the help of the grace of the Holy Spirit."[8] The good future is assured because in hope one has already joined himself to God. Therefore, one always meets any difficulty in life through deepening one's union with God. Hope assures that whatever the details of any potential outcome, the believer lives in personal and sound newness because he or she is already joined to God through hope. Emptiness will not have the last word, God will.[9]

Hope enables us to meet the bleak experiences of life with resiliency rather than despair, whether we face job loss, family dysfunction, illness, dryness in prayer, the ills of society, or any

---

8. *CCC,* no. 1817.

9. See Pope Benedict XVI, *Spe Salvi,* 2, 7.

other problem. Our despair usually masquerades in the hectic guise of busyness. Hope is the opposite of despair. The resilience of hope comes from knowing Jesus. He is the one who has overcome all. We trust Jesus not because he will make things happen exactly the way we want them to happen, but because he himself *is* the way, and whatever he chooses will eventually lead to life and blessedness.

Hope provides the ultimate basis for following Jesus. Hope strengthens the believer in a way that nothing else can. Through hope, the Christian becomes united with God in the very act of waiting for God. Just as it did for Job and Jeremiah, the *waiting* associated with hope becomes itself a substantial bond and sign of fidelity with God. Waiting wears away our self-will and opens us to discover again the faithfulness of God. Waiting is the training ground of *trust*.[10] The one who truly hopes does not become concerned about *time*. Concern about time draws us into the worry trap. Once in the trap we distract ourselves. One of the principal ways we distract ourselves is noise. How do we emerge from all the clamor and the busyness? We do so through hope. The one who hopes understands in a personal way, in a way explained by the Holy Spirit himself, that all time belongs to Christ. The one who hopes rediscovers silence and the importance of communication, that all sound should in some way praise Christ. The future is only an opportunity for God to show his creativity and fidelity. He holds the future. Hope realizes that whatever our circumstances, desperate as they may be, God has been here before. In the long suffering of Christian history, God has stood in the most painful and unfinished of places, and he knows what

---

10. For a reflection on the significance of waiting, see Adrienne von Speyr, *The Victory of Love: A Meditation on Romans 8* (San Francisco: Ignatius Press, 1990), 69–70.

to do. He will be faithful. Hope teaches that union with God in the waiting is sweeter than having things turn out exactly as we wanted them to.

Hope affords one the strength to deal with the unpleasant realities of life. Hope enables the Christian to profit from difficult situations, using them as opportunities to unite oneself to God by waiting for him to act. Hope looks to a future good that is difficult to obtain, yet possible. Insofar as we hope, our hope already unites us to God himself.

One who hopes in God is already united to him. The hope-filled person relies on God's mercy and is more concerned with God than the thing desired. When one leans on God, one attains God. Hope is more than wishing for a smooth drive at rush hour. Hope is more than positive thinking about something we want, for example, that a meeting will go well. Hope is the virtue of the pilgrim who journeys from the city of the world to the city of heaven. Hope is the center of gravity in the heart of the believer. Hope gives us the resilience we need when we encounter the daily and sometimes prolonged difficulties, burdens, and temptations of living the Christian life. Hope enables us to persevere into the future through union with God: ". . . hope does not disappoint, because the love of God has been poured out into our hearts through the holy Spirit that has been given to us." (Rom 5:5). By this hope the believer is joined to God himself in times of difficulty. Hope unites the Christian to God himself, and therefore shapes and forms the Christian to be like God. This hope is placed in God who has saved us through his divine power.

Hope opens the way for the Christian to cling to Christ and rely on God's mercy even in the face of sin, and to await his omnipotent power: Christ has made our hope firm. Hope is the word that leads to salvation: "For in hope we were saved" (Rom

8:24). Hope therefore brings a youthfulness to the believer which renews the inner man every day (cf. 2 Cor 4:16). Today, countless people rely on extracts, surgery, and wrinkle removers that restore only the appearance of youth. Hope is the fountain of youth that God applies directly to the heart: "They that hope in the LORD will renew their strength" (Is 40:31). Even the most distressing and painful events of life only serve to illumine the true character of hope. Job said that even if God would slay him, he would still trust in God (cf. Jb 13:15).

When it meets an obstacle, a fountain relies on patience and perseverance. The patience of the fountain is a combination of its substance and its pressure. A fountain wears down even the largest boulders by continued pressure. The fountain erodes the boulder over time as water flows faithfully over the huge rock. A fountain actually *creates* new ways around an obstacle. Similarly, by its very nature, hope *creates* a new way. Christian hope is in for the long haul. Creation takes time. Hope does not give in to momentary gripes in the form of complaints and criticism. Such ailments easily harden into self-centered attitudes that block the fountain of self-giving love, which is meant to surge from within no matter what obstacles stand before us. This is the momentum of the gift of self. The outpouring of Jesus on the cross comes to live inside of us as a gift of self and seeks to be expressed in our attitudes and actions. This is the patience and force by which God gradually transforms the world.

Temperance

Temperance is the virtue that strengthens the believer to integrate and sanctify the appetites in the pursuit of holiness. The *Catechism* teaches that, "Temperance is the moral virtue that moderates the attraction of pleasures and provides balance in the use of created goods."[11] One cannot reach the fullness of chastity simply by sheer determination. One must rely on God's action as found in the first surge of the spiritual life. The struggle with the appetites is so basic that the early action of God already prepares us for the task of intergration of the appetites. Fear of the Lord leads us to understand that God has created and ordered the human person in a profound and beautiful way toward that which is truly good. Sin disturbs this inherent tendency and turns us away from God. Sin is based on the proposal that we can usurp the power of God. Grace invites us back to the proper path, in particular through temperance and hope.

Hope and temperance have much in common. For instance, hope and temperance both are focused on perseverance: the ability to wait. Waiting is not the passive inability to get what we want. When we wait for something we *learn* from the delay. Waiting is *active*. Waiting is growth's second name. Experience itself is a form of waiting; from the most routine to the most profound, experience is punctuated by waiting: one waits for a sunrise, a sunset, an ocean wave to crest, the seasons to change, and, most of all, for pregnancy to give way to birth. Beauty is the crescendo of waiting. Because it looks forward, waiting already begins to illumine *trust*. Love matures in waiting's pause as a substantial bond is forged that opens ways into God of which we never dreamed. As we wait for God, something is revealed about him that can never be revealed in any of our achievements.

Waiting is a school of deprivation that unites us to Jesus in his deprivation. The momentary delays of life become rehearsals for waiting for God: when we wait at the post office, the

---

11. *CCC,* no. 1809.

doctor's office, for an elevator, at the grocery store, or in traffic, rather than being upset and frazzled at the delay, we have a practice session in learning the patience of hope. When we wait in an argument and surrender rather than get in the last word, when we refrain from talkativeness, we allow God to create a place where we are united to him. When we wait behind as others frantically rush forward as they turn the pleasures of creation into the demands of the world, something actually *happens*. We are left behind the crowd, and in this silence and stillness, even in the ache of uncertainty about what we should really be doing, *someone* emerges. At this moment, waiting can become prayer, a secret door that was always there right in front of us, in an obvious place but overlooked for so long, that leads to God. A word emerges in the waiting: charity.

The waiting of hope introduces us to the Lord himself: "I waited, waited for the LORD; who bent down and heard my cry" (Ps 40:2). Waiting is a kind of light by which God illumines us to see the nature of his life and our own. Waiting *locates* us. In waiting we can see more clearly the chaos, neglect, daily assaults, and carelessness of our lives and the simple order to which God summons us. The author of the Book of Lamentations writes, "Good is the LORD to one who waits for him, to the soul that seeks him; it is good to hope in silence for the saving help of the LORD" (Lam 3:25–26). In waiting and patience we see our thoughts from a new distance of discretion and discernment. We detect how little room our quick thoughts have left us to be ourselves. Instead of accepting who we are with patience, we were off trying to please someone else, to gain distinction, to assert influence, to win, to see others lose.

The secret places of the heart become visible in slow motion through patience and waiting.[12] Waiting opens up the

---

12. See John Cassian, *The Conferences* XII, VI, 5.

kingdom of heaven. The kingdom finds us. We are not like the busy, rushed, and frantic crowd trying to get more. We settle for less in terms of the world. We prepare well to treasure that which we do receive from God. Waiting demonstrates the poverty of those who are poor in Spirit.

Gluttony

Hope forms the senses, reminding the person that the senses do not exist for their own pleasure, but for the communication and reception of the authentic gift of self. Hope counteracts the temptation to satisfy the senses through the tactile pleasures associated with gluttony and lust. The one who worries about the future will frequently be tempted to take refuge in the natural comfort that food and sex afford.

The temptation to gluttony is more about thoughts than about food. Gluttony is not characterized simply by overeating. Gluttony deceives the believer into relying on food for comfort and into abandoning moderation and nourishment. This temptation thrives on the illusion that food is not about bodily health, but about satisfaction through a variety of flavors and tastes. Gluttony makes sugar into medicine rather than a condiment. Gluttony does not so much expand one's stomach, but attempts to soothe one's spirit. In this context, food becomes a business. Neon signs and enhanced commercials regularly beckon the family away from the dinner table to the fast food eatery.

The true meaning of food is visible at the family table in the home. Food is about unity and nourishment; eating is about loving preparation and gathering together. When one eats at the family table one learns conversation skills, stories, family traditions, concern for others, how to share, dependency on the gifts of creation, and how to integrate taste with hunger. In the fast food line, orders are given without complete sentences; one learns impatience, speed, bargains, the rush to satisfaction, and the primacy of the appetites. Once the appetites are transformed to serve virtue, the goods of creation follow: "He who practices virtue and speaks honestly . . . [shall have] food and drink in steady supply" (Is 33:15a; 16b).

Lust

Lust is the deception that the urges to touch and experience sexual release are really about my own personal need rather than a gift of self. Lust subverts the perennial attraction between man and woman by reducing touch to pleasure, rather than a gift of self. In the world of lust, flirting turns into control, and relationships turn into manipulations. Lust makes sex into an industry. Lust must reduce meanings inherent in human sexuality. The permanent, faithful, and fruitful union of one man and one woman in matrimony is the only proper context for the physical expression of human sexuality in the sexual act. In the Old Testament, God invites his people to conversion and respect for the marriage vow: "You shall not covet your neighbor's wife" (Ex 20:17; cf. Dt 5:21). Jesus deepens this invitation to conversion, locating it in the heart of the person: "But I say to you, everyone who looks at a woman with lust has already committed adultery with her in his heart" (Mt 5:28). The temptation to lust seeks to overturn conversion of heart through subverting our appetites, so that we treat another or ourselves as an object to be used for pleasure rather than an irrepeatable and irreplaceable gift.

Sexual acts, of their very nature, are meant always and only to manifest a complete gift of self. Sexual acts are immediately related to the meaning of the body, love, marriage, family, relation, and unity. The gift always creates and unites. The culmination of creation and unity occurs when a child is conceived. Even for married couples who may not be able to conceive a child, the sexual act retains all its procreative and unitive meaning. Lust short-circuits the person's awareness of the meaning of human sexuality, the human body, love, marriage, family, relation, and unity. Advertising, media, and entertainment delude us into thinking that sex is simply recreational. The intensity and immediacy of bodily intimacy is privatized in lust and centered on the self rather than on the other in permanent, faithful, fruitful love. Lust reduces sex so that it is no longer about love, but merely about the satisfaction of personal erotic needs. The person's mental energies and bodily appetites become associated with seeking out what appears to be best and most comforting for the self rather than in making a gift of self. Separated from love, human sexuality is no longer about children and marriage. Lust is ultimately a frustrating illusion that never brings what it promises.

The gift of Fear of the Lord strengthens the virtues of hope and temperance. These virtues unite to make clear the real purpose of the five bodily senses: sight, hearing, smell, touch, and taste. These five senses serve our interior intellectual perception and inform the soul. The senses can actually perceive God's power and glory through natural signs. Instead of running from unpleasant realities, one now deals with these through the gift of self. One begins to understand that the body, food, human touch, and sexuality are gifts, not entitlements to be used and manipulated. Gluttony and lust arise from the failure to live with hope that pleasure delayed is not a slow form of suicide. Delaying pleasure trains us to treasure the gift of self. A new appreciation grows in the believer to respect the identity of the human person.

From the beginning, the human person is created as a union of body and soul. Body and soul are both good. The beauty of the body is meant to reflect the beauty of the soul. The powers of the soul, reason and free choice, are good. So too, are our appetites or passions. According to the *Catechism*, the "principal passions" are: "love and hatred, desire and fear, joy, sadness, and anger."[13] The influence of sin pits the appetites against reason. Sin presents counterfeit goods and apparent truths, and dupes us into pursuing these forgeries.

In the modern understanding of the nature of the body-soul relation, society frequently separates body and soul in the pursuit of happiness. So many people, especially the young, are duped into believing that life is made up of partying, sleeping, and working. This attitude wounds the soul and imperils the body. Once body and soul are separated in our understanding, we easily tilt to one extreme or the other. Either the body is emphasized to the neglect of the soul, or the soul is favored, disregarding the dignity of the body. Materialism focuses on the body to the exclusion of the soul. Spiritualism emphasizes the soul to the exclusion of the body.

The reduction of the meaning of soul or body happens because we are afraid of either the soul or the body. We quickly come to fear what we cannot control. With its varying moods, attractions, needs, and desires, the body is not easily controlled and appears to thwart our best intentions. The soul, with its deep capacities, mystery, and meaning is not easily charted. We are influenced by deep desires and longings. We experience faults, but also the impulse for forgiveness. We stew and hold grudges for years, but also can relent at the mere smile of an old friend. We keep score over the silliest things and find meaning in the briefest and most unexpected moments. The

---

13. *CCC,* no. 1772.

powers of the soul can lead us on as many twists and turns and ups and downs as can the body.

The Holy Spirit works through the gift of Fear of the Lord so the Christian does not dread the powers of body or soul, but respects each and believes the words of the psalmist in deeply personal ways: "I give you thanks that I am fearfully, wonderfully made" (Ps 139:14). The soul is not isolated in the body, but permeates it. The Spirit leads the believer to understand that the body is not a restrictive container of the soul, but reverently expresses the soul and the person. The virtues help us properly understand the identity of the human person as the integral *union* of body and soul. Temptations against chastity can alarm us. Many people of goodwill struggle with such temptations, often for a long time. The ongoing struggle is not a sign of failure, but an invitation to deeper dedication and humility. The *Catechism of the Catholic Church* teaches, "Self-mastery is a *long and exacting work.* One can never consider it acquired once and for all. It presupposes renewed effort at all stages of life. The effort required can be more intense in certain periods, such as when the personality is being formed during childhood and adolescence."[14] The Book of Proverbs tells us something similar: "The crucible for silver, and the furnace for gold, but the tester of hearts is the LORD" (Prv 17:3). God does not cause our temptations to evil, but he can transform our trials to work for good by his grace and mercy. Sometimes the fountain of all holiness is a fountain of suffering.

The gift of Fear of the Lord forms the first surge of the fountain of holiness. This surge builds hope and temperance in the Christian and leads to poverty of spirit. As these develop, the believer begins to be purified of the tendency to indulge

---

14. Ibid., no. 2342.

gluttony and lust, which can so easily weaken the will. Perseverance begins to build in the heart as poverty of spirit begins to glow.

Poverty of Spirit

Poverty or becoming poor in spirit is the first step of Christian transformation. In order to be filled with the Spirit of Christ, one must become empty of the spirit of the world. One is freed from the self-taking of the world only by the great reversal brought about by self-giving love. *Giving comes only through poverty. Only poverty can truly give the self away.*

Poverty finds its origin within the eternal life of the Trinity. Poverty thus begins in God himself. In one eternal act, the Father gives himself, in the love of the Holy Spirit, entirely in the begetting of his Son. God the Father gives the divine Substance to the Son. In this complete giving of himself in love the Father *is* the Father. In the same one and eternal act, the Son not only receives the fullness of his divinity from the Father, but he also gives himself entirely, in the love of the Holy Spirit, to the Father. The Father, in the love of the Holy Spirit, gives himself completely to the Son so that the Son shares in the fullness of the Father's divinity. The Son, in turn, through the same Holy Spirit gives himself completely to the Father so as to be fully united to the Father's divine being. It is in this giving of himself in love that the Son *is* the Son. This eternal complete self-giving of the Father to the Son and of the Son to the Father is in the love of the Holy Spirit, thus the Holy Spirit proceeds as complete love of the Father for the Son and proceeds as the complete love of the Son for the Father. Here we find the divine poverty of the Trinity. None of the Persons hoards the Godhead, but they eternally and mutually surrender themselves to one another in love.[15] We are called through the grace of the Holy Spirit to join this exchange of love and to give ourselves to God and one another.

Saint Peter's words to the crippled beggar at the gate of the temple reveal the importance of poverty: "I have neither silver nor gold, but what I do have I give you: in the name of Jesus Christ the Nazorean, (rise and) walk" (Acts 3:6). Poverty is so important because *it makes room* for the full exercise of the gift of love. In our materialistic world we cannot say to the crippled "rise and walk," because we cannot say "I have neither silver nor gold." The miracle itself is a sign of self-giving, not a privilege or prerogative given arbitrarily. One can receive the deep capacity for the gift of self even if one does not receive a physical healing. Poverty heals and creates. The room created by poverty now allows space for *acceptance* of the gift. Acceptance of the gift of love is belief in the nature of love itself. Faithfulness to love is the adamant refusal to play by the old rules of self-centeredness, subtle manipulation, and entitlement brought about by the refusal to love, which is inherent in the fear and disorder of sin.

Poverty is first a spiritual reality. It is much more than a social or economic class. In its fullness, it cannot be determined by my bank balance, income level, credit rating, expenses, or debts. Spiritual poverty does not make me eligible for assistance programs as determined by income, inflation, and costs. Poverty is not a spiritual consolation prize that helps me to cope with being born outside of a wealthy area.

Poverty is not the opposite of wealth; it is the opposite of greed. The greedy actually have nothing, for they never rest

---

15. See Hans Urs von Balthasar, *Christian Meditation* (San Francisco: Ignatius Press, 1989), 25.

content in what they have. They continue to need and to want the next thing.[16] All that comes within their grasp slips away, as if through a sieve, and never really satisfies them. The poor, on the other hand, may not have much, but value the meaning of what they do have. The poor have more than the greedy. Poverty is not what I am left with when I have lost my money or things, but the first thing I truly have ever had that is my own. Poverty is not a measure of what I do not have, but of who I am regardless of what I may have.

Jesus proclaims: "Blessed are the poor in Spirit, for theirs is the kingdom of heaven" (Mt 5:3). God is so rich that our total poverty is the response. We give all away to make room to receive his love. The psalmist proclaims that the Lord hears the cry of the poor (cf. Ps 34:7; 10:17). The Lord then acts on behalf of the poor: "For the poor who are oppressed and the needy who groan I myself will arise. I will grant them the salvation for which they thirst" (Ps 12:6). Poverty is not defeat, but a resilient scarcity that deals only with the substance of reality. Poverty of Spirit is acceptance of the deep designs of God. Because poverty is trained in reality and reliance upon God, it can recognize the tricks and illusions of the world. The authority of poverty resides in the capacity for self-abandonment.[17]

Poverty frees the person to have the interior room necessary to make an authentic gift of self that is the essential movement of love. Poverty frees the person from the many layers of illusions about the self. Freed from illusions, the person is free for the gift of self. Poverty brings about freedom

---

16. Simon Tugwell notes the possibility of real danger indicated by prosperity in the way the world defines it. See Simon Tugwell, OP, *The Beatitudes: Soundings in Christian Tradition* (Springfield, IL: Templegate Publishers, 1985), 17. A very similar notion is indicated by Daniélou, *Advent*, 106.

17. See Balthasar, *The Glory of the Lord VII*, 247.

from possessions. This freedom is the sign and the effect of the Holy Spirit as he gains greater access to the Christian's heart. Poverty is therefore not a human creation. Poverty is founded upon the poverty of God the Father who has *given up,* that is, *handed over,* his only Son in love for our salvation. Poverty is founded upon the Son of God, who carried out his mission in *complete obedience* to the Father. Since the Son of God became poor for our salvation, poverty itself is transformed into the deepest wealth of the human person.[18]

Poverty lightens the load. Unnecessary things pollute and weigh down life, obscuring its meaning. Poverty provokes spontaneous receptivity within us. This receptivity opens us for the gift of self. Poverty renews the naturalness of childhood within us, a childhood we have long forgotten.

Poverty of spirit is therefore the human disposition, formed by the Holy Spirit's action in the believer, of one who understands that the meaning of life and human identity is to make a gift of self in sacrificial offering. The grace of the gift of self from the inmost depths of the Trinitarian God pour forth to dwell in the heart of the Christian.[19] Poverty is the freedom to continue to give space to the life received from God himself, by which the Holy Spirit configures the believer to Christ through the transformation wrought by grace.

The self-taking ways of the world are the subtle, tricky enemy of love. Self-taking cannot be conquered by resolutions, mental discipline, reading the latest guru's bestseller, or mastering a spiritual technique. One can only *be freed* from self-taking. If one "conquers" self-taking attitudes by one's own measures or efforts, the original self-taking leaves its roots and seeds in the vanity of the assurance that one has finally

---

18. Ibid., 391.
19. Ibid., 309–310.

"fixed oneself." Unfortunately, such persons next try to "fix" others, and the pain multiplies.

The Holy Spirit purifies us from all the debris that accumulates in our lives due to sin. In battling sin, many Christians attempt to overcome it through the force of will. They resolve not to do a particular sinful action again. They swear off gossip or foul language. They promise they will refrain from sexualizing or cheating. The resolution of the will may be worn down over time and they repeat the sin and feel frustrated. This is due in part because in trying to remedy sin, they are only concentrating on the expression of sin. The nature of sin is that it overflows from preoccupation with the self to the subtle exclusion of God. The action of sin then actualizes and expresses this self-centered focus.

A new basis is required to live the life of holiness. The fountain of God's grace must flood the self-centeredness of sin and purify the deepest parts of the person's heart. As the fountain of God's grace surges into our hearts, it directs us to make a gift of self in the face of the hurt and sin of the world. The world has been telling us for so long to fight back that when the grace of God directs us to love, we feel disoriented and confused.

As the Spirit's gift of Fear of the Lord breaks through the hardness of our heart, the water of grace and the fountain of his love rise forth. As the first movement of the fountain emerges, it moistens the dryness of our hearts. Even now, his love dislodges and pushes sin, faults, and bad habits out of the way of its surge. Fear of the Lord has brought hope and temperance so that we can live life at a new pace: that of the poor in Spirit. The new perspective that hope brings allows us a new vision. Though we still move about in the old world in which we used to be a slave to painful patterns, unrealistic expectations, and sin, the force of the water begins to bring new life. This new life is delicate. Any flirting with temptation or collision with sin can begin to block the upward flow of God's grace.

Purgation is the first burst of the fountain of grace that clears away the debris of sin. The opening of the way allows for a stronger influx of grace in the heart of the believer. This purification is needed due to the wounds and effects of sin. The person, originally intended for the gift of self, has accumulated much rubble and debris from focusing on the self. All purification proceeds from the cross. The gift of grace cleanses us of this debris, so that God's illuminating light may shine into the deep places of the heart.

Chapter Six

The Second Surge of the Fountain: Blessed Are the Meek

In the second surge of the fountain, the gift of Piety leads the believer to internalize the virtue of justice and to further internalize temperance. Justice heals the wounds of envy and greed so that Christians may be strengthened to become meek and humble.

The Gift of Piety

The poverty of spirit given us by the first surge of the fountain may take years to reach the surface and purify an individual's actions. The Holy Spirit works diligently and persistently to remove the layers of sediment deposited by sin, which often cover and obstruct our hearts. He continually displaces old attitudes and creates new paths that lead from his depths to our hearts, and then from our hearts to our actions. The process often proceeds very slowly, for many things distract us.

Once the gift of the Fear of the Lord has begun to flow freely in the believer, the Holy Spirit bestows his gift of Piety. This gift does not refer to outward postures of prayer or a devout external demeanor. Rather, through Piety, the Holy Spirit transforms our hearts, enabling us to realize that just as we are children of God, other persons are *also* children of God.[1] And if we are all children of God, then we are brothers and sisters to one another. In loving God we are also directed to love one another: the virtue of justice is central to life in Christ.[2] The teaching of Jesus on the love of God and love of neighbor begins to stand in bold relief for us (cf. Mt 5:21–22; 22:36–40). The call to love God and neighbor is not split in two, as if once we have started to love God, then we must begin to love others. The love of neighbor is not added as a secondary duty that the Christian must perform after loving God. The internal form of love of God is love of neighbor. Similarly, the internal form of love of neighbor is love of God. Our love for God can therefore never be isolated from our love for neighbor.

Just as the Holy Spirit's work of Fear of the Lord can take years to build hope in the Christian, so too the Holy Spirit's action of Piety can take a long time to work in our lives. God appreciates the time it takes to heal, forgive, integrate, and take risks again on the path to holiness in our relationships. Our wounds often prevent us from treating one another as brothers and sisters. The Holy Spirit labors intensely in the deep places of our hearts to heal patterns of pain, abuse,

---

1. See John of St. Thomas, *The Gifts of the Holy Ghost*, 183.

2. See John Paul II, *Evangelium Vitae*, 7–8, 10, 19, 25, 40–41.

dysfunction, and bitter memories, which very often influence our own actions and sinfulness. But no automatic cure or magic exists to dispel such wounds. If we could only see the many ways the Holy Spirit seeks daily inroads into our pain, we would realize the mercy he longs to apply to our hearts. So often, in our pain and misunderstanding, we turn away from him and flinch as he draws close.

Through the gift of Piety, the Holy Spirit heals the wounds that divide us and leads us to treat one another with justice.[3] We develop a new, deeper sense of justice toward others. Justice is thus not merely a legal measurement or juridical category. Justice is formed from the awareness that God has created every person and loves them uniquely with a vast love. Piety enables the believer to live the virtue of justice: to give every person his or her due as a child of God. The Holy Spirit transforms us to understand that our family members, friends, strangers, and even enemies are children of God.

Before we can become servants of justice we must be the patients of justice. We must receive its medicine before we dispense its influence. As we become children of God through the gift of Fear of the Lord, so we become brothers and sisters of one another through the gift of Piety and the virtue of justice.

Justice and Temperance

The prophet Habakkuk describes the healing properties of justice: "The rash man has no integrity, but the just man, because of his faith, shall live" (Hb 2:4a). The Holy Spirit seeks continuously to bring the mercy of God to our hearts,

---

3. See John of St. Thomas, *The Gifts of the Holy Ghost,* 182–183, 188.

prompting us to respect others and to take the risk to forgive. He holds our hands as we move forward and forgive. Mercy surges into the remote places of our hearts, and we discover anew how God can turn the painful experiences of life to our benefit.

Justice is not simply about a social cause of which one is supportive. It is not merely the ability to measure out proper amounts and distribute goods equitably. Justice is first and foremost a disposition of the person that emerges from familiarity with God's faithfulness. The just person knows long-suffering and shares this as a sign of God's fidelity. As the psalmist says, "Neither in my youth, nor now in old age have I ever seen the just abandoned or their children begging bread" (Ps 37:25). After a long period of healing, the person develops an ever-greater capacity to act justly. The virtue of justice helps us relate to others and to the community at large. The *Catechism* teaches that, "Justice is the moral virtue that consists in the constant and firm will to give their due to God and neighbor."[4] In particular, justice orders the way we make use of material things. Through justice, we become aware that due to our frailty, we easily value things instead of people. Justice reminds us that the best things in life are not things. Justice restores our attitude to treat people with respect, and not as objects to be used. As such we must respect the authentic rights of others and fulfill our legitimate duties toward them. More than an obligation, justice is a *vocation* that invites the special guidance of God: "Therefore the wicked will not survive judgment, nor will sinners in the assembly of the just. "The LORD watches over the way of the just" (Ps 1:5–6). Justice recognizes the worth of the person in every situation. Justice is not a contemporary movement. It is the original gesture of

---

4. *CCC,* no. 1807.

man. This is why the psalmist can proclaim: "God will never allow the righteous to stumble" (Ps 55:23). We are to give others their due not simply because they deserve it, but because this is the way to be human. Forgiveness is the ultimate manner of giving the other their due. As we begin to treat one another with justice, then the words of the prophet Amos are fulfilled: ". . . let justice surge like water, and goodness like an unfailing stream" (Am 5:24).

The gift of Piety and the virtue of justice also further the work of the virtue of temperance within us. The gift of Fear of the Lord laid the foundation of temperance. Yet, the human appetites are so much a part of life and love that Piety also continues to form them. According to Pope John Paul II, piety leads us to treat justly our bodies and the bodies of others.[5] Saint Bonaventure also indicated that piety assisted in temperance.[6] When the Trinitarian love of God met the most ferocious actions of man in the death of Jesus on the cross, God responded with forgiveness and mercy. Jesus on the cross responded to the anger of his accusers and executioners by forgiving them. Paradoxically, the meekness of Jesus Christ conquered Satan's rage. Becoming children again means letting go of anger. Piety in particular begins to train the heart in new ways to let go of anger.

Anger

When people perceive that they have been treated unjustly, not given their natural and legitimate due, they become angry. When an injustice happens early in life, particularly if it is

---

5. Pope John Paul II, *Man and Woman He Created Them*, 353.

6. St. Bonaventure, *Collations on the Seven Gifts of the Holy Spirit* (New York: Franciscan Institute Publications, 2008), 80.

chronic, the chaos and fear experienced burrow deep into the person. Layers of denial protect them from painful or crushing memories. In fact, some people can only feel by being angry. They may react in a number of ways. Some may sooth themselves through bitter and resentful withdrawal. Others may lash out in spite and aggression. Our emotions can become attached to the memories of unforgiven and unhealed past wrongs. When we act on those emotions, we tend to hurt others through gossip, teasing, or yelling. Anger does not have an expiration date. Anger is born of fear, because fear keeps alive the energy of old hurts. Unforgiven grievances generate an anger that does not decease in energy until the grievance is truly forgiven. Many people still choose fear over forgiveness and so the anger remains.

Many people walk around every day with a heavy burden from their long history of slights, abuse, and mistreatment. The effects of pent-up, unhealed anger can easily poison our modern society: road rage, domestic violence, gang violence, school shootings, bullying, and hate crimes erupt daily in what should be safe places. Instead of responding in love, the person may seek retaliation. Others may put up with it for years: a father who bossed them around, a teacher who belittled them, a coach who yelled at them, a bully who insulted or teased them. Rage results.

Rage is not mere anger. Anger can be justified and appropriate when used as a tool. We can use anger in a constructive way against an unjust aggressor who seeks to mistreat others. Rage is anger that never learned to speak up. Rage is compounded and fermented anger. It is anger without aim or direction. Oddly enough, anger often hides behind heightened sensitivity, masked in the excessive desire to please and control others. Masks can make us seem polite. Yet, when the masks come off, rage arises in a split second. Rage depends on a camouflage that it does not even realize it is wearing. The sin of rage can take various shapes. Considerable rage can conceal itself behind the most routine things, until one day a painful circumstance causes it to accelerate and rear forth.

Rage is allergic to logic. Rage feels the sting of those painful, undeserved, and unjust past events as if they are still going on. The angry person may have long forgotten the details of past slights and pains, but still clings to the verdict. Painful emotional memories that remain unhealed can exert a strong and often unconscious influence. The pain is still very much remembered and alive. The present day slight forms an immediate link to the pain of long past, but unforgiven, injustice. The angry person believes the past event is still going on. The coach who yelled may now be retired, suffering with Alzheimer's in a nursing home; the teacher may be deceased; the parents may live far-away in Kansas; and the bully may now be a gentle yoga instructor. But the person with unresolved anger never left the schoolyard, field, classroom, or family home. Overreactions to present-day events are often rooted in past hurts. These overreactions can become invitations for us to notice any extremes in our behavior and to seek forgiveness and healing. The original pain of the mistreatment, and every mistreatment following, is thus connected to the current and seemingly unrelated circumstance. This is why there is such rage over a parking place, arguments, the little-league umpire calling my son out at third base, or a loud radio. The energy of the past pain is hot-wired directly to the current situation. The trigger is pulled. This is because the angry person sees the stakes of the past as riding on the present. If he wins this time, all the past pain will be healed, because for the angry person the past is never really the past. Anger is its own time machine. If one did not learn how to work it out then, he or she will sooner or later act it out in the present. This is why the angry person, whether in the mode of acting out or not, finds transparency and accountability tedious. If a situation has clearly established boundaries and requires such a person to be accountable for actions, the anger is more difficult to justify and will be found out all the more easily.

As noted earlier, the seven deadly sins are related one to another and rarely occur as vices isolated from the other sins. The seven form an overlapping network of disorder and have particular alliances among themselves. Involvement with one of the sins leads to an engagement with others. One deadly sin feeds off the others. Anger and lust are often closely aligned. Non-conjugal sexual acting out is often more about anger than it is about lust.[7] This is true in particular for men. Many men who battle with lust are actually battling with anger. Sex and aggression are closely linked in men even at the hormonal level. Because of the relatively intense, rapid, and physical nature of the male sex drive, men can unconsciously use their sexuality as an explosive outlet for the amorphous and undetected anger. Fear can make human sexuality a conduit of anger. Fear makes the car an extension of the person and results in road rage. Fear makes fashion part of the fabric of one's being and results in arrogance. Fear makes spending become one's worth and results in greed.

Anger waits many years to be released, and its energy is compounded the longer it waits. While it waits, anger is visible in many ways. The classic signs of anger are the visible manifestations of rage such as shouting, shaking, verbal threats, ultimatums, or physical violence to self or another.

There are also covert signs of anger. The phenomenon of body piercing arose very quickly only recently in the West. In

---

7. See John Cassian, *The Conferences,* XII, VI, 1.

some cultures, body piercing is an art or a sign of status; in the West, however, there is no cultural heritage from which this act emerges. The speed with which piercing entered Western culture makes one wonder about its roots. We pierce what we hate or what we want to kill. Many young people have been taught to hate their bodies, their looks, themselves.

Another sign of anger is a display of extravagant luxury. People who must surround themselves with fine things are communicating a message to the world. Since they do not experience the gift of self on the inside, they must constantly find security and affirmation through things on the outside. Angry people must see, discuss, and call everyone's attention to the extra-special finery around them, so that others never see *them*. This is the meaning of the saying, "Living well is the best revenge." Angry people use possessions as an attempt to prove to others how important they are and, at the same time, to protect themselves. Yet no matter how much crystal or china they purchase, no matter how many designer fashions they wear, stocks they trade, new cars they polish, acres they own, or first class tickets they buy, the value of the things never quite fills the emptiness. The hunger remains and deepens. The fear is never far away. In fact, the ineffectiveness of opulence to fill the void only deepens the anger.

Anger hides in a million places. The percussion of heavy metal music keeps perfect beat with the throbbing sensation of rejection and anger so many young persons experience. Souped-up, loud automobile engines are yet another attempt for a tired and overlooked young man to say, "Here I am . . . please . . . would someone finally notice me?" The drive of perfectionism is the attempt to counteract the fear of rejection with good grades, good looks, and good reports. Chronic criticism and gossip can destroy another's reputation. People can only criticize and gossip about others after they have finished the long litany of self-criticism based in self-hatred. The way we treat others reflects how we feel about ourselves.

Oddly enough, anger is a form of relationship, an inversion of friendship, which is learned over time and is marked by explosiveness. Anger ferments. Grudges fester. Negativity irritates. Anger and bitterness build up in the heart over the years. When angry persons meet someone more powerful than they, be it a parent, boss, or administrator, and the angry persons perceive that they have been treated unjustly by this person, they react in anger. The unique wisdom of a perceptive mentor can teach us to use anger as a tool. As Solomon said: "The fool gives vent to all his anger; but by biding his time, the wise man calms it" (Prv 29:11). Such wisdom comes only through replacing denial with acceptance, projection with acknowledgment, and blame with forgiveness. These movements only arise from the suffering of fear transformed into love.

Anger, unintegrated through suffering, distills into depression. Depression is anger with tenure. Anger thus follows a continuum: disturbance leads to annoyance, to temper, to a grudge, to the desire for revenge, to wrath, and finally, to rage. In anger, one seeks power out of fear. Ironically, the power that one wants to achieve eventually rears around and attempts to destroy the one who seeks the power.

Greed

To let go of anger one must be healed of the greedy experiences one has encountered. The Holy Spirit's gift of Piety begins to heal the wounds of greed. Though the greedy have a tendency to personalize money, greed is not simply the attitude of the Scrooge-like miser. It is true that if money becomes the way we show love, then we have made money the meaning of our existence. From the earliest times, the Lord reminds his people that just as he has given them the land he promised, so too, they must give and be generous: "If one of your kinsmen in any community is in need in the land which the Lord, your God, is giving you, you shall not harden your heart nor close your hand to him in his need. Instead, you shall open your hand to him and freely lend him enough to meet his need" (Dt 15:7–8). The psalmist advises: "Though wealth increase, do not set your heart upon it" (Ps 62:11b). Jesus emphasizes the subtle tendency of greed to corrupt the heart: "Do not store up for yourselves treasures on earth, where moth and decay destroy, and thieves break in and steal. But store up treasures in heaven, where neither moth nor decay destroys, nor thieves break in and steal. For where your treasure is, there also will your heart be" (Mt 6:19–21).

Money is a tool. In the case of greed, preoccupation with money is a symptom of a deeper malady. But one can be greedy with more than money: "Take care to guard against all greed" (Lk 12:15). The psalmist speaks of "Those who trust in their wealth and boast of their abundant riches" (Ps 49:7). One can be greedy for love, affection, and kindness. Greed can also prevent a person from giving another the room that he or she needs to grow. Like anger and the other deadly sins, greed is based on fear: the fear of generosity. Ironically, no matter how much greedy persons attempt to possess, they actually *have* nothing. They cannot sustain the experience of worth. The feeling of being worthwhile keeps slipping away from them like a balloon floating up to the sky, so they must continue to grab and accumulate the next thing that will make them feel worthwhile. The one who has embraced poverty, on the other hand, actually does have something, and in this small amount finds the meaning, worth, and contentment that escape the greedy.

The greedy may in fact be philanthropic. It is not that the greedy cannot give; they cannot *receive*. They have been wounded by a series of daily encounters with selfishness from the earliest age. They have stored so many wounds in their hearts in the feverish race to fill up their pain with things. The intense chase never rewards; it only deepens the wounds. These wounds make it difficult for them to generously accept others. Deprived of the experience of the gift, they possess themselves by disqualifying others. In the greedy, the human hunger for the gift of self has been realigned with self-taking: they want to control the television channel, the remote control, the steering wheel, the attention of the crowd, and the opinion of colleagues. The greedy hoard their own ability to be human. Manipulation replaces the authentic way to life. The greedy cannot receive because they think all other persons are like themselves—greedy. So they mistake competition for relationship.

The greedy do not have friends; they have contacts. They do not have conversations; they have interviews. They seek to impress other by name-dropping: restaurants, brands, clubs, vacation spots, and celebrities. The greedy do not dream. They wish. Greed wastes the present by fantasizing about what might have been: getting into the market at the right time, being known as an expert, acquiring power and popularity. Greed does not enjoy other persons, but attempts to use them. Greed thus leads to a pattern of fraud and deceit.

Greedy persons need to continually convince themselves of their worth and importance. Since they cannot find their own internal value, they seek it externally in their lifestyles. The greedy generate their own non-stop reminders of self-importance. They attempt to impress others with their lifestyle or knowledge, hoping to be thought sophisticated. But tragically, instead of living from the inside-out, the person lives from the outside-in: the external markers of importance that the person relies on for a sense of self can never lead to internal worth. Their longing to receive the gift of love becomes an unmet, chronic need.

Meekness

Jesus announces that meekness is one of the great secrets of his heart: "Take my yoke upon you and learn from me, for I am meek and humble of heart" (Mt 11:29). The meek are not hapless and naïve persons who shrink from any risk or vulnerability. The prophet Joel proclaims that the meek man shall be a warrior (cf. Jl 4:10). Meek persons are not passive. Rather, they have not only learned the ways of the world, but they also have seen too much of the world. They know the signs of deception, negativity, and falsity. At the same time, their way of thinking is gentle and childlike.[8] Meekness is a special and rare form of love. It is love that has been purified of anger.[9] Thus, meek love is steadfast love that forebears in an active sense, that endures in a vigorous and positive way. Meekness is strength. The meek have moved from complaints to accountability. They understand that many of our roadblocks are self-established. The waiting that we learned from Fear of the Lord becomes a sustained, dynamic patience in the meek (cf. 1 Cor 13:4). They realize that the wisdom learned from daily life is more valuable than winning any lottery. The meek rise early in the morning, realizing that an hour in the morning is worth two at night. They seek the

---

8. See Pinckaers, *The Sources of Christian Ethics*, 92–93.

9. See Gabriel Bunge, *Dragon's Wine and Angel's Bread: The Teaching of Evagrius Ponticus on Anger and Meekness* (New York: St. Vladimir's Seminary Press, 2009), 74, 81–82, 102, 110.

lowest place, knowing they can find there the mystery of God. Humility and powerlessness do not lead to dead ends, but to secret openings. For the meek, simplicity means that they are indivisible and uncomplicated. The meek have not simply learned from their mistakes, but have been *healed* from those mistakes by risking the lowest place. It was only after Moses lost his high position in Egypt that he could actually learn meekness. What seemed like a setback to the world is a step up in the eyes of God. Thus, after Moses was exiled, the Book of Numbers states: "Now, Moses himself was by far the meekest man on the face of the earth" (Nm 12:3). The meek are not afraid of the ordinary, and they do not rush away from the threatening, nor cling to the familiar. They have watched as God has worked to transform their mistakes into wisdom.

God transforms mistakes into blessedness only in the school of suffering.[10] Meekness bears up under evil. The humility of the meek flows from the Spirit's action within their own long-suffering. They bear hardships and sustain difficulties not as a kind of toleration, but because their principles lead them to the deepest good. They are willing to accept and carry more than their share of suffering only because of the charity of Christ. The meek feel their suffering completely, and while the feeling pains them, in faith they realize that suffering actually unites them to a deeper good—the good for which they suffer and, ultimately, therefore, to God.

Only the meek are truly at home in their own skin. They are at rest because they have nothing to prove. The natural credibility of the meek is a relief from the excuses and entitlements of the proud. They show wisdom, though not in a know-it-all, arrogant manner. This is why the meek are easily

---

10. See Pinckaers, *The Sources of Christian Ethics*, 25, 119.

missed. They do not compete in the rat race. For them, competition always remains recreation. Daily life is too important to value it only for advancement and gain. Incomplete skill or knowledge is not a threat to them, but a sign of their own dependence on love. They know the feeling, deep in their psyche, of gradually trusting their own once hidden strength. They know that this strength belongs first to God.

If others do notice the meek, they are threatened by them because they do not want the same things these others chase after. Therefore, they cannot control the meek and must label them to be safe from them. But even here, the meek rest: others think about them more than they think about these others.

At this second surge of the fountain the gifts of Fear of the Lord and Piety have coalesced to nourish the Christian in the virtues of hope, temperance, and justice, and to further dislodge attachment to sin. These strengthen the believer to live as one who is poor in spirit and meek.

Chapter Seven

The Third Surge of the Fountain: Blessed Are Those Who Mourn

The transformation and conversion central to the Christian life ordinarily take time. The primary path God uses to accomplish this conversion is the grace that flows from the sacraments, which fills our hearts with the Gifts of the Holy Spirit. The gifts, in turn, strengthen the virtues, and the virtues lead us to live the Beatitudes. The merits of Jesus, the example and intercession of the Blessed Virgin Mary and the saints, Scriptural prayer, spiritual direction, and the natural gifts of prudent counseling, healthy friendships, and the example of good persons coalesce to direct us to the sacraments.

The third surge of the fountain consists of the gift of Knowledge, which strengthens the virtue of faith in the believer. This virtue helps to heal the pain of envy and leads the believer to the healthy mourning that animates those who desire God. Thus far, the Holy Spirit has sought to gain deeper access to our hearts as his gifts of Fear of the Lord and Piety form the virtues of hope, temperance, and justice in the believer. The Christian has been discovering a new strength as he or she realizes more deeply what it means to be a son or daughter of God. The person has more access to the heart, where the Holy Spirit has been long at work to strengthen the Christian. This strength does not bring entitlement or bravado, but the power of humility.

The layers of debris from the ill effects of intemperance and injustice had blocked the Christian from the pure waters of faith and virtue. As the Holy Spirit cleanses the Christian's heart from selfishness, pleasure, anger, and greed, new places open, so that the Christian can more deeply receive the truths of faith. Saint Bonaventure points out that the gift of Knowledge opens the mind up to the knowledge of grace for the reception of the truths of faith.[1] The fountain inside the believer gushes ever higher. Previously, when the person attempted to live the life of faith, the desire for worldly things pushed the truths of faith away. They seemed too heavy, unrealistic, or demanding. Now, the energy that formerly went into chasing the things of the world is channeled to an authentic gift of self. This gift takes on a new depth and directs the Christian to live more deeply the life of grace and virtue.

The Gift of Knowledge

The gifts of Fear of the Lord and Piety have restored childlikeness in the believer and renewed his or her sense of proper relationship with self, others, and God. The truths taught by the Holy Spirit through the Church become a living

---

1. See St. Bonaventure, *Collations on the Seven Gifts of the Holy Spirit*, 83–85.

principle within the Christian, who begins to understand that the Church is much more than an institution. The Christian discerns the intimate bond between Jesus and the Church.[2] This unity strengthens the believer, whom the Holy Spirit now prepares to guide further into the mystery of Jesus. The Holy Spirit's gift of Knowledge helps the Christian to grasp the teachings of the Church. The truths of faith are less likely to be hindered or blocked by the person's preoccupation with pleasures and busy activities. The believer may have heard these teachings many times before. He or she may have found them one dimensional, flat obligations and duties, or as mere man-made, abstract laws, and perhaps even rejected them.

Through the gift of Knowledge, the Holy Spirit enables the believer to receive these same teachings anew. As we navigate our relationships, we discover that we are not totally dependent or independent. We are *interdependent*. We grow in our knowledge of God as we come to terms with our own contingency and limits, which teach us to rely upon God.[3] This gift of Knowledge is not necessarily the fruit of formal education. In fact, the person might never have had a formal religious education class in his or her life. This knowledge arises through God acting in the Church, in such a way that God's goodness begins to impart knowledge to the soul. The knowledge of God grows in the soul through the Holy Spirit's action.[4] The Christian mourns that more time and space is not available to know God's goodness.

Moving from meekness to mourning, the Christian cries out with the psalmist: "Teach me wisdom and knowledge"

---

2. *CCC*, no. 789.

3. See Hans Urs von Balthasar, *Theo-Logic: Theological logical Theory I: The Truth of the World* (San Francisco: Ignatius Press, 2000), 52.

4. See Torrell, *Saint Thomas Aquinas: Spiritual Master*, vol. 2, 97–98, 109. See also John Corbett, OP, "The Functions of *Paraclesis*," *The Thomist* 73 (2009), 96–102.

(Ps 119:66).[5] This mourning is actually a kind of longing for
the Holy Spirit to teach the soul directly. The Spirit now
casts light on what the believer was taught years before. Even
the most hardened of atheists have a thin layer somewhere of
the capacity for faith. Layers of pain may cover it, especially
the pain of abandonment. These pains wound the capacity to
entrust oneself to another, the docility necessary for faith.
Lack of faith is more about pain in this life than thought-out
conclusions about eternal life. The gifts of Fear of the Lord
and Piety heal the person's capacity to trust and to believe.
Discernment and docility are the signs that the Holy Spirit
is at work within the soul.[6] Through the gift of Knowledge
the Holy Spirit works inside us, in a way we are often not
aware of, to help us understand the deep meaning of God's
actions, which we hear in Scripture and witness in the world
around us.[7]

For example, God casts a light and makes plain his saving
presence in various moments that he alone chooses. God may
choose a particular verse of Sacred Scripture that we hear proclaimed one Sunday in church or read before we go to bed. We
may have heard or read that verse dozens of times before.
Then, one day, as we hear it or read it, it stands out. The words
sound different this time. They do not simply describe our
lives or tell us what to do. The experience is deeper than that.
In hearing the words, we experience a *closeness,* and we feel the
presence of God through faith.

The gift of Knowledge works on the lessons we have been
taught about the faith by parents, priests, and catechists. This

---

5. See St. Bonaventure, *Collations on the Seven Gifts of the Holy Spirit*, 101.

6. See Torrell, *Saint Thomas Aquinas: Spiritual Master,* vol. 2, 209.

7. See Hans Urs von Balthasar, *Engagement with God* (San Francisco: Ignatius
Press, 2008), 97.

knowledge translates ordinary thoughts and affections into deep *realizations* that resonate in our souls and confirm in our hearts the truth of God. The gift of Knowledge also develops in the believer through homilies and good catechesis.

The Holy Spirit uses many instruments to work this conversion in our lives: a reading, a homily, familiar prayers heard in a new way, quiet moments in which he touches our hearts, an adult education class, a sacramental preparation night. The Holy Spirit does not work automatically. He engages the Church in an active and immediate manner. Those who preach and teach the message of salvation need to make time for prayer and preparation. Homilists and catechists proclaim the authentic teaching of the Church with faithful originality in a living context. Their teaching becomes more fruitful when they pay close attention to the pastoral needs of those whom they serve. Preaching and catechesis will be effective to the extent that they lead us to the sacraments and assist us in living the grace received in the sacraments.

As the Holy Spirit acts through the gift of Knowledge, the words or concepts of an early religious education class resound anew in us, or we hear the words of a homily with a new depth. As the *Catechism of the Catholic Church* teaches, "The Holy Spirit gives a spiritual understanding of the Word of God to those who read or hear it, according to the dispositions of their hearts."[8] By means of the gift of Knowledge, the Holy Spirit leads us to understand that the mysteries of Christianity are credible, consistent, and have an effect in our lives.[9] The Holy Spirit actually moves within the soul, directing and inspiring it to move to holiness.[10] He uses the instruction of catechists,

---

8. *CCC,* no. 1101.

9. John of St. Thomas, *The Gifts of the Holy Ghost*, 68, 77.

10. See St. Bonaventure, *Collations on the Seven Gifts of the Holy Spirit*, 99.

teaching of priests, reading of Sacred Scripture, and lives of the saints to help people internalize knowledge of holy things. The gift of Knowledge moves prayer beyond words to shape the person's disposition. The believer who was previously distracted by superficial realities now experiences a new firmness of mind for the things of God. The gift of Knowledge draws the believer to appreciate the teachings of the Church. The Holy Spirit unlocks the meaning of Sacred Scripture and the experiences of the person's life, enabling him or her to make right judgments about what is to be believed. Grace internalizes the teaching of the Church in the heart of the believer as personal *beliefs*.

Baptism and Confirmation

Sound preaching and catechesis are inspired by the Holy Spirit and prepare the ground for the Spirit's further action in the believer. In particular, instruction on the meaning of our Baptism and Confirmation can bear great fruit. The plan of God is already taking place deep in the hearts and lives of the baptized. The action of God is not foreign to us or withheld from us; neither can we earn it. Baptism is not simply a ceremony that happened long ago in our lives, for many of us as infants. Baptism is a decisive moment in which we experienced, through the action of the Holy Spirit, the event of salvation in such a way that we were changed forever. The *Catechism* refers to Baptism as "the gateway to life in the Spirit." [11] The mark of Baptism is not simply the crinkled, yellowed certificate in the bottom drawer of our parents' dresser. It is an indelible mark on our soul.

---

11. *CCC,* no. 1213.

Baptism and Confirmation begin the initiation of the Christian into the cross of Jesus by the action of the Holy Spirit. Initiation is the moment when we receive the mystery of Christ with an inward commitment and external witness that makes us joyful. In Baptism, as the water is poured and the Trinitarian formula is spoken externally, something happens internally in the soul of the one being baptized: God confers grace on the person, who is really and truly conformed internally to Jesus Christ through a permanent seal on the soul. The person is forever meant for a blessed Kingdom. This blessedness takes the form of a life of communion that emerges through the gift of self in love. The initiated are entrusted with the mystery. While our individual Baptism is a fact of history, it is never past in terms of its effects. The mark of our Baptism is a living reality etched indelibly in our hearts. The believer's direct perception of the real continuity with the foundational act of God nourishes communion with God. The believer then does not rely on the self, but on God. This distinction is crucial in the spiritual life.

This means that at every step of our journey, the next step is already inside of us waiting to be discerned: the passion, death, and glorious resurrection of Jesus. Our Baptism means that we have met Jesus in his death and resurrection, that he has driven away sin and made us the adopted sons and daughters of God in the midst of his Church. The baptized are thus inserted into the mystery of Jesus's death and resurrection: they die with him, are buried with him, and rise with him. A unique openness to the things of God now animates their spirit. This openness leads to return to this source—the death and resurrection of Jesus, which is celebrated explicitly in the liturgy and in every self-gift made in love. They are therefore drawn in freedom to worship God, strengthened to love as his sons and daughters. This realization and the grace it brings are always near to us, even if at church the homily is too long, the music is not very good, we are distracted by children misbehaving and babies crying, and some people seem to be "more holy" than us so that we wonder why we even try. Even the random thoughts that come to us can become invitations to love God. When we turn and recall that we are marked permanently and irrevocably by God's love, we are strengthened to turn to that love anew by remembering that we have met Jesus in his death and resurrection. This is the reason to avoid sin: because we are wedded to Christ in the depths of our souls. So as we wait for Mass to continue, whether in a moment of silence or distraction, we can still reach across this space where the veil between heaven and earth almost allows us to see through it.

Noah and the Flood

We can realize what God has done for us in Baptism by reading the biblical account of Noah's Ark. Baptism saves us in a way similar to the way God saved Noah and his family through the ark (cf. 1 Pt 3:18–21). God created the world to be good: "God looked at everything he had made, and he found it very good" (Gn 1:31). After original sin entered the world, sin, chaos, and disorder began to spread. Just before the flood, the Genesis account notes: "God saw how corrupt the earth had become" (Gn 6:12).

God longed to save the world from sin. He did so through a magnificent act by which he not only destroyed sin, but also saved and delivered Noah and his family. God used water to accomplish this.

God intervened in the evil of the world. God always intervenes by *creating*, but in a world of sin and self-taking, his creating is first experienced as a *destruction*. God preserves those who cling to him in the midst of this destruction preservation is his *plan.* The distinction here is crucial: it seem that all the world is crashing down around us. We may feel abandoned and lost. Yet, God sustains us when everything around us collapses.

Faithful to the word of God, Noah begins to build the ark. How odd this must have looked to his neighbors. Notice that the creation of the ark is actually a miniature of the creation of the world. Creation has three levels (the sky, the land, and the water) and the ark has three levels as well (see Gn 6:16). The world is created at God's command, and so is the ark. Creation contains all creatures; the ark also contains all creatures. Man and woman, the pinnacle of creation, are called to fruitfulness. So, too, the married couples who are saved via the ark are called to fill the earth. Thus the ark echoes the original creation.[12] Noah listens to God when chaos abounds. The fountains that burst upon the world as the negative, shapeless chaos of the first verse of Genesis returns so that the world may be created anew.[13]

God then recalls Noah and the ark (cf. Gn 8:1–5). The Lord sends the dove over the waters, as the spirit hovered over the waters at creation. Noah's opening the window of the ark parallels the creation of light.[14] Releasing the birds from the window parallels the creation of the sky. The return of the olive branch to Noah reminds us of the creation of land and plants. The Lord establishing seedtime and harvest after the flood

---

12. Thomas Brodie, *Genesis as Dialogue*, (New York: Oxford University Press, 2001), 167.

13. Gn 7:11. See A. Dillman, *Genesis: Critically and Exegetically Expounded* (Edinburgh: T. & T. Clark, 1897), 278. See also C. Westerman, *Genesis 1–11* (Minneapolis: Fortress Press, 1994), 433. See also W. Eichrodt, *Theology of the Old Testament*, vol. II (Philadelphia: Westminster Press, 1967), 93.

14. Gn 8:6. Brodie, *Genesis as Dialogue*, 173.

can be compared to the lights that divide the day and seasons in creation. The Lord then reestablishes the animal world. He reinstates man, and he gives him the command to be fruitful and multiply just as in Genesis (cf. Gn 8:15–9:7).

In a similar way, God uses water in Baptism. The flood waters are like the waters of baptism. The water makes us think of cleanliness and refreshment. But water also symbolizes destruction and birth. In Baptism, the Holy Spirit incorporates the person, body and soul, into the passion, death, and resurrection of Jesus. From the depths of the Triune God an uninterrupted stream of love flows through the sacraments into the Church. In this stream of love, the Holy Spirit makes Christ and the effects of his passion, death, and resurrection present to us through grace. The grace of the sacraments conforms our entire existence to the gift of self Jesus makes in the passion and resurrection. The self-giving that goes on in the Triune God as an eternal event of love flows into time and space through the action of the Holy Spirit in the Church. This gift of self from God becomes a fountain in the believer.

A fountain surges up toward the heavens because of pressure from deep within the earth. So too, from the deepest places of our hearts God's grace enables us to reach to heaven. Jesus renews the capacity of even the most hardened sinner to make a gift of self. By this association with the sacrifice of Jesus, the person becomes like Jesus, a son of the Father. By joining with Christ in his sacrifice, the person is consecrated for the gift of self and freed from sin and the power of evil. The inclination to sin, known as concupiscence, still remains in the baptized, though it is now weakened. The baptized will experience temptation, the suggestion and pressure to put self first rather than make the gift of self. But God's own self-giving love comes to their aid. The baptized must call to mind that they are a new creation in Christ, changed and strengthened by the cross of Jesus to imitate his self-gift of love. Thus, the baptized who walk across the parking lot and up the steps to church each week do not walk alone; God acts in them. They walk not simply to fulfill an obligation or maintain a duty. Above all, they attend because the love of Christ draws them to this place: joining in the communion of the Church is always the next step in the life of grace and virtue.

The Sacrament of Confirmation strengthens the bond of the baptized with Christ and deepens the effects of Baptism. Just as Baptism uses the symbolism of water, Confirmation uses the symbolism of oil. It is a natural symbol of strength and light. Wrestlers in the ancient world would cover themselves with oil so they could slip out of the grasp of a foe. Oil can also make one's body reflect the glistening brilliance of light. In Confirmation, the Holy Spirit infuses the believer with the grace of Christ, strengthening him or her to live the baptismal identity of an adopted child of God.

Jesus is the one who is filled with the Holy Spirit: "The Spirit of the Lord is upon me" (Lk 4:18). Jesus promises to give him to the Apostles (cf. Lk 12:12; Jn 14–15). The pouring and anointing with oil is the sign of the descent of the Holy Spirit: "You will receive power when the Holy Spirit comes upon you, and you will be my witnesses" (Acts 1:8; cf. Lk 24:49). This anointing must be honored and recalled, for it is the strength of the Christian: "As for you, the anointing that you received from him remains in you, so that you do not need anyone to teach you. But his anointing teaches you about everything and is true and not false; just as it taught you, remain in him" (1 Jn 2:27).

The Holy Spirit permeates the one who is anointed with oil in the Sacrament of Confirmation, transforming the person to be a strong bearer of light (cf. Jl 3:1; Is 44:3). The oil used in biblical times came from the olive tree. Various interior walls of the temple of Solomon featured the strong cedar wood (cf. 1 Kgs 6:31, 33, 36). Yet the doors and two cherubim of the inner sanctuary were made from olive wood, which is more durable than cedar. The prophet Hosea proclaims of the one who follows God's ways: "His splendor shall be like the olive tree" (Hos 14:7). The Lord began his saving Passion in a grove of olive trees in the Garden of Gethsemane. That garden is like the Temple in which God dwells. The permanent promise of God grows more palpable as one nears the heart of God's dwelling. The oil of the olive tree is meant to signify the unshakable, durable, and permanent change that takes place in the heart of the believer through the Holy Spirit's action: "Like olive plants [shall be] your children around your table" (Ps 128:3). The confirmed can cry out with the psalmist: "But I, like an olive tree in the house of God, trust in God's faithful love forever" (Ps 52:10).

The Christian must call on courage and strength daily: to respond to a co-worker who criticizes Church teaching, to forego revenge, to spend time with one's children, to make time for family dinner, to get up and go to church on Sunday. The strength to follow Christ in these instances comes from Christ himself. The fidelity, justice, and mercy of God sustain our courage and trust as we surrender ourselves to him in concrete actions that the world considers foolish. As we surrender to God, we abandon our own egotistical standards and refuse to concentrate on opposition from the world.

Faith

The gift of Knowledge enables the virtue of faith to grow. Faith makes our thoughts holy, which further unites us to

God himself. We no longer see our Catholic beliefs as just a list of required teachings. The *Catechism* explains that, "Faith is the theological virtue by which we believe in God and believe all that he has said and revealed to us, and that Holy Church proposes for our belief, because he is truth itself."[15] The virtue of faith joins us to God himself as the one who is the ultimately faithful witness to the truth. God does not and will not deceive us. He reveals himself to us, and the response of faith sanctifies our intellect. When God communicates with us, he does so by casting the light of his truth into our minds. This light is cast in its most authentic form by the ministry of the Church. God uses many instruments to cast this light: the words of Sacred Scripture, of a homily, of a catechist, or of a conversation. By his light, we are led more deeply into the mystery of God. We respond to this light through the assent and obedience of faith, by which we participate in the very life of God. The faithful assent to all that God has revealed is not only our affirmation that God exists, but it is also the assent to all that God reveals about himself. Above all, our faith is *in* God.

God *unites* us to himself by that which is believed. When we assent to belief, we are united to God. The character of knowledge is changed. What was once merely a rationalistic procedure of increasing knowledge, now captivates our minds with the beauty of God's truth, which leads us to cry out in love, *Abba,* "Father!" (cf. Rom 8:15). The search for truth becomes second nature as we develop an innate sense to discern the effect of God's action in the world. Nothing less than God will satisfy our minds.

The light of faith scatters the darkness of previous attachments. God strengthens the soul and illumines reality so that

---

15. *CCC,* no. 1814.

the soul begins to see with its entire being. Then we can see and understand the world in terms of the clarity of God's light rather than through the veil of self-centeredness, which so often results in envy.

Envy

Those who mourn are the opposite of the envious. The first Book of Samuel presents the classical biblical account of envy. When Saul was the king of Israel and David a mighty champion who had slain many Philistines, Saul and David returned home to a victory celebration. The women came out to meet the king and they sang, "Saul has slain his thousands, and David his ten thousands" (1 Sm 18:7). When Saul heard that the women attributed "tens of thousands" to David and only "thousands" to him, the king immediately noted the difference and grew envious.

Notice the nature of envy. Saul and David have defended Israel and were enormously successful and victorious. Saul is already the king and a veteran of many conquests. They are enjoying a day of celebration. Yet that one *detail* sounds in Saul's ears above all else. He obsesses over the small variation in the song of the women: "Saul has slain his thousands, and David his ten thousands." Saul's past honors, his privileged position as king, and the reveling in the latest victory all fade. It is as if they were all drained of meaning. Instead of savoring the triumph, Saul grows angry (cf. 1 Sm 18:8). The one detail in the song of celebration overrides all else. Saul fears that David will ascend to the kingship while he, Saul, descends to inadequacy. The account indicates that "From that day on, Saul was jealous of David" (1 Sm 18:9). The Douay Rheims translation of this verse reads: "From that day on, Saul *looked hard* on David." The envious person *watches*.

Envy does not simply take in the surroundings. Envy scans the world with radar-like precision, taking in the differences between oneself and others. Envy measures the world with radar-like precision, taking in with one glance the differences between self and others. Envy measures in a two-fold way: First, it disregards all that is positive about the self, and second, it hones in on one detail in which the other seems to excel. Envy does not see beauty or diversity in the talents or good fortune of others. Envy detects one perceived flaw in the self that fails to measure up to the apparent blessing of the other. Then, on that basis, the envious person builds an obsession.

Envy is not limited to a single moment or a passing emotion. When envy hones in on the details, it begins a pursuit that continues to search, measure, compare. Envy is born in a moment and then nurtured over weeks, months, and years. Envy flares up in the momentary furtive glance in which one notices the good that belongs to another person. Envy then continues to notice, resent, and plot ways to tear down the good of the other through stealthily sowing seeds of contention, gossip, and defamation. This is the toxic pain of envy. It is both drawn and repelled at the same time by the same object or person. The envious person fears the one thing that he or she is convinced will bring them success. In envy, the fear and the wish collide in a maelstrom of despair.

The envious do not have relationships as such. Instead they have a series of continual and ongoing comparisons. Envious persons torment themselves every time they see others succeeding. Conversely, the envious are glad when others suffer a setback or diminishment. Envy is sorrow at the other's good. Envy churns on to anger, bitterness, and then despair.

Envy is a unique sin akin to pride. The two are the premier sins of Satan: he was cast out of heaven for his pride, while it was through his envy that sin entered the world (cf. Wis 2:24). As an angel, Lucifer enjoyed perfect knowledge. The Fathers of the Church developed the teaching that Lucifer, in the first moment of his existence, foresaw that the Son of God would become incarnate in flesh.[16] The sin of Lucifer is pride (1 Tm 3:6). In his pride he could not abide that God would bypass angelic nature and take human nature in the Incarnation. Then, cast out from heaven, through his envy he sought to destroy man and woman through sin. What he could not have in heaven he would destroy on earth.

The gift of Knowledge is the antidote to pride and envy. This gift turns us away from ourselves so that we are awed by the mysteries of God. Knowledge builds on the foundation begun by the gifts of Fear of the Lord and Piety. The virtue of faith augments the strength the believer has internalized through the practice of hope, temperance, and justice. The Christian who has learned to be a child of God and to be steadfast in meekness now senses in a direct way that the world is made for God. The gift of Knowledge builds the virtue of faith in the Christian. The *Catechism of the Catholic Church* explains that faith is the free submission of the intellect and will to God.[17] By faith we cling to the truth that God has revealed about the One he has sent, the Lord Jesus Christ. And Jesus points us to his Church. Through the gift of faith,

16. See Jean Daniélou, *The Angels and Their Mission According to the Fathers of the Church* (Westminster, MD: Newman Press, 1957), 44–46. See also, Gabriel Bunge, *Dragon's Wine and Angel's Bread: The Teaching of Evagrius Ponticus on Anger and Meekness* (New York: St. Vladimir's Seminary Press, 2009), 29–31.

17. See *CCC,* no. 143.

the Holy Spirit assists us to understand what the Church teaches. Faith begins to dislodge skepticism, doubt, and previous error. The Holy Spirit acts in the believer to reveal that faith is not about the self, but about God. This witness will now require courage.

Blessed Are Those Who Mourn

With this new insight into the life of faith, a sobering knowledge also comes to the person who now mourns for past errors. This mourning is not a depression or lament. Rather, the mourning is a type of seasoning, a solemn yet earnest dedication. Saint Paul speaks of this mourning and sorrow: ". . . for you were saddened in a godly way, so that you did not suffer loss in anything because of us. For godly sorrow produces a salutary repentance without regret, but worldly sorrow produces death" (2 Cor 7:9a–10). The person mourns the lack of time and space to make known the beauty and truth of God's goodness. The one who mourns understands faith as knowledge, which connects his awareness of everything and leads him from what he encounters in the world back to God. And in this he finds reasons for mourning. If only everything would achieve all it was meant to as a manifestation of God. He mourns that the world is so caught up with its business that it would fail to see the beauty of God. The mourning person grieves missed opportunities to follow all the events of life back to their ultimate cause. This mourning is not the pang for nostalgia, it is a strength for the future, a resolve to look for the next opportunity to learn about God.

The Christian also mourns because the world neglects the way of God, as the psalmist lamented: "My eyes shed streams of tears because your teaching is not followed" (Ps 119:136). Yet, the Christian mourns the world in a robust sense, rather than a pitiful sense. The person mourns not what is lost, but what can be, that the words will not come quickly enough to express how the Holy Spirit has acted in his life. The mourning is tempered and forged by the Holy Spirit, who quickly brings consolation so that sorrow does not redirect the believer's gaze to the self. Like the artisan who heats the metal in the forge, molds it, and then quickly cools it in water, so to the Holy Spirit forms and shapes our hearts. The Holy Spirit enlivens the person to see more clearly how to use creatures rightly and to order love properly. The gift of Knowledge helps the Christian to advance in prayer and to make it a habit.

At this third surge of the fountain, the gift of Knowledge has begun to forge the virtue of faith so that the believer adheres to the Person of Christ and begins to see the many opportunities to share knowledge of his Word of life.

CHAPTER EIGHT

The Fourth Surge of the Fountain: Blessed Are Those Who Hunger and Thirst

The journey to holiness ordinarily does not take place overnight. The Christian is a pilgrim who journeys through life in search of a closer relationship to God. Many gifts and virtues are needed to make this journey. Temptation never ceases in this life. The world is always attempting to lure the Christian to abandon the quest for holiness and return to vain attempts to acquire pleasure quickly. Grace guides and protects Christians from these attacks. The Holy Spirit's gift of Courage is the next surge of the fountain. Courage builds the virtue of fortitude which battles against the sin of sloth. The courageous Christian does not simply go through the motions, but begins to feel deep within the hunger and thirst for righteousness. The believer begins to do the good not simply out of duty. Rather, the Christian now seeks the way of holiness because it is the natural follow through to his deepest impulse.

The Gift of Courage

After the gift of Knowledge and the virtue of faith have revealed to the believer that the world is made for God, the Christian quickly recognizes that the world often fails to acknowledge God. The Christian's initial response is to mourn this deficit. Mourning summons the Holy Spirit who moves swiftly to the deep places of the heart. When the Spirit's comfort meets mourning, he bestows his gift of Courage. Courage turns the knowledge of God into *hunger* for God. In fact, hunger is the strength by which we are led to the fourth Beatitude: "Blessed are they who hunger and thirst for righteousness, for they will be satisfied" (Mt 5:6).

The world is often confused about the true nature and source of courage. The prophet Isaiah locates our courage in the Person of the Lord himself: "My strength and my courage is the LORD, and he has been my savior" (Is 12:2). The psalmist witnesses to this fact: "Not with their own swords did they conquer the land, nor did their own arms bring victory; it was your right hand, your own arm, the light of your face for you favored them" (Ps 44:4). Therefore the psalmist acclaims: "I love you, LORD, my strength" (Ps 18:2). Saint Paul deepens the mystery of Christian courage: "The weakness of God is stronger than human strength" (1 Cor 1:25). Saint Bonaventure calls our attention to Joshua and Caleb as two persons to whom the Lord gave great courage. [1]

---

1. See St. Bonaventure, *Collations on the Seven Gifts of the Holy Spirit*, 117–118. Cf. Sir 46:1, 11; Num 13:7, 17.

The gift of Courage moves our minds in a way that surpasses momentary bravado or mature and ordinary determination. This courage is not stubbornness, fanaticism, or a steamroller approach to religious witness. The Holy Spirit moves the Christian through a new, confident, and consistent firmness of mind to be devoted and faithful to that which is good and to remain strong in the face of evil. Courage bolsters the Christian to bear hardship and to advance against any threat when this is called for by the Holy Spirit.[2] The world is a dangerous place, in which serious difficulties can overwhelm the believer. Sickness, pain, disappointment, and evil all deliver the message that fidelity to the goodness of God is one option among many. Simply watching the evening news can tempt a person to a kind of gradual despair, to give in to the ways of the world, to question the effort required to live the Christian life.

Our everyday lives seem so mundane, a predictable mix of events even when familiar tensions, disagreements, or obstacles arise. We easily reduce ourselves to a measure of our histories, genetics, and circumstances. When we begin to doubt our deepest identity as sons and daughters of God, the Holy Spirit acts to renew the mind. The Holy Spirit's gift of Courage strengthens the Christian, just as Moses strengthened the Israelites as they faced their opponents: "Have no dread or fear of them. The LORD, your God, who goes before you, will himself fight for you" (Dt 1:29–30; cf. 20:3–4; 31:6.). Similarly, the Lord strengthened Joshua with these words, "I command you: be firm and steadfast! Do not fear nor be dismayed, for the LORD, your God, is with you wherever you go" (Jos 1:9). Above all, the Holy Spirit reminds us that through his cross and resurrection, the victorious Lord Jesus has

---

2. See John of St. Thomas, *The Gifts of the Holy Ghost*, 68, 189ff.

conquered our greatest tragedy: sin and death. The Holy Spirit longs to continuously draw the Christian into the saving effects of Jesus's life-giving sacrifice of love. The cross and resurrection of Jesus fill us with courage. From this inexhaustible source, the Holy Spirit infuses into our hearts a new measure of the grace of the Lord Jesus.

The crucifix reminds us of the Spirit's gift of Courage. When I was growing up, two distinct places in our home had a crucifix. One was hung on the wall in our living room where the archway opened toward the dining room, and the other was in my parents' bedroom. As children, my siblings and I had smaller ones near our beds, as well. We also had the practice, still common during Lent, of carrying a small crucifix in a pocket, so that when we reached in for change, we were reminded that the gift of Jesus is the center of every moment of life.

This awareness moved us to realize that the smallest of sufferings *meant* something. We were journeying, and still had not arrived at the Kingdom. In our journey we would suffer. When even small hardships arose, something deeper was happening. When we could not find a seat on the subway, when the weather was too hot, too humid, too cold, when the menu was not exactly what we liked, we were learning that we did not have our own private right-of-way in the world. We did not always get our way because *other* people also lived in the world. Our call was to love these people, not control them to our benefit.

The Christian knows well that evil and sin still lurk in the world, which is so caught up and hurried with its own affairs and its busy crowds. People make choices that cause great harm. In the midst of this the Holy Spirit longs to convince the world that even in the darkest events, the cross of Christ always holds the high ground. Through personal witness, the believer arouses the world to be aware of God.

The believer does not need to become frustrated and shout to win arguments, but simply to drop hints about God in a conversation that would otherwise not make any connections with God. The Christian is more an invitation to mystery than a polemical response to an argument. The gift of Courage helps the believer to realize that hardship is no reason to complain and make excuses. Instead, it spurs us to get down to the real work of confidently enduring the buffeting of the world so as to witness to the strength of Jesus Christ. He summons us to take up our cross daily not simply because the world is a difficult place, but because the cross *is* the path through the world (cf. Lk 9:23; Rom 8:36; 2 Cor 4:16). It is the only way through.

The gift of Courage reveals the treasure of powerlessness and weakness. Saint Paul said that he was "content with weaknesses" (2 Cor 12:10). The world is caught up with notoriety and fame. The constant commotion around celebrity, power, self-advertising, and success is actually, when seen in its true light, a frantic race away from the self. Self-surrender is always the most direct route to authenticity, and can only take the form of a gift. The authentic gift of self is not feverish dedication to work or an attitude of service. The gift of self is a way of being human, the only authentic way. A gift never says, "Look at all I have done." A gift is never an excuse to indulge the pleasures of the world. The old things that used to satisfy us, things we used to look forward to, begin to lose their luster in the light of the gift of self. The authentic gift of self always leads to the next surrender.

The world cannot understand the beauty of the undistinguished life of simplicity. Jesus was counted among the most common of his day. There was literally *no room* for him from the very beginning to the very end. He was born in a stable and buried in a borrowed tomb. He had no place to lay his head. He did not accustom himself to the expectations or status of the world. He was sovereign in his powerlessness. When the crowds offered him a crown of power, he escaped into the mountains. When they offered a crown of thorns, he bowed his head. This is the Holy Spirit's gift of Courage that leads us without the illusion of idealism through the wiles of the world.

Fortitude

Courage begins to form the virtue of fortitude in the believer. Fortitude helps us to resist obstacles that would otherwise turn us away from what is truly good. Well-meaning people often fail to reach Courage because they confuse it with anger. It is perfectly natural to encounter conflict in the world, even with other well-meaning believers. The mature Christian will have to cut his teeth on a disagreement or confrontation. Growing pains are natural and help us to sharpen and mature. Yet we often avoid these and turn back, withdraw, and internalize anger rather than act with courage. Turf wars, flashes of anger, and passive-aggressive resistance are all signs that the person has not learned how to handle healthy disagreements. Fortitude integrates and refines our natural aggression into purposeful assertiveness.

Fortitude is developed at a crucial moment, when the fountain's momentum is growing stronger. The Christian has begun to live as a son or daughter of God and to treat others with justice. Faith has grown and taken on deeper meaning. When one begins to internalize these realities, both the world and the devil take notice. One is living contrary to the world, so the world will necessarily cross the path of the believer. A showdown awaits. This confrontation can easily overwhelm the beginner who has advanced somewhat. Through adversity, temptation, or assault, the world seeks to make the believer grow fearful. Sensing the power and corruption of the world, the beginner may then turn back to old ways of seeking comfort and escape. It takes skill and practice to resist the assault and to defend all that has been gained through Fear of the Lord, Piety, and Knowledge. The believer needs strength to stay on the road of integrating the appetites. The Spirit provides Courage to make the Christian determined to live a truly good life.

The gift of Courage forms fortitude in the believer, providing the means to hold up against and move past worldly fears. In confidence one begins to dare to risk a deeper fidelity. This is not a bold, impulsive, or reckless risk. The *Catechism* teaches that, "Fortitude is the moral virtue that ensures firmness in difficulties and constancy in the pursuit of the good."[3] Fortitude is not brute offensiveness or rash response. Fortitude is a confident, ready, and purposeful approach that perseveres in the long haul instead of seeking the quick fix. Fortitude is bravery, patience, and persistence in enduring suffering, hardship, and persecution for the good that is Jesus Christ and his Church.

Fortitude is best viewed as the bravery of the martyr, who is strengthened to bear witness to Jesus in an extraordinary manner. The martyr confesses Christ and so faces persecution in the midst of conflict with Satan.[4] The world's persecution does not reveal the martyr as a type of celebrity action hero who advances on the merits of his own resolve. Rather, as the martyr faces persecution, the Holy Spirit conforms him to the

---

3. *CCC,* no. 1808.

4. See Jean Daniélou and Henri Marrou, *The Christian Centuries: The First Hundred Years* vol. 1 (New York: McGraw-Hill Book Company, 1964), 125ff.

passion of Jesus by granting him a share in the death and resurrection of the Lord. The passion of Jesus won the victory
over Satan. The martyr conquers Satan by clinging to Christ
in his death and resurrection. In the martyr's ordeal, the Holy
Spirit again reveals the image and the victory of Christ (cf. 1
Tm 3:16). The martyr is conformed to Christ by sharing in the
passion of Christ. The Holy Spirit strengthens the person for
this conflict through the gift of Courage.

The martyr imitates the self-giving love of Christ to such
an extent that it transforms him into a sign of the strength of
Jesus Christ. The martyr stands out not because of a firm will,
but because the Holy Spirit has enabled the person to cling to
Jesus alone in utter faithfulness.

The martyr suffers yet does not pout. The sacrifice that
becomes a way of life for the martyr actually summons the life
of God into everyday events. The martyr rejects narcissism and
sees the entitlements of the world as the illusions they are.
Getting ahead and having power are cartoon caricatures to the
real-life union with God that the martyr enjoys through the
grace of Jesus Christ.

The martyr bears a special kinship to the prophet. Pope
Benedict XVI notes that prophets often fail.[5] Like the martyr,
the prophet is often rejected by the world. The system finds
the prophet to be too much and, therefore, must expel him
rather than follow the way of truth. The prophet, however,
does not think in the worldly categories of success or failure.
The prophet knows the Lord and speaks from this knowledge.
The gift of Knowledge so assimilates the believer to Jesus that
the prophet is sent to announce a word that is not his own, but
the Lord's. This knowledge arises from an intimate life with
Christ in the Church. The prophet cannot bear to see the

---

5. See Pope Benedict XVI, *Jesus of Nazareth*, 189.

Gospel remain hidden. The prophet feels impelled to proclaim the Gospel; he cannot hide from or disguise the message. It flows from his very being. Courage is the energy of both the prophet and the martyr.

Sloth

The believer realizes that the politics, back-room deals, compromises, and betrayals found in the world often arise not out of direct ill-will, but from sloth. The world gives in to the temptation to take the shortcut and to give up. The path to God through faith, hope, and justice is one of patience and entrusting the self to God. The world is afraid and in such a hurry that it flees the hidden fountain, or does not seek it out in the first place. So many emotions require much energy, and the internalized fear provokes the person to fix things rather than to heal patiently. Sloth is a slumbering danger. Sloth is the melody of fear which lulls us into routine. It is not that sloth is simple laziness and therefore we may be caught unawares. Rather, sloth is laziness about the things of God: when we realize the cost of living contrary to the world, we take shelter in the routine of the world. The slothful live by the secularist creed, "Fake it until you make it." The slothful just try to fit in and go through the motions so that the world will reward them.

Even the holiest of God's chosen ones can fall quickly and easily to the sedentary reward of apparent accomplishment. When we confuse our dedication to God with the business of our efforts on his behalf, we are forming the pothole that will make us stumble: sloth. It says, "I have done enough, let someone else work at it now." Even after the attachment to anger and the preoccupation with greed diminish, sloth may still remain. Sloth can reignite the appetites one has thought to be long conquered. King David is a prime example. God had chosen David as king, and the prophet Samuel had anointed him. David had won campaign after campaign in service to God's plan. The king had brought the Ark of the Covenant to Jerusalem, and he had defeated Goliath through God's might. David's faith was strong, and he had seen the most evident signs of God's favor. If anyone knew God was with him, protecting and guiding him, it was King David.

Yet David sinned (cf. 2 Sm 11:1–26). David takes Bathsheba, who is the wife of a soldier named Uriah, and commits adultery with her (cf. 2 Sm 11:4). In fact, David does this while the soldier is away at battle for a long time on David's behalf. Bathsheba becomes pregnant with David's child. If she is pregnant on his return, Uriah will know this is not his child, and Bathsheba will be found guilty of adultery and liable to be sentenced to death. David orders Uriah home and induces him to spend the night with Bathsheba (cf. 2 Sm 11:6–13). But Uriah is dutiful and will not engage in relations with his wife during a time of battle. So David arranges to have Uriah placed in the midst of fierce fighting and abandoned by his comrads (cf. 2 Sm 11:14–17). Uriah is killed, and David takes Bathsheba as his wife (cf. 2 Sm 11:17–27).

What exactly is the sin of David? Some say his sin is adultery, others say it is murder. But what sin of David came first, which paved the way for the other sins of adultery and murder? We find it in the first verse of chapter eleven, long before the adultery or the murder: "At the turn of the year, when kings go out on campaign, David sent out Joab along with his officers and the army of Israel ... David, however, remained in Jerusalem" (2 Sm 11:1). David's first sin, the sin that opened the way for the others, was the sin of sloth. David stayed at home during the time of year when kings are to go out with their armies. Despite all his previous heroic accomplishments, something wearied David and weighed him down. This weight inclined him to sin. At first, he simply stayed at home and took a nap. When he awoke, he was bored and started to look around.

Sloth turns us away from the goods that lead us to God. It makes us believe that doing things for God, such as attending Mass, frequenting the Sacrament of Penance, obeying the Commandments, praying, and doing good works would be tedious and fleeting. We then begin to seek material goods and use them in unreasonable ways. Sloth is not waiting an additional day before mowing the lawn, or sleeping an extra hour on a holiday. In fact, sloth more often hides in busyness and activity than in laziness. Even something as apparently insignificant as talkativeness arises out of sloth. Proverbs tells us: "The fool's mouth is his ruin; his lips are a snare to his life" (Prv 18:7). The sins of language are not limited to foul language or profanity. Idle talk and unnecessary words are a sign of sloth. Masters of the spiritual life use strong words to describe the dangers that idle talk and gossip pose to the spiritual life.[6] The remedy of silence brings us close to God. As the writer of Proverbs says: "He who guards his mouth protects his life; to open wide one's lips brings downfall" (Prv 13:3).

Hunger and Thirst for Righteousness

To avoid falling in love with material things requires real work. The finer things in life appear to bring great comfort. Yet when one pulls back the curtain, one sees that luxury leads us to a road that never truly satisfies. The more one gets of the

---

6. See Pope Benedict XVI, *Jesus of Nazareth*, 189.

fine things, the more one wants, and the less these things satisfy. If the finer things in life brought happiness, why would the rich and famous need rehab as often as they do? Courage gives us the strength to love true goods and to endure the absence of apparent pleasures. The one strengthened by the gift of Courage hungers for righteousness. Courage is not satisfied by crystal or filled up by the latest fashions. Courage treasures the patient pursuit of the unique and rare life of virtue itself.

Courage helps us to resist and overcome the complacency that attempts to set in from time to time. Courage rekindles our perseverance and desire. Pope Benedict XVI notes that this Beatitude speaks to a type of holy longing in man.[7] This is the good type of restlessness that directs us to the deeper meaning of human life. Fortitude frees us from what would otherwise weigh us down in despair so that we can follow authentic desire in a holy and mature manner. In fact, our desire, our hunger and thirst, when purified from the path of sin, actually become an internal radar that helps to detect the traces of the kingdom waiting to emerge.

---

7. Ibid., 90–91.

Chapter Nine

The Fifth Surge of the Fountain: Blessed Are the Merciful

The journey of transformation in Christ continues for the Christian. The influx of God's grace has led the believer to appreciate in a new way the meaning of being a son or daughter of God. The early steps of piety, of treating one's neighbor with justice, have led to a deepening of the life of faith. At the same time, the believer senses a more profound awareness of the desire to share the faith and to invite others to drink from the fountain. The believer does not make this invitation with a lot of fanfare, but with a matter-of-fact, unadorned simplicity. Faith practice through the gift of Courage is not extreme; it is neither a purely private matter or a fanatic insistence. The ordinariness of the example and invitation is attractive and refreshing. As the world continues to attempt to deter the journey, the believer begins to rely on the fifth surge of the fountain: the gift of Counsel, which strengthens the virtue of prudence. Prudence leads the believer to be merciful and to treat others with compassion.

The Gift of Counsel

Each surge of the fountain cleanses the wounds of sin and erodes the resistance that has built up in the believer due to the effects of sin. Those who practice their faith more regularly begin to discover an emerging pattern. Over time, seemingly routine practices begin to open new and unexpected sources of meaning and strength in the believer. This emergent pattern is not a perfect ideal. It is not something done for display. In fact, the struggle always remains, for the Christian life is never easy. Yet, at the same time, a new strength grows in the heart of the believer. This new strength emerges not from some unique grace held out for the few. It emerges often enough from suffering love, responding to daily trials from a depth that one only gradually learns, a depth by which one loves not for selfish reasons, but for the good of others. One learns, over time, that there is nowhere else to turn than God. The moment the Christian learns to trust, he discovers the hinge of conversion. Whoever places his or her ears to the trail of existence will hear the message and rhythm of existence itself: *Trust, even if you have been hurt in the past when you have trusted. God will open a new place, and you can only enter by fully trusting him.* Such suffering love is the seasoning by which the Christian life becomes an instinctive response.

New inroads to moments with God emerge. Arriving for Sunday Mass fifteen minutes early, sitting in a quiet church and closing one's eyes to think of Jesus is the same as digging in the ground in search of the fountain. Pausing at nighttime to kneel by the bedside to pray one of the mysteries of the

Rosary can lead down the path to the hidden wellspring. Deciding to look up the confession schedule and to go to confession for the first time in many years creates an opening for the Holy Spirit to fill with God's very life. Taking the miraculous medal out of the dresser drawer and wearing it is a reminder of God's provident care. Pausing during lunch hour for seven or eight minutes to pray a novena to the Blessed Mother reestablishes a foundation in the plan of God. Forgoing evening appointments with clients to go to the parental information night for a child's first Penance or first Holy Communion may pivot a parent's life in a new way toward God. We may think that we have discovered God, but he actually *finds* us.

The fountain of grace heals us and strengthens the life of grace by guiding the flow of purest love to the deep recesses of the heart. So often we forget the depths for which we are created. We rush through the day from one thing to another, without realizing the meaning available in this very moment. As the Holy Spirit moves within us a change takes place and an interior conversion emerges. The mysteries of the faith more easily suffuse the soul's most original depths. The heart itself becomes contoured to receive a deeper influx of the life of grace. Like a fountain, the Holy Spirit generates his love from the very center of our existence. This is not automatic or without difficulty. We do not become immune to the ups and downs of life, but we find a deeper stability and purpose in them. A fountain is always transcending itself by giving itself away, pouring itself out. Through grace, the Holy Spirit's gift of love encounters our weaknesses, our faults and bad habits, our secrets, and also our sins. The Spirit's love transforms us so that today, in this time and space, our love can be renewed. We will still feel the same pressures and stress. We will still encounter difficulties and burdens. But we will discover a new momentum, a new spaciousness opening up even in anxious moments. This newness invites us to respond with love where we used to become upset, flustered, or angry. This new momentum comes from grace and prompts us to make a self-giving sacrifice of obedience by which we live the life of virtue on the way to salvation.

After the gift of Courage has strengthened us to speak of faith at work, in our neighborhoods, or on the sports field, the Holy Spirit provides his gift of Counsel. Through this gift, the Holy Spirit guides the believer in making decisions regarding concrete situations. The Christian grows more sensitive to the voice and summons of the Holy Spirit and can distinguish between what comes from the self and what comes from the Spirit. The gift of Counsel strengthens the capacity to perceive humbly the direction made known by the wisdom of God. The Lord tells us through the psalmist, "I will instruct you and show you the way you should walk, give you counsel and watch over you" (Ps 32:8). Elsewhere, the psalmist rejoices at the guidance of God: "I bless the LORD who counsels me; even at night my heart exhorts me" (Ps 16:7). God longs to guide his people. Counsel discerns a course of action on the basis of right reason.[1] Counsel guides the believer in day-to-day, moment-to-moment decisions, so that the Christian applies the truth of the Gospel in practical matters. Counsel helps us discern what will lead us to avoid sin and to honor the beauty of God. Counsel is at work when we speak up effectively to defend the Church's teaching on controversial issues such as human embryonic stem cell research, euthanasia, immigration, abortion, and contraception. The gift of counsel is not automatic. As the Book of Sirach says, "Let

---

1. See St. Bonaventure, *Collations on the Seven Gifts of the Holy Spirit*, 146.

your acquaintances be many, but one in a thousand your confidant" (Sir 6:6). Counsel is not mere rational knowledge. It is the fruit of a seasoned and tested guide who is familiar with the path to the hidden wellspring. As the Book of Job asks, "But whence can wisdom be obtained, and where is the place of understanding?" (Jb 28:12). Job describes how man can find many things in life. We can find gold or silver deep in the earth. We can search out crystal, jasper, and topaz. But the path of Counsel, the path that leads to wisdom and understanding is hidden (cf. Jb 28:21). Job concludes, "God knows the way to it; it is he who is familiar with its place" (Jb 28:23). Counsel guides us when we realize that anger at another driver is futile and ineffective, when we set proper boundaries in dating, when we form our conscience to vote according to the inviolable dignity of all human life. Counsel guides us when we raise our hand in a classroom to acknowledge we have thought about becoming a priest or religious, when we decide to study and prepare for an exam, when we realize a late night of partying does not fit with an early morning shift at work. Courage and Counsel work together to channel our boldness in following Jesus into effective strategies for Christian living. Through Counsel, we do not do these good acts simply to conform to the law of charity. Rather, the gift of Counsel brings the law of charity into our hearts so that it becomes not simply a guidepost, but an internal principle indistinguishable from our hearts.

Prudence

The gift of Courage strengthens and perfects the virtue of prudence in the Christian. Prudence is not acting with good manners: folding the napkin properly, walking with correct posture, and saying please and thank you. Prudence is also not a cautious attitude toward action.[2] Prudence is not calculating how many evils are acceptable in order to carry out a good action. Prudence concerns the visible and ongoing growth of faith from deep within. Prudence enables us to bring our history of faithfulness to God into our daily decisions. The *Catechism* teaches that, "Prudence is the virtue that disposes practical reason to discern our true good in every circumstance and to choose the right means of achieving it."[3] This virtue is like an internal compass that discovers and clarifies the proper ways and means to do good and avoid evil. Prudence thrives on the vision of the true character of things. Through the virtue of prudence, prayerful docility of heart intersects with sound reason, reflective insight, seasoned study, and our memory and experience. Prudence guides us to make good choices in daily life. Prudence governs our desires and inclinations as we face difficulties. The virtue helps us to weigh and consider our motives as we choose a course of action.

Two things in particular help this virtue grow: patience with oneself and learning from the seasoned experience of good teachers. First, patience with oneself sustains us as we try to overcome the bad habits we can so easily and quickly absorb from the world. It can take a long time to replace bad habits with good ones. Second, having good teachers, spiritual directors, and perceptive confessors is crucial. We need to learn the ways of virtue. The best spiritual guides are those who have been tried by the world and have learned how to be faithful to the true and lasting good.

The world offers many seductive illusions. The chaos of day-to-day life can easily prey on the weaknesses of sinners.

---

2. Torrell, *Saint Thomas Aquinas: Spiritual Master*, vol. 2, 270–271.

3. *CCC,* no. 1806.

For instance, we may feel that gossiping with our neighbor draws us closer. But reason alerts that someone who will gossip *with* us will easily gossip *about* us. Right reason can see through the illusions the world offers. Prudence is practical reason that enables the heart to judge accurately the folly of the world and the frailty of human nature. Prudence teaches us authentic discernment. It helps us weigh all the dimensions of a course of action, both the ends and the means, so that we may pursue what is truly good.

The spiritual director or mentor teaches us that this world is meant to move us to the world to come. The director provides a voice of sanity in the midst of the world's chaos and helps us strip away illusions and learn humility: the truth about oneself. The mentor becomes especially important when we move from Courage to Counsel. Courage without Counsel can easily lead to the "ready . . . fire . . . aim" backfire of our own strength. Counsel does not stifle action, but forms it. Prudence works through all the virtues, yet the gift of Counsel works in a particular way through the spiritual director or mentor. According to the old saying, "When the student is ready, the teacher will appear." The director's wisdom helps us to internalize the gift of Counsel and grow in the virtue of prudence. The mentor teaches from a strategic point, distant yet close, and must appear at precisely the right moment.

The beginner has advanced a great way from the time he or she first internalized the identity of being a child of God through the gift of Fear of the Lord. The virtues of hope, temperance, justice, and fortitude have grown. The beginner has known many struggles and victories, confronted his or her own recklessness, felt the surge of courage, and has, at times, fallen back, misused courage, and acted too quickly. Often the mentor appears when the student has gone as far as he can on his own initiative. Turning to a mentor is crucial. Accounts of the mentor-student relationship fill much literature: *The Mark of Zorro* and *The Count of Monte Cristo* are two examples of stories in which the beleaguered and defeated hero meets the seasoned and wise sage, who also appears to have every reason to be downcast and rejected. In the Christian life, the sage knows the ways of the world and has the capacity to bring all things together: skill, knowledge, street smarts, a seemingly innate knowledge of human nature, and personal familiarity with the mysteries of Christ. It is up to the student to pull the wisdom from the teacher.

In the various legends of Zorro, after the great sword fighter has been in exile many years, his possessions and family decimated, he meets a young thief about to recklessly attack a soldier. The old Zorro intervenes and begins to train the young vagabond, imparting wisdom gained from his years of experience. He trains the young man to be the new Zorro. The training is based on the practical wisdom that the young man should begin by considering only those things that come into his circle, those things that enter in and affect him.

Similarly, in *The Count of Monte Cristo*, the young man Edmond Dantès has lost his possessions, good name, and freedom. He has been betrayed and seems to have no escape. In the terrible prison Château d'If, he meets an old priest who tunnels into his cell and begins to teach him how to live. Over time the priest imparts a lessons on everything from the classics, to sword fighting, to manners, to the ways of human nature. He is the voice of experience.

Similarly, a mentor trains us to attend to the practical actions of our lives and to drill down into the many layers of our daily actions and find a new path, that of counsel and prudence. The wisdom of seasoned guides relies on principles that respect the nature of things. Prudence relies on the memory of good decisions based on sound reasoning and judgment. This method of careful pause, refusing to react impulsively to a complex situation, rewards us in the long haul. Acting on impulse never resolves a complex situation, but careful consideration can lead us to discover effective solutions. Over time, one can more quickly weigh complexities and make good judgments. Prudence is the refusal to set aside all God has done for us when we turn to act in the world. Prudence always acts with mercy, because it emerges from the joining of Courage and Counsel. The prophet Hosea notes that prudence opens us to the next two gifts of the Holy Spirit, Understanding and Wisdom, to be treated later in this work: "Let him who is wise understand these things; let him who is prudent know them. Straight are the paths of the LORD, in them the just walk, but sinners stumble in them" (Hos 14:10).

The Merciful

The journey of hope, temperance, justice, fortitude, and prudence can sound idealistic at first. Yet, our docility to the movement of the Holy Spirit through his gifts demands great sacrifice. At times, life does not make sense. We encounter temptation, hardship, pain, adversity, and loss. Difficulties and conflicts easily escalate. Accidents and even tragedies occur. Though we seek to follow the Christian way, we still sometimes refuse to talk to one another and even betray one another. The words of the psalmist become our own: "Has God forgotten mercy, in anger withheld compassion?" (Ps 77:10). Christian prayer, in the form of the Liturgy of the Hours and the Divine Office, responds at every hour, with at least two of those hours explicitly including the reference to mercy. In the great Gospel Canticles of Morning Prayer and Evening Prayer, the *Benedictus* and the *Magnificat*, the Church calls to mind the compassion and mercy of God. In the morning we pray the Canticle of Zachariah: "because of the tender mercy of our God by which the daybreak from on high will visit us" (Lk 1:78–79). In the evening the Church prays with the Blessed Mother: "He has helped Israel his servant, remembering his mercy, according to his promise to our fathers, to Abraham and to his descendants forever" (Lk 1:54–55). Mercy is a daily reality for the Church. We must bring it to mind at both the beginning and close of every day.

Pope John Paul II taught about the mercy of God. The Holy Father's encyclical letter, *Dives in Misericordia*, focuses on the mercy of God the Father.[4] John Paul taught that man always has a special need for mercy. The search for mercy, the special power of God's steadfast love, is the quest of every person. Jesus himself is the definitive fulfillment of the mercy of God. The sacraments and the celebration of the mysteries of the life of Christ communicate mercy. Confession is a fountain of mercy. The Sorrowful Mysteries of the Rosary, and the celebration of Divine Mercy Sunday point immediately to the mercy of God in the Sacrament of Penance. Many who have been away from the Sacrament of Penance actually strongly desire to go to confession, but they are afraid. It is important to remember that the desire to receive this sacrament, even the mere thinking about it, is itself an action and invitation of the Holy Spirit. If he invites us, he will lead us at every moment. The hardest part is opening the door to the confessional or reconciliation room. After that God takes over.

---

4. Released the first Sunday of Advent, November 1980.

Going to Confession

In the darkened church, the line of people sitting along the wooden pews now shortens, whittled off . . . the thrill of sin so far removed, the stain so close, the reason for this risky business. The door to the confession room closes behind us and another seal surrounds us, far more permanent and unbreakable. Yet the cloistering of this conversation seems at times not to have any effect on the high-anxiety of this meeting. So many take those last few steps toward the confessional still filled with stress. They worry about such topics as, *How do I start? Do I stay anonymous or sit more directly? Will I remember the Act of Contrition? Will I sound nervous? Will I remember everything?* Notice the subject of each interjection—I. Each of these tracks begins a line of thought that raises blood pressure and decreases confession lines. These inner movements may be the last ditch effort of the Evil One to undo a far more splendid movement toward grace, however awkward it may be. For this covert activity he puts forward his best operative—the ego—to plead with us lest we enter the world of Christ.

Turbulence still agitates this darkened locus of grace in which we sit. While the seal closes this conversation for all time, it simultaneously can open the hidden passages of the heart. As priest and penitent cross that perimeter, they cross something in themselves—another line deep within. Not only do they converse, but one *world* meets another, uncovers another. The process begins when they start to speak. Despite the fear that goes with telling one's sins, the penitent displays a certain strength, the strength of confidence. In telling the sad story of sin, the emphasis switches from the penitent's ability to "say everything" toward what he or she is really saying behind the words: "I want to go deeper. . . . *My actions are not far removed, like random satellites, but reflect and announce the inmost movements of my person. How can I get in touch with this profound connection?* This conversation goes beyond listing the times we lost patience, got angry, sinned sexually, cheated, stole, or took God's name in vain. Behind the well-memorized list of thoughts and actions, a pattern of wounding emerges. Sin is the symptom of a buried recklessness. We can play it safe and let the ego drive by merely skimming God's grace, making this encounter as short as possible, if not avoiding it all together. Or we can overthrow the ego and meet Christ, trusting beyond the shallows.

As we explore we see into our deeper self. Impatience speaks of an inner neglect—we are not taking care of ourselves and have spread ourselves too thin. Then, under pressure, we rip. We even think *What's the matter with you? You really ripped into him.* The answer to impatience is not to summon some strength next time, grit our teeth, and be nice, but to re-examine our style of life and our belief system. *Did I, in subtle pride, think I could do it all, and then find out with a crash that I could not?* Likewise, sexual sin is often a symptom of an unaddressed neediness in our life. We ignore the hole in our hearts, and try to fill the void with sex. Again, pride roams free—we cannot admit our own neediness so it comes forth disguised.

Unlike the therapy office where behaviors meet diagnosis, in Reconciliation a person meets Jesus Christ. Infallibly. And Christ is the Truth. Trusting him, especially in our own anxiety, will lead to honest discernment. Our actions will cease to be faults we only want to be *absolved from,* and instead will announce a profundity to be *reconciled with*: the love of God. We sinners are in effect *confessing* that there is more to us, and however noble our efforts, there is a place within us that can only respond to Christ. The opening sentences of confession are the first motion of the sacrament. We admit particular sins as if to say: "I specify this for God, and in so doing, I am simultaneously *confessing* my faith in God, inviting him to enter the tangle." God then goes into the inmost places and works undisturbed. That focus can easily slip in these early moments. We are on a bridge to grace, and, as we know, bridges freeze before roads. The penitent may be tempted to make excuses for the conflicts, repeated slips, or deliberate hurts that he or she confesses. Pause and listen beyond all that. In confession the penitent is not merely telling sins, nor is the priest just hearing sins as if either could organize, alone, the exhaustive event of Calvary. We let Christ touch us in the power of the Spirit by the medium and instrument *he* has chosen. And it is amazingly difficult to allow him to do this. So many objections are raised today about confession: *Why do I have to go to a priest? Can he really understand my sins?* Ultimately, whether or not the priest *understands* our sins is irrelevant. Confession is not about the experience of the priest, it is about Jesus Christ working through his chosen instrument, however imperfect. To be unduly caught up with these questions shows that old trick of preoccupation with the self, which is the very reason to go to Reconciliation. Our ego endlessly seeks to sabotage this encounter.

When we speak honestly about ourselves we free ourselves, and in confession we speak more than our sins. They are the means by which we say, "God is the One whom I trust as I enter his sacrament." Unconsciously we try to shield ourselves from our fear of abandoning ourselves to God with an honest confession. Perhaps the Sacrament of Penance demands more participation of the one who approaches than any other liturgical experience. We can go to Mass and be bored, never allowing ourselves to be called forth. Rarely can one say that the Sacrament of Penance is boring. If you have never had an awkward experience of confession, perhaps you have missed a step of the sacrament. Admitting our sins is never a simple task initially, even though through confession we may grow into the most comfortable of relationships. The penitent at first dredges up tough, complicated material. As soon as we do this, our hidden defenses begin to operate, trying to dissect, deny, explain, or organize. The forgiveness consists not merely in the penitent's telling of sins, or in the priest's hearing of them, but in the fact that these activities specify the matter that the person is placing before God to forgive, and before oneself to amend.

In the Eucharist, the bread and wine are designated for the action of the Holy Spirit through the words of institution. In Ordination, a baptized male is, by the laying on of hands, designated for the Holy Spirit's action in the prayer of consecration. In Penance the telling and the hearing are a kind of designating activity, which the Holy Spirit acts on in the moment of absolution. Not only do penitents remember the Act of Contrition, but priests also remember the words of absolution—the moment when forgiveness is given—without fail. The next time we stand in line for confession, we ought to refuse to be brought low by anxiety. Instead we should realize that we are in the upright posture of the resurrection, and reach out to God, open the door to our hearts, peek in the darkness, and see what he is already doing.

The Compassionate Heart

Mercy intensifies love and is always found in the midst of suffering. Courage and Counsel, and fortitude and prudence forge mercy as the ultimate response to the illusions and backroom deals of the world. The suffering love of mercy transcends all previous attempts to describe love. Love is not affection, a basic attraction, having things in common, or dividing up the daily chores. Love is a gift of self for the good of the other, a gift that is willing to pour itself out to the extent of suffering and sacrifice in the face of pain, difficulty, and hardship. Mercy is the second name of love.

To experience another person's suffering evokes something in us. To see a grieving mother who has just lost a child or a father suffering with cancer evokes empathy. We begin to feel with our compassionate heart (*miserum cor*). This heart *unites* us to the one who suffers. We grieve over their distress. Saint Paul speaks about this in his Letter to the Colossians: "Put on then, as God's chosen ones, holy and beloved, heartfelt compassion, kindness, humility, gentleness, and patience, bearing with one another and forgiving one another . . ." (Col 3:12). This "heartfelt compassion" flows from sharing in the mercy that is proper to God. Mercy brings the grace of union with the poor and arouses a spirit of sacrifice within us.

Mercy is not sentiment or sympathy. Mercy is not letting another off the hook or giving them a second, third, or fourth chance. Mercy prompts us to generously give to another from our own reserves of the Spirit's gifts of Fear of the Lord, Piety, Knowledge, Counsel, and Courage. Mercy is the living opposite of revenge. Mercy goes deeper than the evil that has been done and begins to love from a more profound place: the gift of self. Mercy does not teach a lesson or take the higher road; it is a new beginning of goodness. Mercy springs from deep inside the Christian. It flows from the stalwart depths of faith, hope, temperance, justice, prudence, and fortitude in the form of the gift of self. It does this even in the face of evil. This is compassion: to make a sacrificial gift of self in the face of evil, and thus to join with Christ's sacrifice. In this way he creates a new beginning of goodness right where evil has attempted to do its worst.

Chapter Ten

The Sixth Surge of the Fountain: Blessed Are the Pure of Heart

The first thing the world tries to do to Christians is dismiss them. If it cannot dismiss them outright, it must reduce them to a caricature so as to lessen their influence. Christians who respond to the call of Christ to live and practice the faith are not naïve holy rollers. Believers make a free response to the God who has called us to follow him in his Church. We may have for a time forgotten or grown cold to the call of God. We may have bought into the world's program to acquire pleasure quickly. No matter how far we may drift from him, God always pursues us with his love. He wants to convince us more and more that life is not about acquiring pleasure quickly, but about giving beauty slowly. No one has ever wanted anything as much as God has wanted to share his life with us. When our hearts soften enough to receive this divine message of salvation we begin with a new moment of faithfulness. Our

inner growth in faith is not about control or outspoken fana-
tacism. It is about conversation and transformation, by which
we turn away from the false promises of the world to the God
who reveals himself in Christ. We discover his movement and
sense his plan. This does not lead to the surety of a perfect life
as the world defines it. Rather, we trust that God is leading,
knows the way, and will supply us with inner strength as we
follow him.

In its five preceding surges, the fountain of new life welling up within the Christian has brought the gifts of Fear of
the Lord, Piety, Knowledge, Courage, and Counsel. These
have given rise to hope, temperance, justice, faith, fortitude,
and prudence. The virtues in turn have given rise to the life of
the Beatitudes: poverty of spirit, meekness, mourning, hunger
and thirst for righteousness, and mercy. As these gifts, virtues,
and beatitudes grow together in the believer, they begin to
flow in fuller measure.

The gift of Understanding develops the virtue of faith
more completely. This new movement of grace clears the way
for purity of heart. As Christian wisdom teaches, purity takes
time. It is not the automatic result of willpower alone. The
clenched teeth, white-knuckle approach to purity usually fails
over the long haul. Chronic repression does not make chastity
flourish, but makes vices fester. Purity emerges from the
believer as the fruit of the gifts, virtues, and Beatitudes. The
gift of Understanding is central to the life of purity.

The Gift of Understanding

Understanding proceeds from the Word God has spoken.
The psalmist proclaims: "The revelation of your words sheds
light, gives understanding to the simple" (Ps 119:130). The

Holy Spirit moves the soul, through the gift of Understanding, to grasp and internalize an intimate knowledge of the sometimes hidden meaning of the Christian mysteries. A supernatural light makes known this meaning. This does not involve an apparition or a voice that tells us what to do. Rather, the Holy Spirit enlightens the mind to dispose us with a special affection to penetrate the mysteries of faith with an interior understanding.[1] This light goes straight to the heart to help it grasp the truths of the faith in an authentic way. The heart, warmed by this light, is also able to see more clearly due to its radiance. For example, recall the two disciples on the road to Emmaus who encounter the Risen Jesus: "Then beginning with Moses and all the prophets, he interpreted to them what referred to him in all the scriptures" (Lk 24:27). After Jesus vanishes from their sight, they joyously affirm: "Were not our hearts burning (within us) while he spoke to us on the way and opened the scriptures to us?" (Lk 24:32). The gift of Understanding operates as the Lord Jesus opens their minds to *understand* the Scriptures. This burning within is the fire of purity that comes from the gift of Understanding. They are now ready to go back to the dangers of Jerusalem despite personal risk, so as to sacrifice for what they now understand. So too, the Blessed Virgin Mary, when she receives the message of the angel that she is to be the Mother of God's Son, asks, "How can this be since I have no relations with a man?" (Lk 1:34).[2] The Blessed Mother asks this not so much for her own benefit, but for ours, so that we may be introduced to the mystery of her perpetual virginity.[3]

---

1. See John of St. Thomas, *The Gifts of the Holy Ghost*, 81, 84–88.

2. Ibid., 102.

3. See John Saward, *Cradle of Redeeming Love: The Theology of the Christmas Mystery* (San Francisco: Ignatius Press, 2002), 218.

The Holy Spirit's gift of Understanding forms the believer to "read" reality by a kind of intuitive grasp of the truths of faith. Through the gift of Understanding, the Holy Spirit, like an internal teacher, guides us through the mysteries of faith that take place in us. This happens even when things do not go right, even at Sunday Mass: when, for reasons beyond my influence, I arrive late; when the lector proclaims the readings poorly; when a baby cries at the top of his lungs or someone slams a kneeler down at the moment of the consecration. Even when a cell phone rings, the microphone fails, and distractions abound, the Holy Spirit is not impeded. He is swifter than the distractions. He anticipates them. The gift of Understanding takes everything into account and guides the Christian to take stock of what we do hear and to go back to the God who stands behind the mystery. The psalmist refers to the gift of Understanding as he prays: "Make me understand the way of your precepts; I will ponder your wondrous deeds" (Ps 119:27). The gift of Understanding moves us through stages of growth. First, we learn the faith from what is taught or preached to us. Then we form a conceptual knowledge of God and his revelation. Finally, we grow in a type of affective knowledge of how we must live now. The gift of Understanding thrives on the various ways we learn about the faith: Bible stories, religion classes, homilies, even stained glass windows. The gift of Understanding makes us supple and flexible in grasping the ways of God. This gift discloses the Christian mystery to the deep places of our hearts, so we may learn more about the saving action of God. We could even say that through this gift, God discloses his own way of understanding existence. By his grace, we begin to share in his knowledge. Under the influence of the gift of Understanding, even secular things trigger the Christian to reflect on the mysteries of God. We begin to use our knowledge not simply to get a promotion, or to make more money, but to learn more about God. The gift of Understanding transforms the scope of our awareness, widening it so that faith begins to inform our entire life: work, recreation, family, and all of daily life.

The gift of Understanding deepens faith by leading the Christian to internalize the saving mystery. The believer begins to learn the value of meditation, and can go quickly into meditation *entrusting* himself to God with daily confidence. Even turbulent events do not offset the believer's affection for God at this stage. The difficulties of life can still cause pain, but the faith-filled Christian guided by the gift of Understanding knows how to wait for the action of God. In fact, at this stage, the Christian is not alarmed by the need to wait many years for God to act. God's apparent delay trains the Christian in a deeper faithfulness and love. At this stage, the Holy Spirit's action frees the Christian from hidden influences and forces. God works undisturbed in the depths of the heart to teach faith as entrustment.

The gift of Understanding surpasses natural reason and introduces the believer to the eternal truths. This gift assists the Christian to penetrate to the meaning of the authentic teaching of the Church. God chooses a mystery to open up to the believer and invites us deeply into his love. The teachings on the Trinity, the Incarnation, or the Church, for example, are all roads he selects to sharpen our intellect to receive his message.

Faith

The gift of Understanding unites us more firmly to God himself as the object of our faith. God tells us the truth. He is always the first to tell us the truth, and he does so through parents, teachers, priests, and the created world. This truth, however, is easily obscured. Faith is the virtue that enables us to understand that God himself is behind all the instruments he chooses to convey his truth to us. When we assent to this truth because it is God who speaks to us, especially when it concerns a difficult truth to receive, we are more firmly united to him in wisdom.

The gift of Understanding leads us to have faith in what is unseen: the God who freely initiates his love for us. This love culminates in the cross and resurrection of Jesus. When we accept the beauty of the cross and the fidelity of God, he makes us faithful, ready to freely and fully entrust ourselves to him. We begin to interpret the events of our lives through the paradigm of God's faithfulness. We understand, perhaps for the first time in our lives, that religion and faith are not an isolated, private dimension of life. Rather, God is the central dimension of life. All leads from him and to him. He is origin and goal. As a result, all of life, all of existence, is God's way of revealing his love in and through the Church. We grasp that just as the mustard seed is a small beginning of God's faithfulness that already holds abundance, so too is the narrative of our lives. This faith brings confidence and joy, not fanaticism and frenetic activity.

The Pure of Heart

The gift of Understanding and the virtue of faith lead us to live purity of heart.[4] The virtues cleanse us of preoccupations, error, and sin. The Christian response that purity is the only valid alternative to promiscuity and licentiousness can easily

---

4. See John of St. Thomas, *The Gifts of the Holy Ghost*, 82.

seem unrealistic and naïve. The world misunderstands purity as a prim way to stifle curiosity. The world labels those who seek purity as victims of an embarrassing prudishness that stays home while others party. To the world, those who seek purity of heart miss out on the fun and are left behind. Purity is portrayed as a sheltered, straight-laced, and naïve denial of the world's pleasures and human appetites.

The world fails to understand that purity alone brings clarity, the capacity to see things as they really are.[5] Purity requires endurance. Such a capacity comes not from our own efforts, but from the light of God. Those who seek purity of heart are not motivated by a desire to prove their own will-power or because of a remote reward. All that they have learned thus far teaches the believer to know the illusions of the world. The world does not bring what it promises. The flashing lights by now are well known as signals of a false path. The pure of heart seek purity, not because they seek only to avoid a loose or wanton lifestyle, but because they seek the excitement of seeing God. God is not in the false promises of the world. The goal of purity of heart is to reach the kingdom of heaven even in the most practical of realities.

Purity of heart is the capacity to distinguish what comes from God and what does not. As Christians, we must carefully examine whatever comes near our hearts. The devil uses hidden snares and illusions to lure us away from God. Satan's goal is not to make us deny God's existence. Satan wants us to deny the existence of Satan. He wants our guard down so that we think we are unbeatable and nothing bad can happen to us. He will attempt to feed off the good like a parasite and try to talk us into something that appears good, but is evil. He tries to lure us from the path of holiness by telling us, "Everyone is

---

5. See Balthasar, *The Glory of the Lord II*, 99–101.

doing it," or "Just this one time." He wants to be merely suggestive, and behind the scenes, to call no real attention to himself until, in the end, he throws off the disguise and reveals the deceit.[6] We must seek refuge in the mystery of Christ. The gift of Understanding guides us deeply in to the mysteries of goodness and salvation. Attentiveness to the word of God expressed in and through the teaching of the Church, and from the prudence of a wise spiritual director is crucial in the day-to-day discernment necessary for peace in the Christian life. The journey is not linear, as if one automatically passes from one surge of the fountain to the next. There are often moments when we return to begin again and to internalize the foregoing virtues through interior trials, weaknesses, fears, difficulties, and faults. God uses these as opportunities to continue to strength his life within us. Saint Teresa of Avila noted that God is very patient, and that he knows how to wait many years for us, especially when he knows that we are attempting to persevere.[7]

---

6. See Féret, *The Apocalypse of St. John,* 113, 117–118. See also St. Teresa of Avila, *The Interior Castle,* 295; I.1.2.15.

7. St. Teresa of Avila, *The Interior Castle*, II:1–3.

Chapter Eleven

The Seventh Surge of the Fountain: Blessed Are the Peacemakers

The Christian life combines quest and adventure in the events of daily life. It is said that the saintly person is not someone who is swept into the heights of prayer by something no one else can see; rather the saintly person is someone who is swept into contemplation by that which everyone can see. The daily ups and downs, ins and outs of our lives are filled with doors to holiness. We often think that holiness is reserved for the few. It is really a call to the many. As the believer interiorizes the gifts of Fear of the Lord, Piety, Knowledge, Courage, Counsel, and Understanding, he or she is prepared for Wisdom. The gift of Wisdom is the seventh surge of the fountain. As the Book of Proverbs teaches: "The source of wisdom is a flowing brook" (Prv 18:4b). This gift forms the virtue of love in the heart of the Christian. Love leads to the Beatitude: "Blessed are the peacemakers, for they will be called children of God" (Mt 5:9).

The Gift of Wisdom

Once the gifts of Knowledge, Counsel, and Understanding have assisted the believer in perceiving the deeper truths of faith in an intimate yet simple manner, the gift of Wisdom enables the Christian to then *act* on this truth. The words of Christ are the way to wisdom: "Everyone who listens to these words of mine and acts on them will be like a wise man who built his house on rock" (Mt 7:24). Wisdom is, in a sense, the fruit of longstanding application of Knowledge, Counsel, and Understanding. Wisdom is truly the gift given to those who are steadfast and tenacious for the things of God. The Book of Sirach compares the wisdom of King Solomon to an overlowing fountain (cf. Sir 47:14–15). The Book of Wisdom says, "Therefore I prayed, and prudence was given me; I pleaded and the spirit of Wisdom came to me" (Wis 7:7). There are two competing wisdoms. First there is the wisdom of the world. This is the path by which we measure ourselves by the standards of the world: who has the most money, the best looks, the most control, power, popularity, and prestige. The world attempts to prove its wisdom through polls, trends, and fads. But these realities can pass in a moment. These are tools, not goals. The Book of Ecclesiastes responds succinctly to the claim that wisdom is found in the power of the world: "Wisdom is a better defense for the wise man than would be ten princes in the city" (Eccl 7:19). Sirach echoes back: "A child or a city will preserve one's name, but better than either, attaining wisdom" (Sir 40:18). All the wisdom of the world is folly before Christ (cf. 1 Cor 3:19). The true school of wisdom is the school of the cross: the authentic gift of self for the true good of the other. As Saint Paul tells us: "For it is written: 'I will destroy the wisdom of the wise, and the learning of the learned I will set aside.' . . . Has not God made the wisdom of the world foolish?" (1 Cor 1:19, 20b). Wisdom is found only in Christ crucified (cf. 1 Cor 1:23). Wisdom teaches us, without flaunting it, the value of spending time thinking about the divine mysteries and using these as the basis to discern daily life. In this, wisdom brings us to union with God. Wisdom is born from the believer's internal experience of God.[1]

The gifts of Counsel and Courage guide this hunger and thirst and enable believers to live in purity of heart. From this purity a seasoned wisdom emerges, which loves freely and makes a gift of self. Wisdom then guides the adopted sons and daughters of God to treat their neighbor with justice and to take the risk to hunger and thirst to transform the world. The only way to do this is by the union with God afforded through Wisdom, so that we can begin to love with the very love by which God loves.

Love

The Second Vatican Council teaches that man can only find himself in a sincere gift of self.[2] This is a paradox. In order to be fulfilled *inside*, we must give ourselves away outside, as a gift. Of its very nature, love wills the true good for the other through the gift of self. The assertion "God is love" (1 Jn 4:8) conveys that in his essence, perfect self-giving love flows among the Persons of the Trinity.[3]

Love is the willing gift of self for the good of the other. For the human person, however, love must often mature from "need love" to "gift love." "Need love" is love that is offered to

---

1. See John of St. Thomas, *The Gifts of the Holy Spirit*, 68, 84–86, 114, 125–135.
2. See *Gaudium et Spes*, 24.
3. See Balthasar, *Theo-Drama V*, 81–82.

the other, not primarily for the good of the other, but for the return such love brings for the self. Such love must be purified of its mixed motives into "gift love." The Holy Spirit purifies our love by reminding us of the sacrificial love of Jesus. When God loves, his love cannot be measured and is never exhausted. We learn this love because God the Holy Spirit strengthens us to love with the very love by which God loves.[4] The *Catechism* teaches that "Charity is the theological virtue by which we love God above all things for his own sake, and our neighbor as ourselves for the love of God."[5] Charity infuses a new degree of divine love into all human actions. Sentiment may or may not accompany this love. The Holy Spirit actually *creates* love and charity in the soul. We begin to experience a movement within us, within our souls, to love others and God in a new way. Jesus says to his disciples, "I no longer call you slaves, because a slave does not know what his master is doing. I have called you friends, because I have told you everything I have heard from my Father" (Jn 15:15). Love is what the Son makes known to us. By charity we attain every good and avoid every evil.[6] God has shared his very self with us, and so we begin to experience God's love: charity.

Purity of heart leads to receiving the gift of Wisdom by which one truly loves the other and desires that person's good. The love that emerges from the gift of Wisdom is charity, the heroic love of agape that joins the believer to God himself. Love has many meanings. It is the most misunderstood one-syllable word in the English tongue. When people speak of love, they often mean an individualistic, transitory, sensual affection. People use the same word to describe their relation

---

4. See Torrell, *Saint Thomas Aquinas: Spiritual Master,* vol. 2, 178, 193.

5. *CCC*, no. 1822.

6. See Melina, *The Epiphany of Love*, 117.

to recreation, work, family members, and spouses. Jesus, however, gives love its full meaning as a gift of self for the good of the other. Love is a self-emptying gift and the very life of the soul. This runs counter to the prevalent contemporary attitude that to be fulfilled, we must acquire and consume everything we want. This attitude infects our work, family life, friendships, leisure, diet, and exercise. Yet this rarely leads to lasting happiness. In fact, it leads to the reverse.

The Child

Love is neither luxury nor recreation, nor is it the result of luck or fate. Love is not a state of mind or romantic magic. The paradigm by which we best understand love is the love of the father and mother for their child: filial love.[7] We first experience love as an invitation, as a gift received. There was a time when you and I did not exist. We did nothing to arrange our being here as citizens of the world and members of the human race. We did not call ahead and arrange to be born in the city or suburbs, in a particular climate or era. We *were not*, and you and I *might not have been*—until the moment of love when our parents, as husband and wife, came together in a bodily act of self-giving love. They came with all their flaws, pains, hurts, and mixed motives. They came with all their genetics, family history, evolution, emotion, and knowledge. They came with their selfishness and generosity, with all they knew and all they did not know. And they made a gift of self to each other, whether they felt fully ready to or not, whether they were fully

---

7. Balthasar notes that for M. J. Scheeben, "The whole structure of the world is, also, seen to derive from a relation of love, a nuptial relation." See Balthasar, *Explorations in Theology I: The Word Made Flesh* (San Francisco: Ignatius Press, 1989), 202.

aware of the tremendous nature of their act or not. They made a gift of self to one another in a personal, bodily, physical, emotional way. And this gift was in a sexual, physical, biological action, which means the gift was total. When my father made a gift of himself to my mother, and my mother to my father, they were so excited by love, by one another, by the gift one made to the other that they were ecstatic. The word ecstatic means "outside the self." They were so totally a gift of self to each other that they were each outside themselves in love. In this they were fully themselves because they made a gift of themselves.

Parents provide the child's first experience of love. The child has done nothing to arrange the time, place, or condition of conception and birth. Conception and birth does not come as a *response* to anything the child has done. No one has yet gazed into the child's eyes, experienced his personality, appreciated his sense of humor, or shared his interests. The child does not come into being on the basis of some reward, recognition, or approval. God does not require anyone to pass an exam to merit birth. The mother loves the child not because he or she will have her favorite color eyes, a beautiful smile, athletic prowess, intelligence, or the ability to provide grandchildren. The potential phenomenon of designer babies is not wrong simply because it is unnatural and presents potential untold risks. The phrase "designer babies" is a contradiction in terms. "Love" that first selects the attributes of a child is not *love* at all, but a transaction, a poor imitation of love. The child is meant to receive life only from the immediate, exclusive, and loving union between mother and father. The parents love the child because the child *is*. Love is always first given; only in this can it be received.

The child receives the love of the mother as the primal and ongoing experience of existence. Despite any faults the parents may have, they are *drawn to a new place by the child.* The child reminds them of the originality and nature of love itself. This is among the first gifts of the child. The child does this simply by being. The child alone transforms husband and wife into mother and father. The child first *gives* identity to the parents through a *gift of self.* This gift of self is a response on the part of the child to the parents' gift of self in the marital act. The child is not a trophy, but a gift. The child is not meant to meet the demands or needs of the parents, but to be the expression of their generous love. The signs of this exchange lead the child to the early intuition that his being is true, good, and beautiful. He then gives this experience back to his mother and father in love. The love we are meant to experience as children can only take the form of a gift of self. This is the irreducible and indispensable element of love. No other attitude, attribute, or disposition can substitute.

The family as a communion of persons is essential to understanding love. At the same time, the family home can often be the scene of pain as well. When betrayal, infidelity, duplicity, or abuse take place in the family, it is so painful because the family is created to be the locus of a unique love. We experience the self-taking of the world through greed, manipulation, indulgence, and infatuation, which masquerade as love. Wounded, we begin to shy away from the gift, to be coerced into choosing fear rather than love. Attacks on marriage and the family, such as same-sex unions, no fault-divorce, free love, cohabitation, pornography, and adultery are attacks on love itself and the very identity of the human person. Healing means returning to the original form of love we were meant to learn as children.

The gift of self makes love visible. Something deep inside us, something we know innately, enables us to respond to the gift of another person. Even those who have known hurt and abuse from an early age still have the ability to love and to make a self-gift. The internal scar tissue of the pain of past relationships may cover our hearts in layers. It may seem as if our old conflicts keep repeating themselves and never get resolved. As long as conflicts are buried, they do not heal. But the heart never forgets the original movement that gave it life, and that movement is love.

Our first memory is love. No matter what happened before or after we were created, love is always the first moment of our identity. This first moment never grows old and is never totally lost. It waits, hidden among valleys of pain in our hearts, beneath old wounds of people who loved us too little, or loved us too much. But it waits, and it longs for the gift. Only the gift of self from another can free the love that waits beneath our wounds. Our wounds are not just injuries, they are *openings*. Where did this love come from that lies, perhaps lost, deep in our hearts? It was *given* to us. This is why only the *gift* can summon love. The mystery of the identity of the human person is the drama of love itself. Love is the authentic surrender of self for the good of the other. For all of our technological advances, we cannot exhaust or grow tired of the discovery of this fundamental truth of love. The Civilization of Love gives rise to peace only when it is seen as the Culture of Life.

In the midst of the responsibilities of life, the human person experiences a desire to reach out for goodness and love: happiness in the classic sense. As people make their way in the world, they long for authentic fulfillment. The first sign of this desire for goodness is the gift is creation itself. A fundamental truth of Catholicism is that the visible world is created good (cf. Gn 1:31). Goodness is not just a feeling of positive equilibrium. Goodness is the union of wisdom and love, which is not a simple, cheerful feeling of easy warmth. Love is authentic acceptance joined to a deep commitment. In its original form, love is self-surrender. The more love fills us, the more we search for it. We are easily confused by substitutes for love, such as infatuation and manipulation. But we have an infinite capacity for love, since our desire for love is linked to infinite love, to God.

One obstacle to belief is that God is invisible. Our modern world tells us that only the visible is real, that all reality must fit into observable and measurable facts. If it does not fit into what we can see, hear, touch, smell, or taste, it does not exist. Anything beyond the senses, anything that cannot be indulged is treated as abstract and arbitrary.

The truth is, however, that many things are invisible and are still completely real. For example, one cannot take love and put it into a test tube, over a Bunsen burner, or on a scale. Love *itself* is invisible. The *signs* of love are visible, but show their preference for the invisible by being hidden: holding hands, gazing into another's eyes, a bouquet of flowers, a wedding ring, a caress, a smile, a silent sense of comfort and security. The more something is hidden, the deeper it goes. Maturity closes the gap between the expression of the authentic sign of love and its reality. The immediate intuition of the visible sign of love and its contact with invisible reality creates an opening, through which we can grasp the essence of faith.[8] The secrets of love intuitively seek the deep places that only faith provides.

It is true that the signs of love are not always dependable and usually involve daring and risk. Signs can be manipulated: holding hands can be done simply to make an ex-girlfriend

---

8. Hans Urs von Balthasar, *The Glory of the Lord: A Theological Aesthetics VII, Theology: The New Covenant* (San Francisco: Ignatius Press, 1989), 371.

jealous, or a man may send flowers so that the recipient will lower her defenses and he can use her. Ulterior motives can hijack and divert the signs of love. Love defies rationality, but it is not unreasonable. Despite love's invisibility and risk, no generation has ever doubted the existence of love, much less abandoned its quest. Invisibility should spur us to search, not to doubt.

Love is invisible in the sense that it is hidden. Like love, God too is invisible and hidden. The invisible God is not the *private* God. He chose to show signs of his presence and action in the day-to-day life of Israel through created realities that served as signs of his presence and action. We know the invisible because its presence shines forth through signs that make it visible. When God revealed himself in history, he became visible in various ways: Jacob's wrestling contest, clouds, wind, small sounds, the pillar of fire, the words of the prophets, and the burning bush. Most of all, God has become visible in Jesus (cf. Jn 1:14ff.). In the birth of his Son, we can see, hear, and touch God. The signs of his presence become visible in and through his saving deeds, reaching the climax in the saving passion, death, and glorious resurrection of Jesus. The experience that Abraham, Moses, and the apostles had of God was not one of a faith versus science argument or an ethics debate. God interrupted their lives. Better still, *he interrupted the interruptions* that filled their lives, with a persuasive and penetrating presence that was living and personal. And they believed; they had faith in this living God.

God's revelation has a direction. God chooses the time and place in our lives and in history to make contact with the deepest places of our hearts. So often we abandon our hearts, because it is too painful to remain there, but the promise of God's love leads us back.

Pride

The gift of self builds humility in the soul and counteracts pride. The proud cannot access their inner world. They live instead in the outer world seeking praise, recognition, and returns. But these never accumulate within. They are spent as soon as they are claimed. The proud confuse external accomplishments with internal worth. Though they appear to *satisfy* the person in the moment, external things never *fulfill* the person. For the proud, the external world never truly strengthens the internal sense of self: the insatiable fear that their inadequacy will somehow block them from a deeper sense of self-worth. The proud do not want recognition for their accomplishments; they want to be *entitled* simply for who they are. The proud do not want to be first in line; they want to be the only ones in line. The proud inflate themselves through exaggeration and name dropping. They seek to impress others and receive all the applause. The proud and vainglorious think highly of themselves, their reputation, and notoriety. They boast that they know better than everyone else. The proud flee silence. They prefer the din of a specific kind of talkativness. The noise of disobedience always begins in stubborn pride that impatiently interrupts others, insists, avoids silence, and promotes themselves in the moment. The proud insatiably cry out for recognition but no victory ever convinces them of their worth. They blame every loss on someone else.

Pride leads to vanity, which is pride internalized and intensified. In the Eastern tradition vanity constitutes an eighth deadly sin distinct from pride. In vanity, the phrase, "What do they think of me?" becomes entwined with one's self-image. Any sense of self or direction depends on what others think, to the point that almost no real self remains in these illusions. The person afflicted with vanity lives on the inside to impress others on the outside. Vanity is the final inverse of the gift of self.

Pride forms the basis for all the other deadly sins. For example, pride and greed are closely aligned. The greedy see the world made up of winners and losers, the proud see the world as made up of *a winner* and all the others are losers. The greedy enjoy competition from their own kind, the proud see competition as an insult. If someone attempts to interrelate on the presumed level of the proud, it is seen as an affront. The greedy get a thrill in chasing after things; the proud get a thrill in winning. The proud cannot endure the chase, for it only causes them anxiety. As a result, the proud sabotage the chase with gossip, backstabbing, lies, and chatter. They indulge in bragging, which by its very nature is external. It never becomes inner strength. As boastful as they are, the proud lack self-confidence. This is why they attack through innuendo and gossip. The psalmist speaks of the plotting of the proud: "The arrogant have set a trap for me; villains have spread a net, laid snares for me by the wayside" (Ps 140:6). The lies of the proud afflict the just person, but even those lies become an opportunity for the believer to trust again in God's Word: "Though princes meet and talk against me, your servant studies your laws" (Ps 119:23).

Herod

King Herod is the textbook example of pride. The Magi walk in one day, laden with gifts, and ask for directions. Herod happens to be in. He is a man easily missed; he could have been out expanding his empire. The Magi tell him that they are led by a presence. This prompts Herod to make three responses, which are not sinister, power hungry, or blood-thirsty. They are telltale signs of resistance common to all of us at times.

First, Herod is "greatly disturbed." His contagious anxiety shows on his face and his hands as he grips his throne. Give him tax problems any day, but not this. Even with his army, political contacts, and operatives, he still needs absolute control. When the least little rumor threatens that reign, his autonomic nervous system takes over.

Second, Herod takes them aside to ask them the exact time of the star's rising. Satan sees another potential rising and fearfully, fitfully enters Herod's way. He takes them aside in his pride lest any word of his ignorance of even the most mundane facts leaks out. With all his parades, conquests, medals, and monuments, he remains unsure of himself and must still proudly defend every token of reputation and respect.

Finally, in the midst of all the nervous adrenaline of this late-breaking (and nerve breaking) news, Herod is lazy. This is the third response he brings to the newborn king. Herod is so fragile in his insecurity he needs the easy way out; he sends strangers to do his dirty work. He tells them to go and find out detailed information about the child. Notice also Herod's twice repeated need for "exact time" and "detailed information," as if knowing it all will impress those who may ask. He runs the familiar yet futile perfectionistic plan. His kingdom begins to suffocate from within. The newborn king thus incurs his first criminal offense, an accusation will be the same as the last: sedition.

This is a most fascinating infant-king. He is given costly gifts of gold, frankincense, and myrrh. One of the first acts of the newborn king is to let these riches go. He does not take the gold and buy the inn and fire the innkeeper. (This has puzzled me ever since I was old enough to see over the pews in church!) Instead, he chooses poverty. He does not form a political alliance with these kings, making them honorary apostles. Even though he could have certainly used their clout later. He flees riches as much as he flees Herod's tirade.

Where do we fit in? A standard for every exploration is to "begin with the end in mind." Often enough we get the journey and the end confused. The wise men didn't. After coming to the stable they gave up on the star and began to follow their dreams. A common misunderstanding of Christianity sees spirituality as stalking our own personal stars. Day by day we travel, magi-like by the light of stars. For some folks the star is status, good grades, a successful career, the perfect family, pleasing someone, or "keeping the peace." These stars are disguised black holes that transform our image of God into a wish-fulfiller or dream-maker who meticulously insures us against tragedy. But when misfortune seeps through and stains our lives we turn on God, whether actively or passively. But God guides us in a much more profound way.

The light for this perplexing way still shines forth no matter how many contrary "lights" burn out. To find what gives the star its light, look at the cross. The path of the star turns into the path of the cross leading to his Father's kingdom. The Magi's purpose is to bring gifts. Their entire journey is predicated on the gift of self. Herod, instead, hides from the journey. He does not take risks. He stays at home so that he can control whatever comes by. His pride and sloth will soon turn to murder with the massacre of the youngest and most defenseless of all: the Holy Innocents. The first ones to be persecuted for the Lord Jesus were children. This is because they are the closest to the kingdom of heaven. If we are childlike, we too will be persecuted by the world.

Peacemaker

In the upward surge of the Christian life within the believer, the next step after purity of heart, which desires to see the world as God sees it, is the resolve to be a peacemaker. Peace is not an abstract ideal or the mere absence of tensions. Peace is an escalation of the life of virtue and its natural effect. In the midst of tension, restlessness, and disturbance, peace calms the deep places of the soul. Peace does not deny the adversity and disquiet, but it understands that the only response is the patience of authentic love, which emerges at the center of the fountain. All of the foregoing gifts of the Holy Spirit, the virtues, and the Beatitudes consolidate to form the basis of genuine peace.

Peace is not a technique or sentiment. It is not power or diplomacy alone. It is not only a witness. It is Christ on the cross. Peace does not emerge from compromise, but through acceptance. Peace is the by-product of living as an adopted child of God and therefore a brother or sister to others. Living well in relation to self and others leads us to explore the knowledge of God. As we proceed from acceptance of self, neighbor, and love of God, we find the courage to face trials with the strength derived from God. Daily decisions are then not arbitrary choices, but true expressions of self. Navigating the world with such realism and genuineness leads one to desire and search out a deeper understanding and wisdom. We then grow in understanding that life is a gift of love. The meaning of life is love, and the meaning of love is life. From this comes peace, even, and especially, in the midst of persecution.

Chapter Twelve

The Eighth Surge of the Fountain: Blessed Are You When They Persecute You

The only response the self-centered love of the world can offer to authentic self-giving love is persecution. Self-centered egoism always crucifies self-giving love. Already in his infancy, the Son of God is persecuted by the tyrant Herod (cf. Mt 2:13). The *Catechism of the Catholic Church* teaches that this early event makes "manifest the opposition of darkness to the light . . . Christ's whole life was lived under the sign of persecution."[1] The Lord Jesus predicted that his own lot was to be that of his followers: "If the world hates you, realize that it hated me first. If you belonged to the world, the world would love its own; but because you do not belong to the world, and

---

1. *CCC*, no. 530.

I have chosen you out of the world, the world hates you" (Jn 15:18–19). Jesus tells us this with care, to strengthen us: "I have told you this so that you may not fall away. They will expel you from the synagogues; in fact, the hour is coming when everyone who kills you will think he is offering worship to God. They will do this because they have not known either the Father or me. I have told you this so that when their hour comes you may remember that I told you" (Jn 16:1–4a).

There are, in the world, two directions. Each person can only choose one direction. There is the way of the world or the way of Christ. The way of the world is a lifestyle defined by some combination of the seven deadly sins: gluttony, lust, greed, envy, anger, sloth, and pride. What first comes as temptation later returns as persecution. At first, the true character of temptation is disguised by illusion. We must learn to discern temptation's true character, persecution, the first time we see it. The seven capital sins operate as a kind of network, as attitudes ingrained, slowly at first, which eventually take on the proportions of a lifestyle. Their effect is to dull the conscience, induce restlessness, and suffocate the life of virtue and the call to holiness. When persecution emerges, we are already led far astray from the life of virtue.

The way of Christ is the path to holiness. This path is marked off by the Beatitudes. This lifestyle is one of purpose and meaning founded upon the gift of self. If we choose the way of Christ we will experience the persecution of the world. It may be the general feeling that we are continually disadvantaged by circumstance and that life is not turning out as we wished. We experience the roadblocks of life, which seem to dauntingly delay our dreams. We may experience physical persecution from others or be exhausted by difficult relationships. Others may look down on us or pass us over because of our commitment to Jesus. They may ridicule us. We may experience conflict, trial, or a depressing decline. We might experience the persecution and pressures of one ideology or another. We also face the persecution of the duplicity, resentment, and contempt of the world. This may tempt us to blame ourselves at times. Our physical suffering may be a type of persecution we endure. Our bodies age and give out on us. Any persecution or pain we experience is not simply meant to be tolerated, but transformed. The persecution of Christians arises because of the ideologies and sin of the world. If the Christian truly lives an authentic witness to Christ, sooner rather than later a conflict will develop with those who view the world through the eyes of materialism, utilitarianism, and egoism. At times, these attitudes and ways of understanding even seep into our fellow Christians. It is one thing for the believer to be persecuted by the world; it is another to be persecuted by fellow Christians who have adapted to the duplicitous ways of the world. Even in this acute hardship, the Holy Spirit leads the believer to understand that nothing can thwart the creative and saving plan of God, who is faithful. In fact, the mystery of the cross reveals that his faithfulness intensifies even more in the midst of persecution.[2] Our response to trial is the simple and persistent day-to-day testimony of the life of virtue.

When we experience inconvenience, much less failure, trial, and persecution, we often respond with resistance, anger, and rebellion. In this way we internalize the pain and allow it to own us. We transform persecution into anger. But we can choose another option. We believe that persecution is the act of something or someone else upon us. But the Holy Spirit teaches us even in times of persecution that persecution does not act upon us; instead, we are called to act upon it. God does

---

2. See Jean Daniélou, *Advent*, 172, 175.

not grant wishes, he does something incredibly more daring: he answers prayers. We see this played out in the calling and life of Moses.

The Burning Bush (Ex 3:1–6; 6:2–13; 6:28–7:7; Acts 7:30–31)

Moses had probably been standing there for a long time, staring into that fire. The passage doesn't indicate that he was surprised to see the fire there. Well acquainted with desert ways, Moses knew that burning bushes can be common in the desert. Shepherds would light a fire at night when the air grew cold. In the morning when they gathered the sheep, they might carelessly leave a fire smoldering. The white-hot ashes, carried on the wind, sometimes landed on dry brambles. The crisp bushes would quickly be set ablaze. Moses had probably seen dozens of burning bushes in the desert, perhaps feeling the embers on his skin as he stirred their crumbled ashes.

The fire in the bush was not the one that first captured Moses' attention, for another fire was burning in the desert: the one inside Moses. He was pretty burned up. After all, look at what he was doing now. He was a shepherd, a nobody, tending someone else's sheep. But Moses also regularly tended and stoked the fire in himself. He was not only a shepherd working in the desert, but he was a shepherd working for his father-in-law. As Moses gazed into that burning bush, he probably thought about the past, the good old days in Egypt. Back then, Moses had been rather close to the Pharaoh. In those days he had influence, money, and power. His future looked bright. But then he made a big mistake.

One day his temper got the best of Moses. He began to beat an Egyptian who was mistreating an Israelite. Moses was so angry that he killed the Egyptian. Having committed a capital crime, he was now cast out of Pharaoh's good pleasure and exiled, just like the Samaritan woman. And, just like she did, he passed by a well. He settled in the land of Midian and met his future wife at a well. So now here he was, working as a shepherd for his father-in-law. Imagine the pain and regret Moses felt. He had gone from Pharaoh's palace to the desert. He had everything and lost it. Angry and resentful, Moses stared at the fire in the burning bush for some time as he had gazed into dozens of others.

And then something starts to happen. Something about *this* fire catches Moses's eye. He sees some movement, a swaying in the branches of that bush. He blinks hard to clear his eyes and gazes into the dancing flames. Whatever he sees is not happening in the *bush* but *within the fire*. Moses sees *fire* within the fire.

Moses did not go over to see a fire. He says that he has to go over and see this great sight. The bush *is* on fire, but the bush is not being *consumed* by the fire. This fire differs from all the rest, for it does not consume the bush (cf. Ex 3:2). Moses wonders why this bush is not consumed by the fire. This fire does not turn things into ash, like all other fires do. This fire is more than a fire; it is a sign of a Presence. Jesus proclaimed: "I have come to set the earth on fire, and how I wish it were already blazing!" (Lk 12:49). *God* is moving in the branches of the bush. He is within the ordinary, making it extraordinary. As we saw in an earlier chapter, the patience to see the supernatural action of God within the ordinary reflects the fruits of the gift of Knowledge that inspires the virtue of faith.

Burning bushes are never far away. We pass them several times a day. The family dinner table, for example, is a burning bush. When I was growing up we gathered every day for family dinner. The time around that table taught me more about conflict resolution than I could ever learn in a class and more about confidence than I have ever learned in a gym or on an obstacle course. No sports practice, play rehearsal, work project, or party could cancel our family dinner. We did not gather around the table to learn manners or because we had nothing else to do. We gathered there because we were loved. Nothing else was as important as that.

So often today the burning bush of the family dinner table is passed by, preempted so that we can attempt to fit in elsewhere: basketball practice, show rehearsal, work, meetings, and friends. The gift of Knowledge must enflame us again to see the extraordinary love within the ordinary customs of daily family life. If we do not spend time around that table as a family every day, then sooner or later the events of our lives start to crumble into ash instead of becoming glowing embers that ignite new and beautiful fires. No family is "typical." One size does not fit all, and never did. Each family has its own share of pains. The pain that bruises our hearts comes in all shapes and sizes. Even the best of families experience pain. An ongoing challenge is the chronic pressure to fit in to a world that has no time for the tradition and communion of the family. Love takes time. The family takes time. The world, however, demands the time that is so often reserved for the family. The infringement of the world on the family is a type of persecution. The world entices us to compare our own families to the ideal presented by Hollywood. The comparison is meant to pry us away from our families and set us out on our own. In the prying is the pain of persecution. Yet, instead of feeling our pain, we often cover it up and avoid it. We usually do this by pretending it does not exist, but pretending scatters us. We pass the burning bush and the anger and pain only grow within us, driving us farther into exile.

Another burning bush is the simplicity of being a child. In childhood we have energy to see what is concrete. Life itself excites us. How sad it is to see a child plunked down in front of a TV set, blankly staring at the screen while his or her imagination crumbles into ashes. How sad it is to see a child pressured during a baseball game that is ruled by coaches' tempers and parents' unlived dreams. This too is a form of persecution. Childhood is filled with vital moments. Such moments in our early years are not meant to be rare. So often, we, perhaps unwittingly, force a child to accommodate to a busy and rushed lifestyle. A child *needs* time. To rush from one activity to another creates a confusing lifestyle. Some children are on the run from the time they are born. They are awakened early and hustled off to daycare, then to aftercare. Later in life they go from school, to sports practice, to rehearsal, and end up with no prolonged center of gravity. Already the secular world presses in to indoctrinate the child into the "acquire pleasure quickly" lifestyle. The ongoing preemption of the vital moments of childhood, even for supposedly good reasons, deprives the child's heart of needed bonds. Many rush so quickly for so long, they later feel their childhood was lost. The bonding moments of early childhood help us to prepare for the later moments of self-giving love. In childhood, there is no such thing as isolated moments of quality time. Rather, for children, a quantity of time *is* quality time. If children learn only to rush, they will likely pass by the burning bushes that light up life.

The concrete and natural imagination of a child is a burning bush. Too often, adults short-circuit children's imaginations by handing them a cell phone or sitting them in front of a TV or computer while the burning bush crumbles into ash. Concrete thinking enriches a child in ways that a computer never can. The virtual reality of computers cannot build our personalities in the way that real-life activities can. Daily activities lead to exploration and wonder: running in a backyard, wading into a rushing stream, gazing at clouds in a deep blue sky, reading a classic novel, competing in sports, doing hard work, making friends, having a spirited conversation.

The practices of the spiritual life, too, are burning bushes. The spiritual life recreates places that we thought were lost to us. Personal prayer, reciting the Rosary, praying a novena, frequenting the Sacrament of Penance, and preparing oneself for reception of the Eucharist are all moments that deepen the life of virtue in us. In these moments, especially in the sacraments, the Holy Spirit does something in our hearts. He introduces us more and more to Jesus Christ and deepens our friendship. We become like Jesus through the life of virtue. Jesus teaches us, above all, the mysteries of his passion, death, and resurrection. He teaches us how to deal with the various persecutions we experience. The spiritual life is not a series of comforting sensations that makes us feel as if we belong. So often Jesus did not fit in. Some of those he came to save rejected him. Rather than giving us a feeling of ease and solace, the spiritual life prepares us for seeing God. Meeting God in prayer doesn't happen by chance. We are able to personally appropriate the revelation of Christian truth only when the action of the Holy Spirit meets our docility, or teachableness. The union of his action and our readiness is the moment of belief.[3]

Sometimes the Holy Spirit speaks to us through the words of a prayer or a memory perceived in a new way. The Holy Spirit may use an empty and darkened church where we sit in silence to show us something about God. The Holy Spirit may use the beauty of the created world, time with our family, or even a moment of suffering. The Holy Spirit never tires of making known the mystery of God and inviting us further

---

3. See Balthasar, *Explorations in Theology IV*, 325.

into his love. The Holy Spirit invites every person many times a day and even within an hour, but we miss the invitations because we are distracted, fearful, and expect God to be somewhere else. But the burning bush is right in front of us, and we pass it by.

The altars of our churches are burning bushes. This reaches its culmination in the Eucharist. The Eucharist immerses the Christian in the self-gift of God, that is, his substantial self-giving love in Jesus. This love nourishes, directs, and strengthens the believer to offer the self-gift of love. We glance at our altars many times, but rarely see the fire that moves within the fire. It may be that we glance at the time on our cell phone more often that we gaze at the altar. Our lives often seem too busy to make time for God. But the fire burns on the altar: the bread and wine on the altar are changed when the words of Jesus are spoken by the priest. The bread and wine are not consumed, but totally changed from within to become the Body and Blood of Jesus. He comes to dwell within us when we receive this sacrament. The embers from that fire on the altar drift up and out and into us as we receive the Eucharist. His presence can then set our hearts on fire. That fire transforms our hearts and burns even more brightly when we return to the pew, to the dinner table, and to the workplace. And someone might see God within us.

As Moses walks over to the burning bush, the embers reach him and he hears the voice of God. The Lord tells Moses that he is standing on holy ground, so he should remove his shoes. It seems that the Spirit of the fire is not confined to the bush. Somehow it has started to spread across the ground, making it holy. Why did God direct Moses to remove his shoes? In that era, shoes were made from the skins of dead animals. God is telling Moses that nothing dead can come between himself and Moses. Success in business cannot come between us and God. Temper cannot come between us and God. Fashion cannot come between us and God. Even our fanciest and most expensive clothes will one day turn into rags. But we were made to last forever.

The spiritual person is not someone caught up in rare and secret divine things that no one else knows. The spiritual person finds wonder in the smallest, most common events and places: the dinner table, a quiet morning, the sound of rain, a wild beach, a busy subway, an empty field, an algebra equation, a Scripture reading, and the sacraments. At the heart of each of these experiences is love. God's love sustains us in persecution.

Love brings close to us what once seemed unattainable. Love does not disappoint. The experience of receiving what seemed unattainable transports us outside ourselves in a gift. This gift is an outpouring of self. This notion of the word *gift* cannot fit into an envelope, wallet, or golden frame, but emerges from the person precisely as a person. When the gift is truly given and received, we *know* it with our whole being. Something is brought about and effected by the gift. The gift is how we experience God and the salvation he offers.

The signs of God's presence often come to us in very ordinary experiences. Yet the ordinary is never boring. The burning bush blazes close to us. We often have no idea how close we are to God, to taking one step closer, receiving the ember and being set ablaze. We find a certain strength emerges only from Jesus Christ in his Church.

In the midst of his self-caused torment and trouble, Moses identified the spark of a privileged moment. His own recklessness and bitterness melted away. It was burned out of him by the purifying presence of the Spirit in the burning bush. As with Moses, so too, the Holy Spirit works within us over time so that our only response to persecution is to cling to the living God in living faith. Jesus was persecuted and in that trial unto death trusted in the love of the Father. Faith transforms persecution into a way of imitating Christ. When we face persecution with faith, this suffering faith grows into charity and is the mysterious movement to resurrection.[4]

Love always comes in the shape of the cross. The height of the fountain is the cross, the total gift of self. Jesus institutes the sacrament of his Body and Blood, the Eucharist, so that we might always draw from his life-giving death and resurrection: "In instituting the sacrament of the Eucharist, Jesus anticipates and makes present the sacrifice of the cross and the victory of the resurrection."[5] The Eucharist is the pristine source of the gifts of the Spirit, the virtues, and the Beatitudes. Those who walk up the steps to church each Sunday are climbing the mountain to the great fountain of life. Trials and temptations will seek to deter us from this ascent. We will face hardship. Yet, assimilation to Christ in his passion begins to root out all sin. Persecution purifies the witness of the Christian. The believer suffers persecution in many ways: by exclusion, rumor, resistance, physical pain, violence, and even death. Herein, however, is the principle of Christian fruitfulness:[6] to lay down one's life in the image of the Son. That is the center of existence for the Christian. That is why we intentionally unite our suffering to that of Jesus. Sacrifice consecrates suffering so that it may be transformed into a gift of self. When the Christian is persecuted, he is most vividly united to Jesus, and hence, most beautiful. Persecution leads back again to the original movement of the fountain, to a new and deeper Fear of the Lord that strengthens our hope.[7]

---

4. See Pinckaers, *The Sources of Christian Ethics*, 119.
5. Pope Benedict XVI, *Sacramentum Caritatis*, 10.
6. See Balthasar, *The Glory of the Lord VII*, 257.
7. See Balthasar, *Theo-Drama IV*, 177.

One seemingly ordinary day when Jesus was on his way from Judea to Galilee, he met a woman. We still do not know her name. We have listened in on their conversation. We have heard the words she heard. We have met the Word whom she met. He offered her a gift of living water, the gift of himself, poured out in love. He gave voice to the psalmist's cry: "There you poured abundant rains, God, graciously given to the poor in their need" (Ps 68:11). He so longed to share that gift of himself with her that he would continue his journey to the heights of the cross and to the depths of death. And from those depths he let forth a stream of love that fills the universe. That day, she met *the thirst of God*.

He passes by us now. He sits down before us and looks at us. He is still thirsty. He longs to speak his word to our hearts. The word that Jesus speaks to the Samaritan woman is a word of revelation. This word reveals himself as the gift of God the Father, as the eternal fountain of the Father's love. The water Jesus gives, literally from the deepest place of his heart, gives new life to the most distant energies and forgotten, long-lasting wounds of the human heart. His word also reveals that all the painful events of the Samaritan woman's life do not have the final word. Instead, these events are themselves transformed by the self gift of Jesus in his cross and resurrection.

After her encounter with Jesus, the woman goes back to the townspeople. She used to fear their gaze. Now, she not only walks in their midst, but she confidently proclaims to them, "Come see a man who told me everything I have done. Could he possibly be the Messiah?" (Jn 4:29). In fact, Saint John tells us, "Many of the Samaritans of that town began to believe in him because of the word of the woman . . ." (Jn

4:39). As we noted at the beginning of these reflections, belief comes easily to the child. On hearing the word of the Son of God, the woman of Samaria has become childlike. The fountain is welling up within her. In a sense, she has now *become the well* for the town, the one who gives the people access to the water of life.[8] She now speaks to the town the word Jesus spoke to her, the word of the Spirit. Her word leads them to *his* word: "Many more began to believe in him because of his word" (Jn 4:41). Jesus evangelizes the entire town through her. Yes, belief comes easily to the child. The people of that town are now childlike as well. The word of Jesus reveals that the gifts of the Holy Spirit, the virtues, and the Beatitudes are not simply lists of abstract theological terms to be memorized. They are radiant conduits of grace that flow from divine actions that take place within us and transform us to be signs of Jesus to a world parched for his presence. His word alone opens the way for the most rare vintage of heroic witness. As he guides us beside "safe waters" (Ps 23:2), his thirst meets ours. The grace of Jesus summons us as it did the Samaritan woman, in the midst of our daily tasks, to receive the gift and reach farther into the fountain of all holiness.

---

8. See Pope Benedict XVI, *Jesus of Nazareth*, 248.

Select Bibliography

Aquinas, Thomas. *Summa Theologiae.* In *Basic Writings of St. Thomas Aquinas.* Edited by Anton C. Pegis. New York: Random House, 1945.

Augustine. *Our Lord's Sermon on the Mount.* Edited by Philip Schaff, DD, LLD. *Nicene and Post-Nicene Fathers,* vol. 6. Peabody, MA: Hendrickson Publishers, Inc., 1994.

Bachelard, Gaston. *The Poetics of Space: The Classic Look at How We Experience Intimate Places.* Boston: Beacon, 1994.

Balthasar, Hans Urs von. *The Christian and Anxiety.* San Francisco: Ignatius Press, 2000.

———. *Christian Meditation.* San Francisco: Ignatius Press, 1989.

———. *Engagement with God.* San Francisco: Ignatius Press, 2008.

———. *Explorations in Theology I: The Word Made Flesh.* San Francisco: Ignatius, 1989.

———. *Explorations in Theology IV: Spirit and Institution.* San Francisco: Ignatius, 1995.

———. *The Glory of the Lord: A Theological Aesthetics I: Seeing the Form.* San Francisco: Ignatius, 1989.

———. *The Glory of the Lord: A Theological Aesthetics II: Clerical Style.* San Francisco: Ignatius, 1984.

———. *The Glory of the Lord: A Theological Aesthetics VI: The Old Covenant.* San Francisco: Ignatius Press, 1991.

———. *The Glory of the Lord: A Theological Aesthetics VII: Theology: The New Covenant.* San Francisco: Ignatius Press, 1989.

———. *Theo-Drama II: Dramatis Personae: Man in God.* San Francisco, Ignatius Press, 1990.

———. *Theo-Drama IV: In the Action.* San Francisco: Ignatius Press, 1994.

———. *Theo-Drama V: The Last Act.* San Francisco: Ignatius Press, 1994.

———. *Theo-Logic I: Truth of the World.* San Francisco: Ignatius Press, 2001.

Benedict XVI, *Jesus of Nazareth: From the Baptism in the Jordan to the Transfiguration.* New York: Doubleday, 2007.

Bernard of Clairvaux. *The Steps of Humility and Pride.* Kalamazoo, MI: Cistercian Publications, 1989.

Bonaventure, *Collations on the Seven Gifts of the Holy Spirit.* Translated by Zachary Hayes, OFM. Vol. 14 of *Works of St. Bonaventure.* New York: Franciscan Institute, 2008.

———. *Commentary on the Gospel of Luke.* In *Works of Saint Bonaventure.* Edited by Robert J. Karris, OFM. New York: Franciscan Institute Publications, 2003.

Bransfield, J. Brian. *The Human Person.* Boston: Pauline Books & Media, 2010.

Brodie, Thomas. *Genesis as Dialogue.* New York: Oxford University Press, 2001.

Bunge, Gabriel. *Dragon's Wine and Angel's Bread: The Teaching of Evagrius Ponticus on Anger and Meekness.* New York: St. Vladimir's Seminary Press, 2009.

Cassian, John. *The Conferences.* Translated by Boniface Ramsey, OP. Mahwah, NJ: Paulist Press, 1997.

Center for Applied Research in the Apostolate. *Sacraments Today: Belief and Practice Among U. S. Catholics.* Georgetown University, Washington, DC, 2008.

Climacus, John. *The Ladder of Divine Ascent.* Translated by Colm Luibheid and Norma Russell. Mahwah, NJ: Paulist Press, 1982.

Congar, Yves, OP. *Christians Active in the World.* New York: Herder and Herder, 1968.

————. *The Mystery of the Temple or The Manner of God's Presence to His People From Genesis to the Apocalypse.* Westminster, MD: The Newman Press, 1962.

————. *The Revelation of God.* New York: Herder and Herder, 1968.

Corbett, John, OP. "The Functions of *Paraclesis.*" *The Thomist* 73, 2009.

Daniélou, Jean. *Advent.* New York: Sheed and Ward, 1951.

————. *The Angels and Their Mission: According to the Fathers of the Church.* Translated by David Heimann. Westminster, MD: Newman Press, 1957.

————. *The Presence of God.* Baltimore: Helicon Press, 1959.

Daniélou, Jean, and Marrou, Henri. *The Christian Centuries: The First Hundred Years,* vol. 1. New York: McGraw-Hill Book Company, 1964.

Dillman, A. *Genesis: Critically and Exegetically Expounded.* Edinburgh: T. & T. Clark, 1897.

Jones, Larry Paul. *The Symbol of Water in the Gospel of John.* Sheffield, England: Sheffield Academic Press, 1997.

Eichrodt, W. *Theology of the Old Testament*, vol. II. Philadelphia: Westminster Press, 1967.

Evagrius Ponticus. *The Practicos: The Chapters on Prayer.* Translated by John Eudes Bamberger. Cistercian Studies Series, no. 4. Kalamazoo, MI: Cistercian Publications, 1970.

Féret, Henri M., OP. *The Apocalypse of Saint John.* Westminster, MD: The Newman Press, 1958.

Forte, Bruno. *The Trinity as History: Saga of the Christian God.* New York: Alba House, 1989.

Gilson, Etienne. *The Christian Philosophy of Saint Thomas Aquinas.* Notre Dame, IN: University of Notre Dame Press, 1956.

Guigo II. *The Ladder of Divine Ascent and Twelve Meditations.* Kalamazoo, MI: Cistercian Studies, 1981.

Hugh of Balma. *The Roads to Zion Mourn.* In *Carthusian Spirituality: The Writings of Hugh of Balma and Guigo de Ponte.* New York: Paulist Press, 1997.

Irenaeus of Lyons. *Adversus Haereses.* In *Ante-Nicene Fathers*, vol. 1. Edited by Alexander Roberts and James Donaldson. Peabody, MA: Hendrickson Publishers, 2004.

John of Saint Thomas. *The Gifts of the Holy Ghost.* New York: Sheed and Ward, 1951.

Marmion, Columba. *Union with God: Letters of Spiritual Direction by Blessed Columba Marmion.* Edited by Dom Raymond Thibaut. Bethesda, MD: Zaccheus Press, 2006.

Melina, Livio. *The Epiphany of Love: Toward a Theological Understanding of Christian Action.* Grand Rapids, MI: Eerdmans Press.

Merton, Thomas. *No Man Is an Island.* New York: Harcourt, Brace and Company, 1955.

Neville, Warwick. "Old Testament Spousal Narratives: A Contribution to the 'Nuptial Mystery.'" In *Dialoghi Sul Mistero Nuziale.* Edited by G. Marengo and B. Ognibeni. Rome: Lateran University Press, 2003.

Pinckaers, Servais. *The Pinckaers Reader: Renewing Thomistic Moral Theology.* Edited by John Berkman and Craig Stevens Titus. Washington, DC: The Catholic University of America Press, 2005.

————. *The Sources of Christian Ethics.* Washington, DC: Catholic University of America Press, 1995.

Pontifical Biblical Commission. *The Bible and Morality: Biblical Roots of Christian Conduct.* Rome: Libreria Editrice Vaticana, 2008.

Ratzinger, Joseph. *God and the World: A Conversation with Peter Seewald.* San Francisco: Ignatius Press, 2002.

Rigali, Justin. *Let the Oppressed Go Free: Breaking the Bonds of Addiction.* Dallas: Basilica Press.

Saward, John. *Cradle of Redeeming Love: The Theology of the Christmas Mystery.* San Francisco: Ignatius Press, 2002.

Speyr, Adrienne von. *The Letter to the Colossians.* San Francisco: Ignatius Press, 1998.

————. *The Letter to the Ephesians.* San Francisco: Ignatius Press, 1996.

————. *The Victory of Love: A Meditation on Romans 8.* San Francisco: Ignatius Press, 1990.

Teresa of Avila. *The Book of Her Life.* In *St. Teresa of Avila: Collected Works* vol. 1. Translated by Otilio Rodriguez, OCD, and Kieran Kavanaugh, OCD. Washington DC: The Institute for Carmelite Studies, 1976.

————. *The Interior Castle.* In *The Collected Works of St. Teresa of Avila,* vol. 2. T translated by Otilio Rodriguez, OCD, and Kieran Kavanaugh, OCD. Washington, DC: Institute for Carmelite Studies, 1980.

Torrell, Jean-Pierre, O.P. *Saint Thomas Aquinas: Spiritual Master,* vol. 2. Washington, DC: Catholic University of America Press, 2003.

Tugwell, Simon. *The Beatitudes: Soundings in the Christian Tradition.* Springfield, IL: Templegate, 1980.

———. *Ways of Imperfection: An Exploration of Christian Spirituality.* Springfield, IL: Templegate Publishers, 1985.

Westerman, C. *Genesis 1–11.* Minneapolis: Fortress Press, 1994.

Magisterial Documents

Benedict XVI. *Caritas in Veritate.* Boston: Pauline Books & Media, 2009.

———. *Spe Salvi.* Boston: Pauline Books & Media, 2007.

———. *Sacramentum Caritatis.* Boston: Pauline Books & Media, 2007.

———. *Verbum Domini.* Boston: Pauline Books & Media, 2010.

Catechism of the Catholic Church, Second Edition. Washington, DC: United States Conference of Catholic Bishops, 2006.

John Paul II. *Christifideles Laici.* Boston: Pauline Books & Media, 1988.

———. *Dominum et Vivificantem.* Boston: Pauline Books & Media, 1986.

———. *Evangelium Vitae.* Boston: Pauline Books & Media, 1995.

———. *Man and Woman He Created Them: A Theology of the Body.* Boston: Pauline Books & Media, 2006.

———. *Redemptor Hominis.* Boston: Pauline Books & Media, 1979.

———. *Veritatis Splendor.* Boston: Pauline Books & Media, 1993.

Vatican Council II. *Gaudium et Spes,* Boston: Pauline Books & Media, 1965.

Also by J. Brian Bransfield

0-8198-3394-0
$19.95

What does it mean to be human? In his theology of the body, John Paul II has made a major contribution to answering this question. Here Brian Bransfield provides a systematic approach to John Paul's teaching, using it as a basis for an integrated moral theology/Christian anthropology that offers practical support in living the Christian life.

"What life-opening pages! Bransfield illuminates John Paul II's vision of the human person brilliantly, fleshing out spiritual insights with an eye to the practical—a combination which opens for us the vocation to love, from the inside out."

— *Carl A. Anderson*
Supreme Knight of the Knights of Columbus

BOOKS & MEDIA

A mission of the Daughters of St. Paul

As apostles of Jesus Christ, evangelizing today's world:

We are CALLED to holiness
by God's living Word and Eucharist.

We COMMUNICATE the Gospel message
through our lives and through all
available forms of media.

We SERVE the Church
by responding to the hopes and needs
of all people with the Word of God,
in the spirit of St. Paul.

For more information visit our website: www.pauline.org.

BOOKS & MEDIA

The Daughters of St. Paul operate book and media centers at the following addresses. Visit, call or write the one nearest you today, or find us at www.pauline.org

CALIFORNIA

    3908 Sepulveda Blvd, Culver City, CA 90230   310-397-8676

    935 Brewster Avenue, Redwood City, CA 9406   3650-369-4230

    5945 Balboa Avenue, San Diego, CA 92111   858-565-9181

FLORIDA

    145 S.W. 107th Avenue, Miami, FL 33174   305-559-6715

HAWAII

    1143 Bishop Street, Honolulu, HI 96813   808-521-2731

    Neighbor Islands call: 866-521-2731

ILLINOIS

    172 North Michigan Avenue, Chicago, IL 60601   312-346-4228

LOUISIANA

    4403 Veterans Memorial Blvd, Metairie, LA 70006   504-887-7631

MASSACHUSETTS

    885 Providence Hwy, Dedham, MA 02026   781-326-5385

MISSOURI

    9804 Watson Road, St. Louis, MO 63126   314-965-3512

NEW YORK

    64 W. 38th Street, New York, NY 10018   212-754-1110

PENNSYLVANIA

    Philadelphia—relocating   215-676-9494

SOUTH CAROLINA

    243 King Street, Charleston, SC 29401   843-577-0175

VIRGINIA

    1025 King Street, Alexandria, VA 22314   703-549-3806

CANADA

    3022 Dufferin Street, Toronto, ON M6B 3T5   416-781-9131

¡También somos su fuente para libros,
videos y música en español!